North America's Top Selling
HOME PLANS

A Letter from the Publisher,

I am very excited about this collection of home designs. This book offers one of the finest collections of home plans ever published. Please take the time to find out for yourself.

Many respected and established designers and architects have contributed to this collection. Their designs are proven winners. As a result, we are confident you will find a first rate plan for North American tastes and building conditions.

Compare for yourself. No matter what your family size, budget, or preferences, you're sure to find a home that suits you. And, you'll save thousands of dollars on the construction blueprints for one of these homes compared to the cost of custom plans.

Today, more than ever, it pays to build "smart". If you're seriously interested in the best home for your lifestyle...if you're seriously interested in maximizing the investment in your home...take a look at this remarkable collection of plans.

Sincerely,

James D. McNair III

James D. McNair, III
Publisher

P.S. To order complete construction blueprints for any design, see pages 316-320.

Cover Design by Anthony Lavorgna
Cover Photography by John Ehrenclou, Cover Plan Contractor Darrin Sherry
© 1994 by the L.F. Garlinghouse Co., Inc. of Middletown, Connecticut. Building a house from a design found in this publication without first purchasing a set of home plans is a copyright violation. Printed in the USA. North America's Top Selling Home Plans is published at 34 Industrial Park Place, Middletown, Connecticut 06457, USA.

Library of Congress Number: 93-080468
ISBN: 0-938708-50-3

First Edition
First Printing, November 1989
Second Printing, January 1992

Second Edition
First Printing, March 1994

Canadian orders should be submitted to:

The Garlinghouse Company, Inc.
20 Cedar Street North
Kitchener, Ontario N2H 2W8
(519) 743-4169
(800) 561-4169

No. 90155

Classic Styling, Exceptional Plan

■ This plan features:

— Four bedrooms

— Two full and one half baths

■ A U-shaped, efficient Kitchen with snack corner separating it from the Breakfast area

■ A sunken Family Room with a brick fireplace

■ A half bath and Mudroom entry from the Garage allowing for clean-up before entering the main living area

■ A Master Suite enhanced by a large walk-in closet and deluxe bath with corner tub and double vanity

■ Three additional bedrooms, two with walk-in closets, sharing a full hall bath

■ An optional basement, slab or crawl space foundation — please specify when ordering

FIRST FLOOR — 1,212 SQ. FT.
SECOND FLOOR — 1,160 SQ. FT.

TOTAL LIVING AREA: 2,372 SQ. FT.

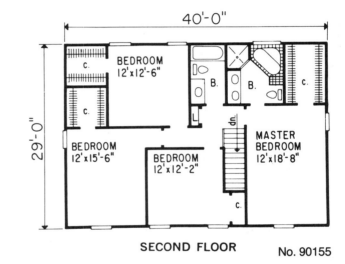

40'-0"

BEDROOM 12'x12'-6"

c.

B.

B.

c.

c.

29'-0"

BEDROOM 12'x15'-6"

BEDROOM 12'x12'-2"

dn.

MASTER BEDROOM 12'x18'-8"

c.

SECOND FLOOR   No. 90155

59'-0"

DINING ROOM 10'-8"x12'-6"

KIT. 9'x12'-6"

snack ctr.

BREAKFAST 9'x12'-6"

FAMILY ROOM 18'-6" x 12'-6"

dn.

28'-0"

LIVING ROOM 17'-5"x14'-6"

c.

dn.

HTR.CLO. PLAN 2

LAV.

w d

37'-10"

shelves

ENTRY

up

MUD ROOM

c.

GARAGE 21'-4"x23'-4"

FIRST FLOOR

No. 92405

Perfect for a First Home

■ This plan features:

— Three bedrooms

— Two full baths

■ A spacious Master Suite including a separate Master Bath with a garden tub and shower

■ A Dining Room and Family Room highlighted by vaulted ceilings

■ An oversized patio accessible from the Master Suite, Family Room and Breakfast Room

■ A well planned Kitchen measuring 12' x 11'

Please note there is no Materials List available for this plan

FIRST FLOOR — 1,564 SQ. FT.
GARAGE & STORAGE — 476 SQ. FT.

TOTAL LIVING AREA:
1,564 SQ. FT.

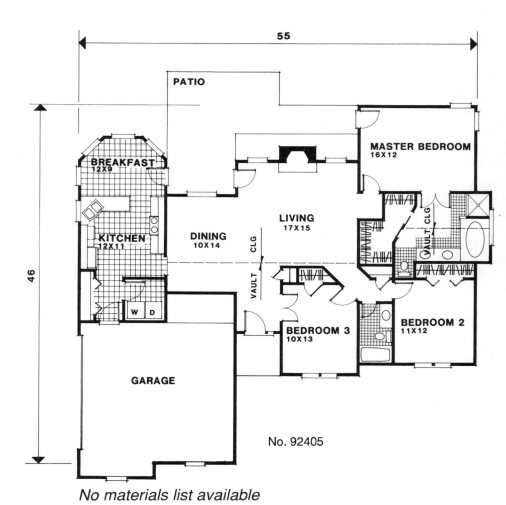

No. 92405

No materials list available

No. 91901

Rich Classic Lines

■ This plan features:

— Four bedrooms

— Three full and one half baths

■ A two-story foyer flooded by light through a half-round transom

■ A vaulted ceiling in the Great Room that continues into the Master Suite

■ A corner fireplace in the Great Room with French doors to the Breakfast/Kitchen area

■ A center island in the Kitchen with an angled sink and a built-in desk and pantry

■ A tray ceiling and recessed hutch area in the formal Dining Room

■ A Master Suite with a walk-in closet, a whirlpool tub, and a double sink vanity

FIRST FLOOR — 1,496 SQ. FT.
SECOND FLOOR — 716 SQ. FT.
BASEMENT — 1,420 SQ. FT.
GARAGE — 460 SQ. FT.

TOTAL LIVING AREA: 2,212 SQ. FT.

No materials list available

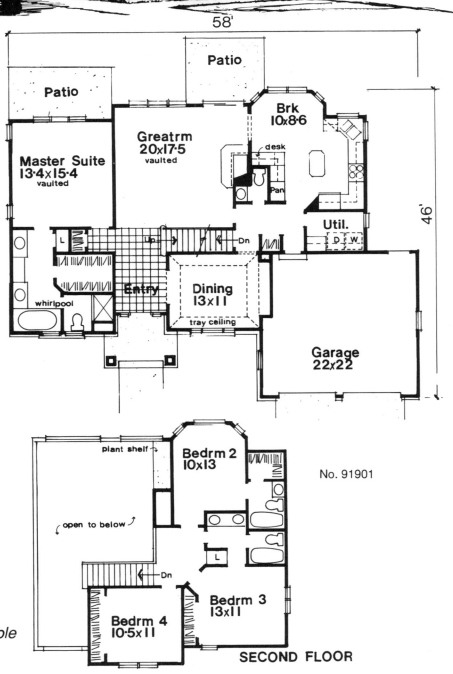

4

No. 91630
Spacious Stucco

■ This plan features:

— Five bedrooms

— Four full baths

■ A Living Room with a fireplace that is separated by columns from the Dining Room

■ A wide-open layout between the Kitchen, Nook and Family Room

■ A Den with easy access to a bath with a shower, making it a perfect guest room

■ A luxurious Master Suite with a spa tub and a walk-in closet

■ Two additional full baths serving the four additional bedrooms

FIRST FLOOR — 1,452 SQ. FT.
SECOND FLOOR — 1,431 SQ. FT.
BONUS ROOM — 316 SQ. FT.

TOTAL LIVING AREA:
2,883 SQ. FT.

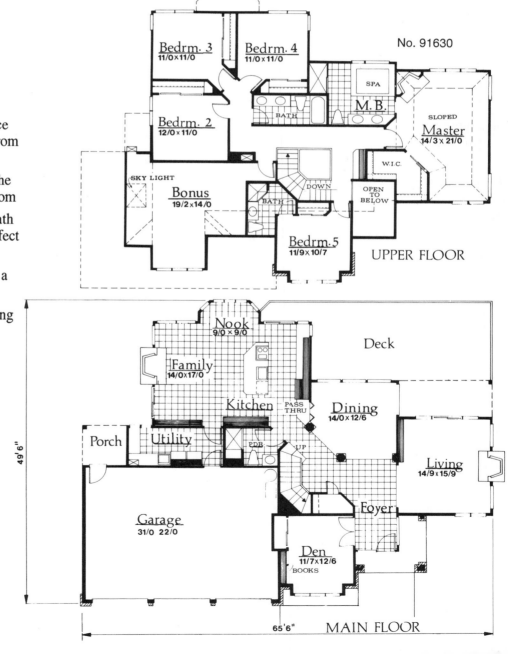

No. 91630

Bedrm. 3
11/0×11/0

Bedrm. 4
11/0×11/0

SPA

M. B.

BATH

SLOPED
Master
14/3 x 21/0

Bedrm. 2
12/0×11/0

W.I.C.

SKY LIGHT

Bonus
19/2×14/0

DOWN

BATH

OPEN TO BELOW

Bedrm. 5
11/9×10/7

UPPER FLOOR

Nook
9/0 × 9/0

Deck

Family
14/0×17/0

Kitchen

PASS THRU

Dining
14/0 × 12/6

Porch

Utility

EDB

UP

Living
14/9 x 15/9

Garage
31/0 22/0

Foyer

Den
11/7×12/6
BOOKS

49' 6"

65'6"

MAIN FLOOR

No. 92013
A Warm Welcome

■ This plan features:

— Three bedrooms

— Two full and one half baths

■ A large, island Kitchen with a built-in pantry, built-in desk and a double sink

■ A vaulted ceiling in the Sun Room

■ A tray ceiling in the formal Dining Room with easy access to the Kitchen

■ A fireplace and a built-in wetbar in the informal Family Room

■ A vaulted ceiling in the Master Suite which is equipped with his and her walk-in closets and a private full bath

■ A barrel vaulted ceiling in the front bedroom

■ A convenient second floor laundry

FIRST FLOOR — 1,336 SQ. FT.
SECOND FLOOR — 1,015 SQ. FT.
BASEMENT — 1,336 SQ. FT.
GARAGE — 496 SQ. FT.

TOTAL LIVING AREA:
2,351 SQ. FT.

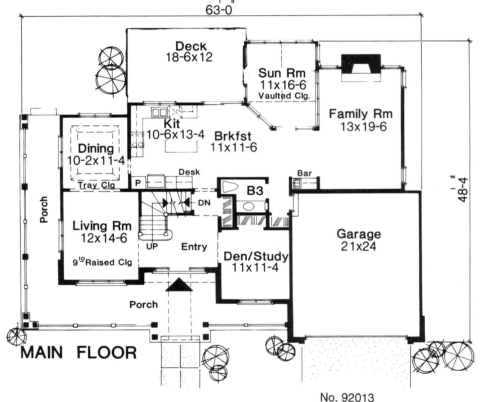

63-0"

48-4"

Deck 18-6x12

Sun Rm 11x16-6 Vaulted Clg.

Family Rm 13x19-6

Kit 10-6x13-4

Brkfst 11x11-6

Dining 10-2x11-4 Tray Clg

Desk

P

B3

Bar

DN

Living Rm 12x14-6 9¹⁰ Raised Clg

UP

Entry

Den/Study 11x11-4

Garage 21x24

Porch

Porch

MAIN FLOOR

No. 92013

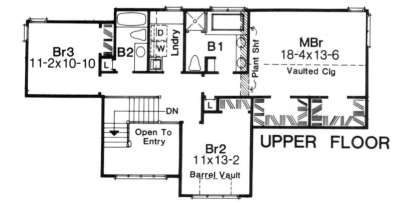

Br3 11-2x10-10

B2

L

D W Lndry

B1

Plant Shf

MBr 18-4x13-6 Vaulted Clg

DN

L

Open To Entry

Br2 11x13-2 Barrel Vault

UPPER FLOOR

No. 91353
Dormer Enhanced Dining Room

■ This plan features:

— Three bedrooms

— Two full and one half baths

■ A vaulted ceiling entry

■ A Living Room accented by a bay window

■ A Dining Room with a vaulted ceiling and two built-in corner china cabinets

■ A large, efficient Kitchen with a peninsula counter, an abundance of cabinets, and a sunny Breakfast bay

■ A Family Room with a cozy fireplace and access to the patio

■ A Master Bedroom Suite with a private Master Bath and a walk-in closet, plus a standard closet

FIRST FLOOR — 950 SQ. FT.
SECOND FLOOR — 683 SQ. FT.

TOTAL LIVING AREA: 1,633 SQ. FT.

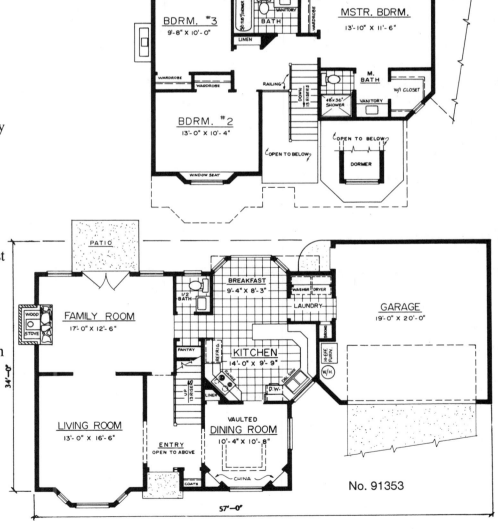

No. 91749
Relax on the Veranda

■ This plan features:

— Four bedrooms

— Three full and one half baths

■ A wrap-around veranda

■ A sky-lit Master Suite with elevated custom spa, twin basins, a walk-in closet, and an additional vanity outside the bathroom

■ A vaulted ceiling in the Den

■ A fireplace in both the Family Room and the formal Living Room

■ An efficient Kitchen with a peninsula counter and a double sink

■ Two additional bedrooms with walk-in closets, served by a compartmentalized bath

■ A Guest Suite with a private bath

FIRST FLOOR — 3,051 SQ. FT.
GARAGE — 646 SQ. FT.
WIDTH — 90'-0"
DEPTH — 82'-0"

TOTAL LIVING AREA: 3,051 SQ. FT.

No. 91749

No. 90653

Angled for Excitement

■ This plan features:

— Four bedrooms

— Two full and one half baths

■ A Family Room that is hexagonal in shape with soaring cathedral ceiling and two-way fireplace

■ A Living Room that is enhanced by the other side of the two-way fireplace

■ A conveniently arranged Kitchen, flanked by a sunny Dining Room and a dinette

■ A Master Bedroom with a walk-in closet and private bath

■ Three additional bedrooms that share a full hall bath

FIRST FLOOR — 2,601 SQ. FT.

TOTAL LIVING AREA:
2,601 SQ. FT.

FLOOR PLAN
No. 90653

No. 91752

For a Growing Family and All its Belongings

■ This plan features:

— Three bedrooms

— Two full baths

■ A Solarium Nook taking advantage of every bit of light possible

■ A wide country Kitchen with an eating bar peninsula, cook-top island and a built-in pantry

■ A built-in window seat in the Living Room and in the Dining Room

■ A cozy fireplace in the Family Room

■ A Master Suite with sky-lit dressing area and a large walk-in closet

■ Two additional bedrooms sharing a full bath and each having walk-in closets

FIRST FLOOR — 1,998 SQ. FT.
GARAGE — 637 SQ. FT.
SHOP — 120 SQ. FT.
WIDTH — 68'-0"
DEPTH — 66'-0"

TOTAL LIVING AREA: *1,998 SQ. FT.*

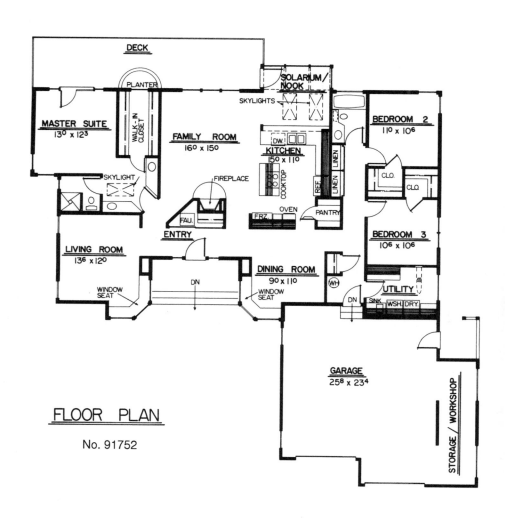

FLOOR PLAN

No. 91752

No. 90689
Formal Balance

- This plan features:
  — Three bedrooms
  — Two full baths
- A cathedral ceiling in the Living Room with a heat-circulating fireplace as focal point
- A bow window in the Dining Room that adds to the elegance as well as the natural light

- A well-equipped Kitchen that serves both the Dinette and the formal Dining Room efficiently
- A Master Bedroom with three closets and a private Master Bath with sliding glass doors to the master deck with hot tub

FIRST FLOOR — 1,374 SQ. FT.
MUDROOM/LAUNDRY — 102 SQ. FT.
BASEMENT — 1,361 SQ. FT.
GARAGE — 548 SQ. FT.

TOTAL LIVING AREA:
1,476 SQ. FT.

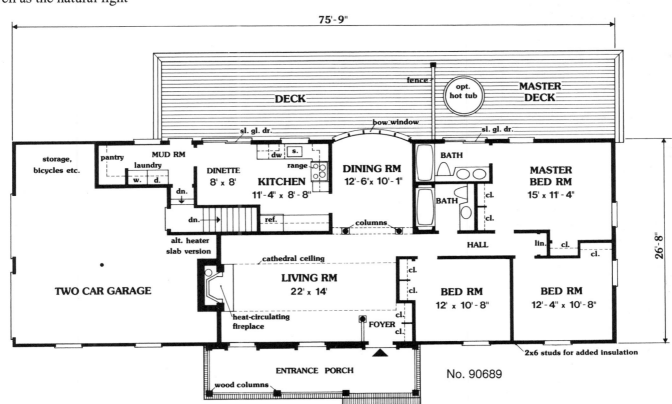

No. 90689

No. 90172

A Tudor-style Gem

■ This plan features:

— One bedroom

— One full bath

■ A private, sheltered stairway

■ Secure storage in the Garage for recreational vehicles or boats

■ A deck off the Dining area for outdoor living space

■ A roomy Living Room that flows into the Dining area for a more spacious feeling

■ A good-sized bedroom

■ Laundry facilities located next to the efficient Kitchen

FIRST FLOOR — 784 SQ. FT.
GARAGE — 784 SQ. FT.

TOTAL LIVING AREA:
784 SQ. FT.

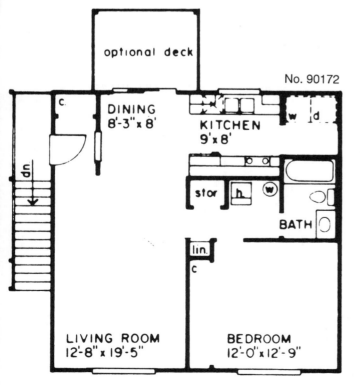

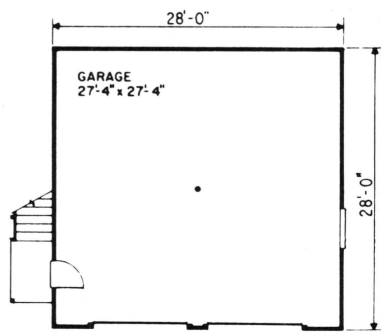

No. 90630

Year Round Leisure

■ This plan features:

— Three bedrooms

— Two full baths

■ A cathedral ceiling with exposed beams and a stone wall with heat-circulating fireplace in the Living Room

■ Three sliding glass doors leading from the Living Room to a large deck

■ A built-in Dining area that separates the Kitchen from the far end of the Living Room

■ A Master Suite with his and her closets and a private bath

■ Two additional bedrooms, one double sized, sharing a full hall bath

■ A crawl space foundation only

FIRST FLOOR — 1,207 SQ. FT.

TOTAL LIVING AREA: 1,207 SQ. FT.

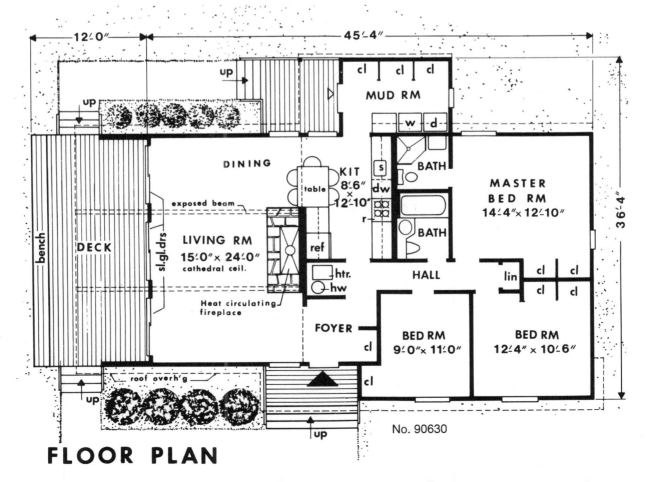

No. 90630

FLOOR PLAN

No. 91011
Indoor/Outdoor Unity

■ This plan features:

— Three bedrooms

— Two full baths

■ A luxurious Master Suite, complete with a spa and a private deck

■ A sunken Living Room with a glass wall opening into the formal Dining Room

■ Expansive windows and sliders in the island Kitchen, Nook and Family Room which has a fireplace

■ An optional basement, slab or crawl space foundation — please specify when ordering

FIRST FLOOR — 2,242 SQ. FT.

TOTAL LIVING AREA: 2,242 SQ. FT.

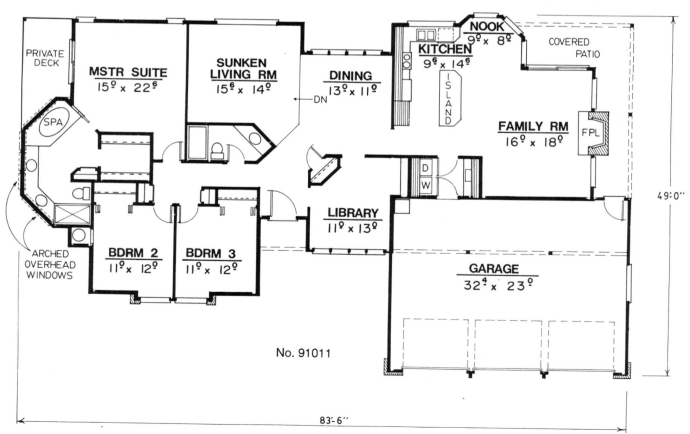

No. 90616

Victorian Touches Disguise Modern Design

■ This plan features:

— Three bedrooms

— Two full and one half baths

■ A Master Suite with a high ceiling, an arched window, a private bath, and a tower sitting room with an adjoining roof deck

■ Two additional bedrooms that share a full hall bath

■ A Living Room accentuated by a brick fireplace

■ A well-equipped Kitchen with a built-in pantry and peninsula counter

■ A sky-lit Family Room with a built-in entertainment center

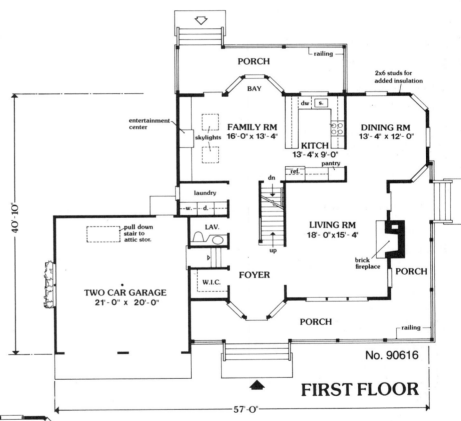

PORCH

railing

2x6 studs for added insulation

BAY

entertainment center

FAMILY RM
16'-0" x 13'-4"

skylights

dw   s.

KITCH
13'-4" x 9'-0"

DINING RM
13'-4" x 12'-0"

pantry

ref.

dn

laundry

w.   d.

LAV.

pull down stair to attic stor.

LIVING RM
18'-0" x 15'-4"

up

brick fireplace

PORCH

TWO CAR GARAGE
21'-0" x 20'-0"

W.I.C.

FOYER

PORCH

railing

40'-0"

57'-0"

No. 90616

FIRST FLOOR

BED RM
11'-0" x 10'-0"

BATH

lin

cl

BED RM
13'-4" x 11'-0"

cl

railing

cl

dn

lin

H

stor.

cl

BATH

lin

DECK

W.I.C.

MASTER SUITE
15'-4" x 12'-8"

railing

TOWER

high ceiling

SECOND FLOOR

FIRST FLOOR — 1,146 SQ. FT.
SECOND FLOOR — 846 SQ. FT.
BASEMENT — 967 SQ. FT.
GARAGE — 447 SQ. FT.

TOTAL LIVING AREA:
1,992 SQ. FT.

No. 91622
Elegant Sophistication

■ This plan features:

— Four bedrooms

— Two full and one half baths

■ A sky-lit entry

■ A back-to-back fireplace in the Great Room and Master Bedroom

■ A sky-lit Kitchen with cook top island and more than ample storage and counter space

■ An elegant formal Dining Room with a coved ceiling

■ A vaulted ceiling in the sprawling Great Room

■ An exquisite Master Suite tucked up a short staircase and a private Master Bath

FIRST FLOOR — 1,758 SQ. FT.
SECOND FLOOR — 549 SQ. FT.
BONUS — 536 SQ. FT.

TOTAL LIVING AREA: 2,307 SQ. FT.

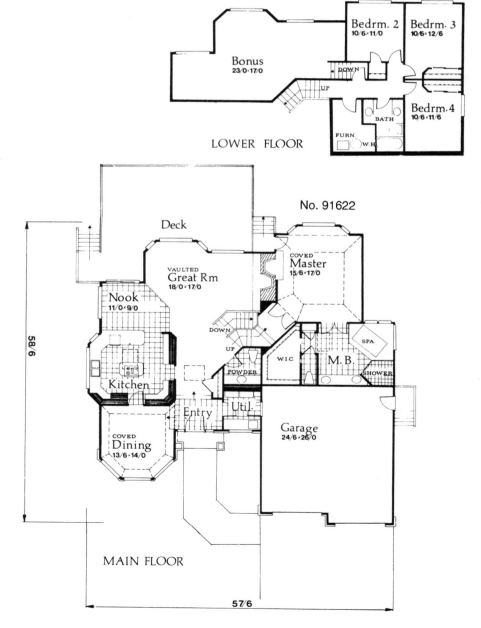

16

No. 90607

Bays Add Beauty and Living Space

■ This plan features:

— Four bedrooms

— Three full baths

■ A heat-circulating fireplace in the spacious, bay windowed Living Room

■ Ionic columns and a semi-circular window wall in the Dining Room giving classic grace

■ A U-shaped Kitchen with a peninsula opening into the Family Room

■ Enhanced by a heat-circulating fireplace, the Family Room has sliding glass doors to the terrace

■ A bayed windowed Master Suite with a walk-in closet and a private Master Bath

FIRST FLOOR — 1,613 SQ. FT.
SECOND FLOOR — 530 SQ. FT.

TOTAL LIVING AREA: 2,143 SQ. FT.

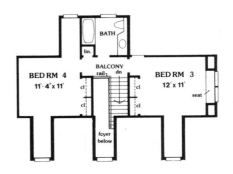

SECOND FLOOR PLAN

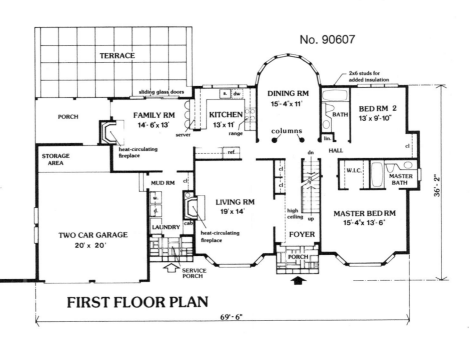

No. 90607

FIRST FLOOR PLAN

No. 90126

Charming and Cozy Rooms

■ This plan features:

— Three bedrooms

— Two full and one half baths

■ A large Family Room with a cozy fireplace and sliding doors to the patio

■ An efficiently organized Kitchen serving either the formal Dining Room or the informal Nook easily

■ A Master Bedroom with a large walk-in closet and private Master Bath

■ Two additional bedrooms sharing a full hall bath with double vanity

■ An optional basement or crawl space foundation — please specify when ordering

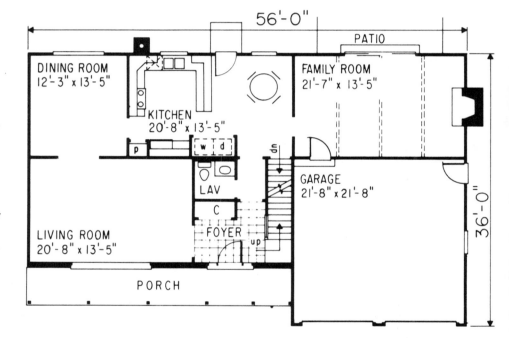

No. 90126

FIRST FLOOR — 1,260 SQ. FT.
SECOND FLOOR — 952 SQ. FT.

TOTAL LIVING AREA: 2,212 SQ. FT.

SECOND FLOOR

No. 90201

A Modern Plan with a Farmhouse Flavor

- ■ This plan features:
- — Four bedrooms
- — Two full and one half baths
- ■ A sprawling covered porch
- ■ A cozy Family Room warmed by a fireplace with a raised hearth

- ■ A formal Dining Room with a large bay window
- ■ A handy Kitchen with built-ins including an eating bar
- ■ A Master Bedroom equipped with a dressing room, two closets and a private bath

FIRST FLOOR — 1,370 SQ. FT.
SECOND FLOOR — 969 SQ. FT.

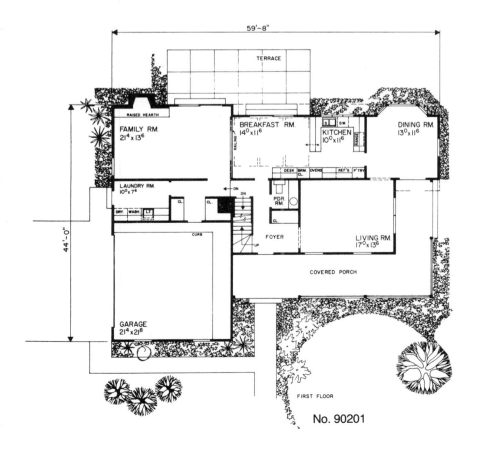

FIRST FLOOR

No. 90201

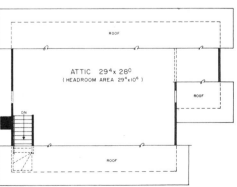

TOTAL LIVING AREA:
2,339 SQ. FT.

No. 99609

Enhanced by Natural Light

■ This plan features:

— Three bedrooms

— Three full baths

■ A two-story Living Room with a heat-circulating fireplace and sliding glass doors to the terrace

■ A formal Dining Room enhanced by a bay window

■ An efficient, well-equipped Kitchen which is separated from the Family Room by a peninsula counter

■ A Family Room with sliding glass doors to the terrace and a heat-circulating fireplace

■ A Master Suite with walk-in closet and private Master Bath with whirlpool tub

■ Two additional bedrooms sharing a full hall bath

FIRST FLOOR — 1,142 SQ. FT.
SECOND FLOOR —978 SQ. FT.
LAUNDRY/MUDROOM — 59 SQ. FT.
GARAGE — 428 SQ. FT.

TOTAL LIVING AREA:
2,179 SQ. FT.

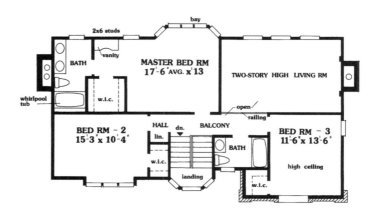

SECOND FLOOR

No. 99609

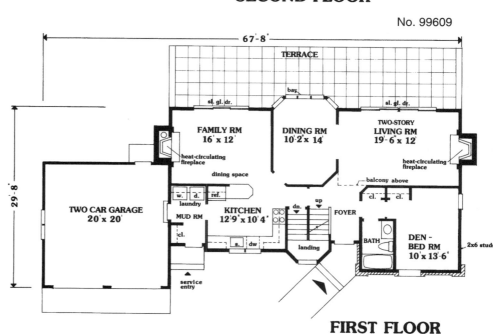

FIRST FLOOR

No. 99373

High Impact Two-Story

■ This plan features:

— Four bedrooms

— Three and one half baths

■ A high impact two-story, double door transom entry

■ A two-story Family Room with a wall consisting of a fireplace and windows

■ A spacious Master Suite with unique curved glass block behind the tub in the Master Bath and a semi-circular window wall with see-through fireplace in sitting area

■ A gourmet Kitchen and Breakfast area opening to a Lanai

■ A Guest Suite with private deck and walk-in closet

FIRST FLOOR — 3,158 SQ. FT.
SECOND FLOOR — 1,374 SQ. FT.

**TOTAL LIVING AREA:
4,532 SQ. FT.**

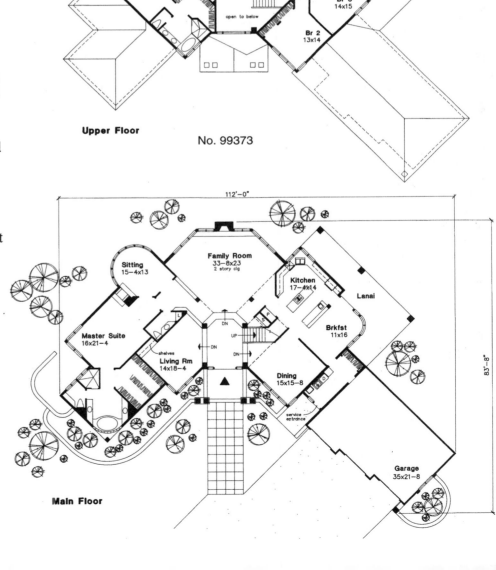

Upper Floor

No. 99373

Main Floor

No. 91662

A Lifetime Home

■ This plan features:

— Five bedrooms

— Three full baths

■ A design that can be modified to accommodate permanently disabled individuals

■ Wider hallways, doors, and low profile thresholds

■ A Master Suite with a coved ceiling and Master Bath with a roll-in shower and grab bars appropriately placed

■ A vaulted ceiling in the Great Room with a fireplace

■ An island Kitchen with a built-in pantry and sunny eating Nook

■ A coved ceiling, and an abundance of windows in the front bedroom

■ A large Recreational Room in the finished Basement

FIRST FLOOR — 2,167 SQ. FT.
FINISHED BASEMENT — 1,154 SQ. FT.

TOTAL LIVING AREA:
3,321 SQ. FT.

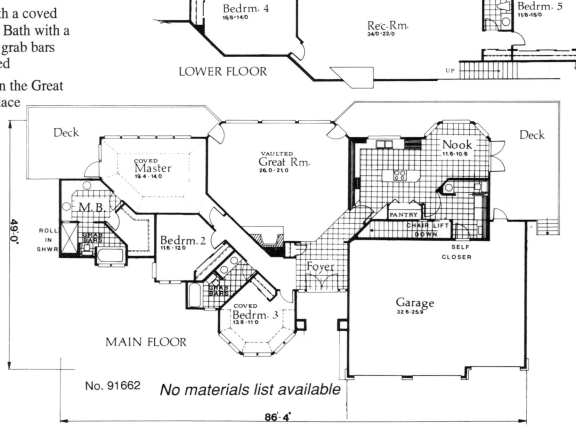

No. 91662   *No materials list available*

No. 91502
Formal Balance

■ This plan features:

— Three bedrooms

— Two full and one half baths

■ A two-story foyer crowned by a towering palladium window

■ A formal Living Room that flows into the formal Dining Room for ease in entertaining

■ A cozy Family Room with a brick hearth fireplace

■ An angular Kitchen with a peninsula counter, a built-in pantry and a sunny eating Nook

■ A magnificent Master Suite with a garden spa, double vanities and a walk-in closet

■ Two additional bedrooms sharing a sky-lit full bath

FIRST FLOOR — 935 SQ. FT.
SECOND FLOOR — 772 SQ. FT.
BONUS ROOM — 177 SQ. FT.

TOTAL LIVING AREA: 1,707 SQ. FT.

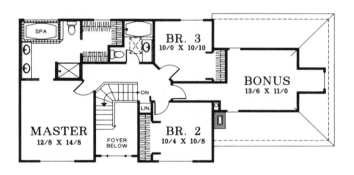

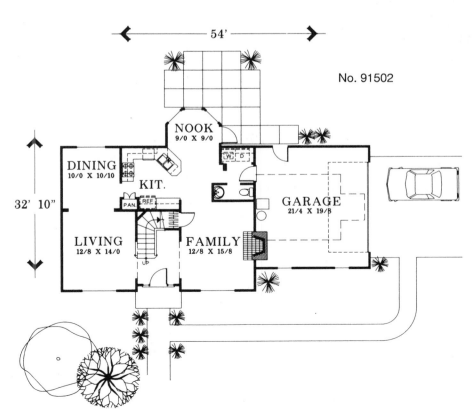

No. 91416
Vaulted Views

■ This plan features:

— Three bedrooms

— Two full baths

■ An expansive, two-story Great Room and full-length deck beyond atrium doors

■ A Kitchen, with rangetop island, flowing into the Dining Room; which has access to the deck

■ A vaulted ceiling in the Master Suite, which includes two walk-in closets, a private Master Bath with garden tub and double vanities

FIRST FLOOR — 1,450 SQ. FT.
SECOND FLOOR — 650 SQ. FT.
BONUS ROOM — 220 SQ. FT.

TOTAL LIVING AREA:
2,100 SQ. FT.

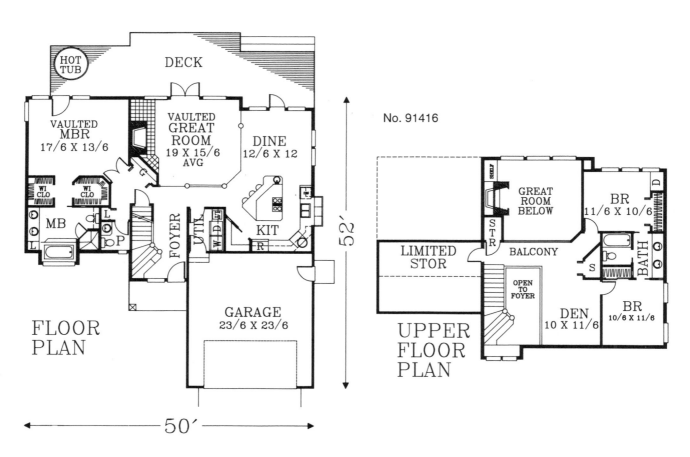

No. 91040

Huge Windows Create Cheerful Atmosphere

- This plan features:
- — Three bedrooms
- — Two full baths
- A modern, efficient Kitchen layout flowing into the Nook and Living Room

- A Living Room, made spacious by an open layout, with a handsome fireplace
- A Master Suite with ample closet space and a private, full bath
- Two additional bedrooms that share a full hall bath

- A crawl space foundation only
  FIRST FLOOR — 1,206 SQ. FT.

  TOTAL LIVING AREA:
  1,206 SQ. FT.

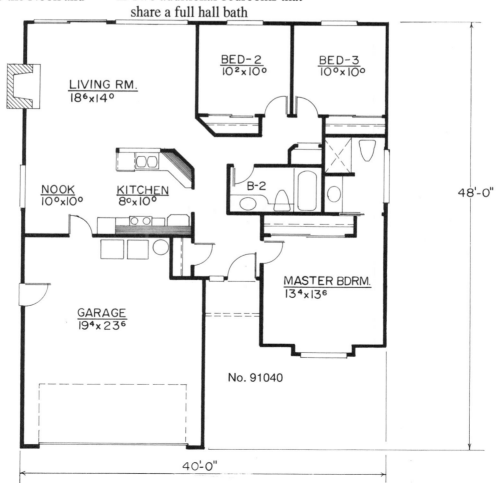

BED-2
10^2x10^0

BED-3
10^0x10^0

LIVING RM.
18^6x14^0

NOOK
10^0x10^0

KITCHEN
8^0x10^0

B-2

MASTER BDRM.
13^4x13^6

GARAGE
19^4x23^6

No. 91040

48'-0"

40'-0"

No. 90671

Adapt this Colonial to Your Lifestyle

■ This plan features:

— Four bedrooms

— Two full baths

■ A Living Room with a beam ceiling and fireplace

■ An eat-in Kitchen efficiently serving the formal Dining Room

■ A Master Bedroom with his and her closets

■ Two upstairs bedrooms sharing a split bath

FIRST FLOOR — 1,056 SQ. FT.
SECOND FLOOR — 531 SQ. FT.

TOTAL LIVING AREA: 1,587 SQ. FT.

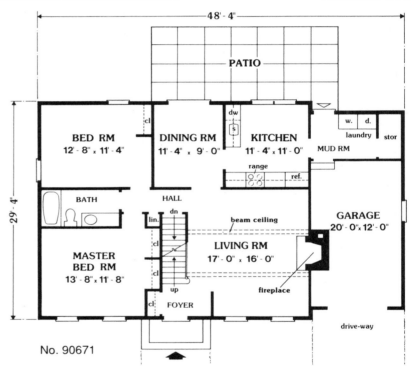

No. 90671

FIRST FLOOR PLAN

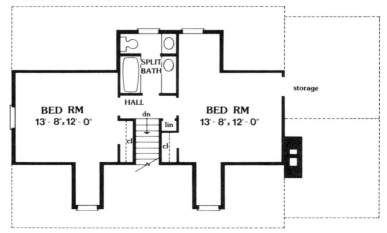

SECOND FLOOR PLAN

No. 90288

Soaring Ceilings Add Space and Drama

■ This plan features:

— Two bedrooms (with optional third bedroom)

— Two full baths

■ A sunny Master Suite with a sloping ceiling, private terrace entry, and luxurious garden bath with an adjoining dressing room

■ A Gathering Room with a fireplace, study and formal Dining Room flowing together for a more spacious feeling

■ A convenient pass-through that adds to the efficiency of the galley Kitchen and adjoining Breakfast Room

FIRST FLOOR — 1,387 SQ. FT.

TOTAL LIVING AREA: 1,387 SQ. FT.

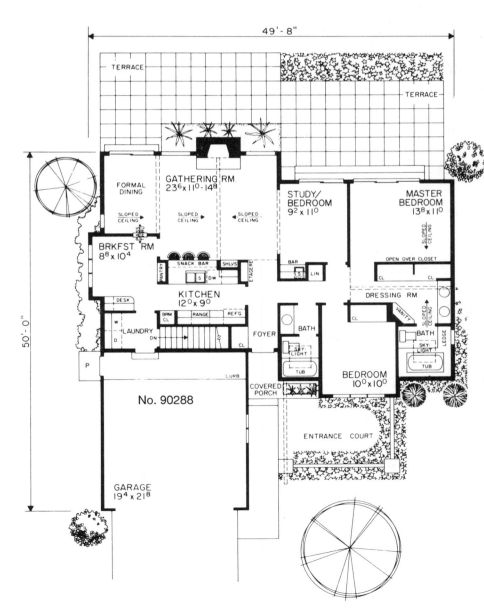

No. 90248

Outdoor-Lovers' Delight

■ This plan features:

— Three bedrooms

— Two full baths

■ A well-appointed Kitchen with snack bar plus ample storage and counter space

■ A huge Gathering Room with a sloped ceiling and fireplace

■ A spacious Master Suite with private terrace access, walk-in closet and full bath

■ Two additional bedrooms that share a full hall bath

FIRST FLOOR — 1,729 SQ. FT.

TOTAL LIVING AREA: *1,729 SQ. FT.*

OPTIONAL NON-BASEMENT

No. 90248

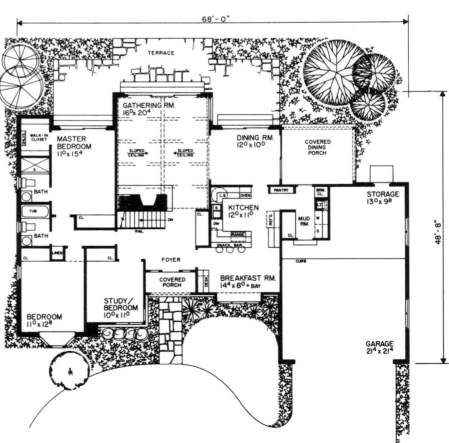

No. 99345

Compact Ranch

■ This plan features:

— Three bedrooms

— Two full baths

■ A Great Room and Dining area with vaulted ceilings

■ A Great Room with a fabulous fire place

■ A Kitchen and sunny Breakfast area with access to rear deck

■ A Master Suite with private full bath and one wall of closet space

FIRST FLOOR — 1,325 SQ. FT.

TOTAL LIVING AREA:
1,325 SQ. FT.

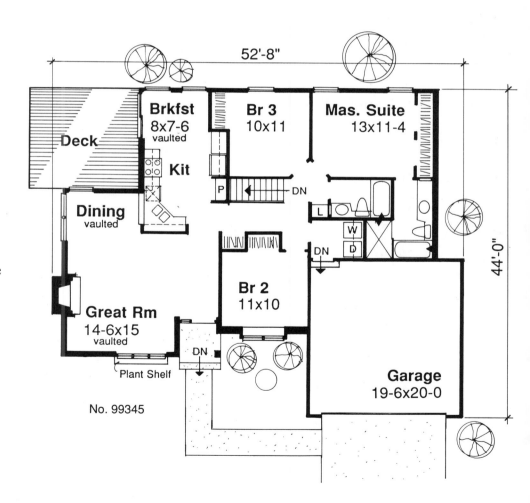

52'-8"

44'-0"

Deck

Brkfst
8x7-6
vaulted

Kit

Br 3
10x11

Mas. Suite
13x11-4

Dining
vaulted

P

DN

L

W
D

DN

Great Rm
14-6x15
vaulted

Br 2
11x10

DN

Garage
19-6x20-0

Plant Shelf

No. 99345

No. 99611

Decorative Staircase Makes for Impressive Entrance

■ This plan features:

— Four bedrooms

— Two full and one half baths

■ A spacious central foyer enhanced by a decorative stairway

■ A formal Living Room with a heat-circulating fireplace

■ An informal Family Room with a heat-circulating fireplace and sliding glass doors to the terrace

■ A solar bay in the Dinette area which flows into the efficient Kitchen

■ A Master Suite with walk-in closet, balcony and private Master Bath

■ Three additional bedrooms, each with a balcony, that share a full hall bath

FIRST FLOOR — 1,134 SQ. FT.
SECOND FLOOR — 1,048 SQ. FT.
BASEMENT — 1,044 SQ. FT.
GARAGE & STORAGE — 475 SQ. FT.
LAUNDRY/MUDROOM — 80 SQ. FT.

TOTAL LIVING AREA: 2,262 SQ. FT.

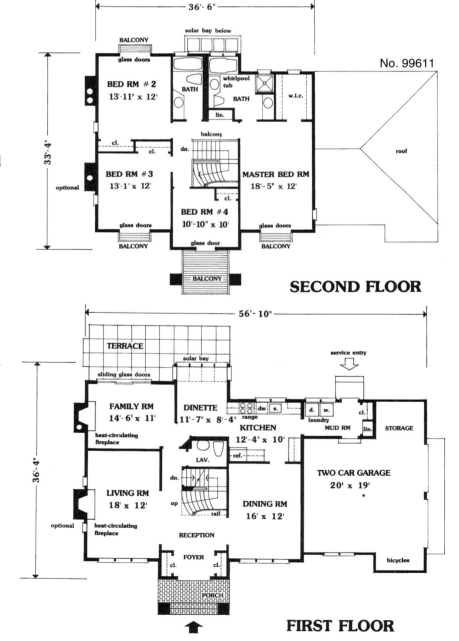

SECOND FLOOR

FIRST FLOOR

No. 99625

Encompassed by the Warmth of the Sun

■ This plan features:

— Four bedrooms

— Three full and one half baths

■ A central fireplace, media center and high-sloped ceiling in the Great Room

■ A formal Living Room with a high-sloped ceiling

■ A large Kitchen, well-equipped and flowing into a sunny Dinette area

■ A second-floor Master Suite with walk-in closet, dressing alcove, and sky-lit Master Bath

■ Three additional bedrooms that share use of a full hall bath

FIRST FLOOR — 1,835 SQ. FT.
SECOND FLOOR — 906 SQ. FT.
GARAGE AND STORAGE — 511 SQ. FT.
LAUNDRY/MUDROOM — 67 SQ. FT.

TOTAL LIVING AREA: 2,808 SQ. FT.

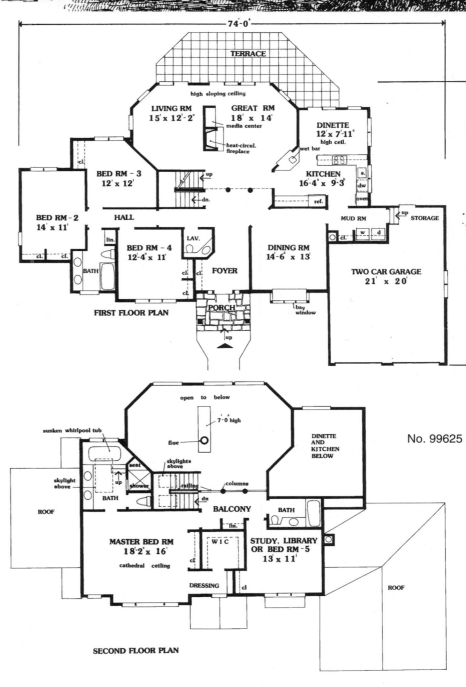

No. 90449

Classic Colonial Style with Modern Floor Plan

■ This plan features:

— Three bedrooms

— Two full and one half baths

■ A large Family Room with a fireplace and built-in book shelves having French doors leading to an outdoor deck

■ A spacious, efficient Kitchen open to the Breakfast Room which has a sunny bay

■ A Master Suite with a large private bath including a garden tub and separate shower

■ A second floor laundry convenient to the bedrooms

■ An optional bonus room so the house can expand with your family

■ An optional basement or crawl space foundation — please specify when ordering

FIRST FLOOR — 1,138 SQ. FT.
SECOND FLOOR — 1,124 SQ. FT.
OPTIONAL BONUS — 284 SQ. FT.
BASEMENT — 1,124 SQ. FT.
GARAGE — 484 SQ. FT.

TOTAL LIVING AREA: 2,262 SQ. FT.

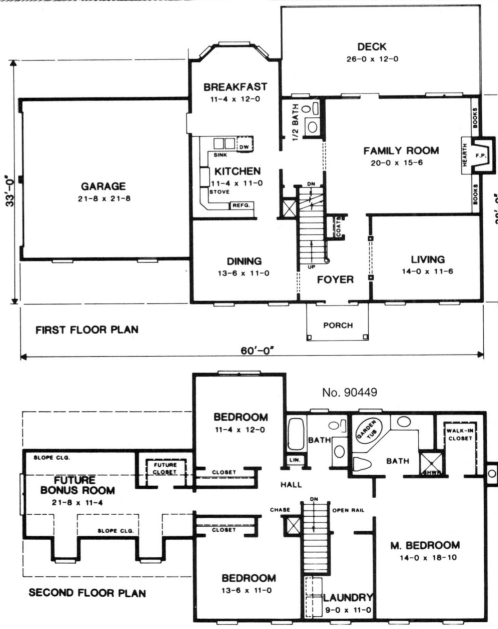

No. 90450
Elegant Brick Two-Story

■ This plan features:

— Four bedrooms

— Two or three full and one half baths

■ A large two-story Great Room with a fireplace and access to a wood deck

■ A secluded Master Suite with two walk-in closets and a private, lavish, Master Bath

■ A large island Kitchen serving the formal Dining Room and the sunny Breakfast Nook with ease

■ Three additional bedrooms, two with walk-in closets, sharing a full hall bath

■ An optional bonus room with a private entrance from below

■ An optional basement or crawl space foundation — please specify when ordering

FIRST FLOOR — 1,637 SQ. FT.
SECOND FLOOR — 761 SQ. FT.
OPT. BATH & CLOSET — 106 SQ. FT.
OPT. BONUS — 347 SQ. FT.

TOTAL LIVING AREA:
2,398 SQ. FT.

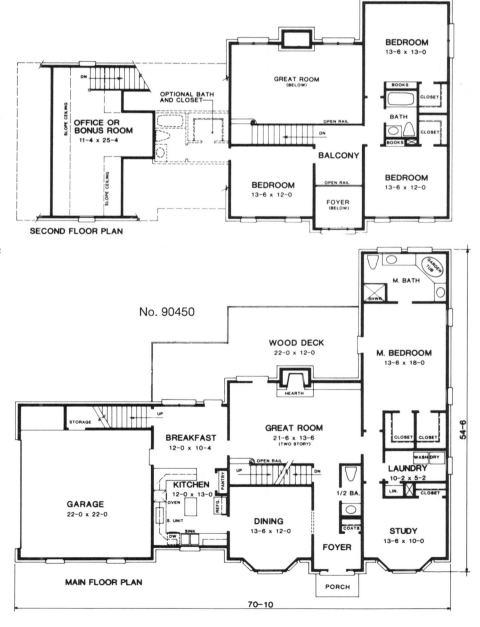

No. 99619

All This On One Level

■ This plan features:

— Three bedrooms

— Two full baths

■ A sky-lit foyer enhanced by a high-sloped ceiling

■ A free-standing, heat-circulating fireplace surrounded by stone to mantel height in the Living Room

■ A formal Dining Room flowing efficiently from the Living Room and easily into the Kitchen

■ An efficient, well-equipped Kitchen with a peninsula counter and informal Dinette area

■ A Family Room with sliding glass doors to the terrace and a heat-circulating fireplace

■ A Master Suite with private Master Bath and ample closet space

■ Two additional bedrooms sharing a full hall bath

FIRST FLOOR — 1,629 SQ. FT.
BASEMENT — 1,457 SQ. FT.
GARAGE — 424 SQ. FT.
LAUNDRY/MUDROOM — 107 SQ. FT.

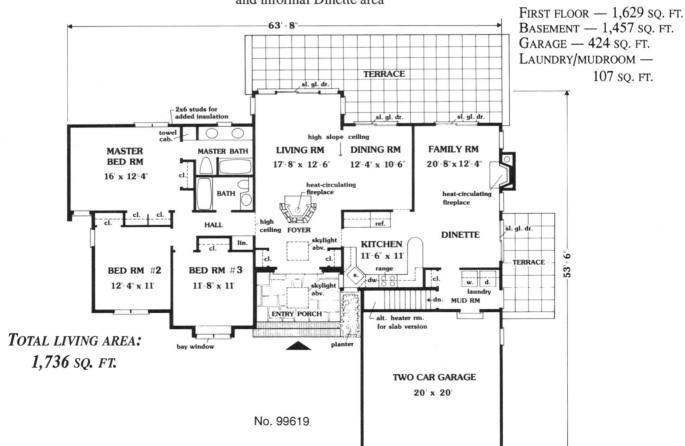

TOTAL LIVING AREA:
1,736 SQ. FT.

No. 99619

No. 99606

Pleasant Trellised Atrium Featured

■ This plan features:

— Three bedrooms

— Two full baths

■ A pleasant trellised atrium entrance

■ A high-sloped ceiling in the Living and Dining Rooms with a heat-circulating fireplace and window wall

■ A Family Room with door-height windows overlooking an atrium on one side and sliding glass doors on the other

■ An efficient fully equipped U-shaped Kitchen that adjoins the Family Room

■ A Master Suite with a large walk-in closet, and a basin in the dressing area

FIRST FLOOR — 1,660 SQ. FT.
LAUNDRY/MUDROOM — 64 SQ. FT.
GARAGE & STORAGE — 471 SQ. FT.

TOTAL LIVING AREA:
1,724 SQ. FT.

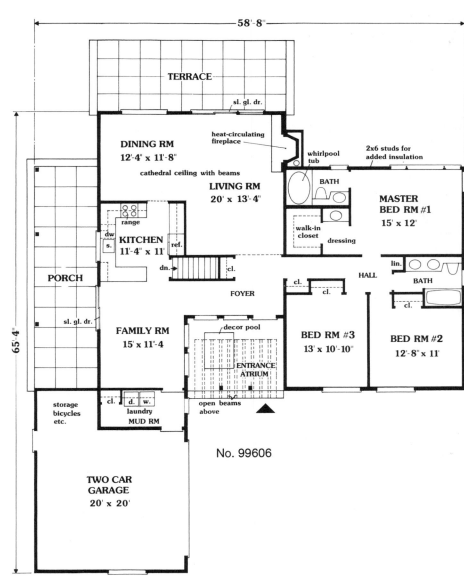

TERRACE

sl. gl. dr.

DINING RM
12'-4" x 11'-8"

cathedral ceiling with beams

heat-circulating fireplace

whirlpool tub

2x6 studs for added insulation

BATH

LIVING RM
20' x 13'-4"

MASTER BED RM #1
15' x 12'

range

walk-in closet

dressing

dw
s.

KITCHEN
11'-4" x 11'

ref.

lin.

PORCH

dn.

cl.

BATH

cl.

HALL

sl. gl. dr.

FOYER

cl.

cl.

cl.

FAMILY RM
15' x 11'-4"

decor pool

BED RM #3
13' x 10'-10"

BED RM #2
12'-8" x 11'

ENTRANCE ATRIUM

storage bicycles etc.

cl.

d. w.
laundry
MUD RM

open beams above

No. 99606

TWO CAR GARAGE
20' x 20'

58'-8"

65'-4"

No. 90098
Elegant English Tudor

■ This plan features:

— Three bedrooms

— Two and one half baths

■ Leaded glass windows, colored stucco, and half-timber creating a castle-like home

■ A tiled entry leading to a split-level combined Living/Dining Room area with an open end wood burning fireplace with raised hearth

■ A spacious Family Room for informal living

■ An efficient Kitchen with an eating bar that flows into the Dinette

■ A private, first floor Master Bedroom with his-and-her closets, dressing area, double vanity and a separate closet

■ Two upstairs bedrooms that share a full hall bath

■ A second floor Den with skylights

FIRST FLOOR — 1,720 SQ. FT.
SECOND FLOOR — 580 SQ. FT.
BASEMENT — 1,720 SQ. FT.

TOTAL LIVING AREA:
2,300 SQ. FT.

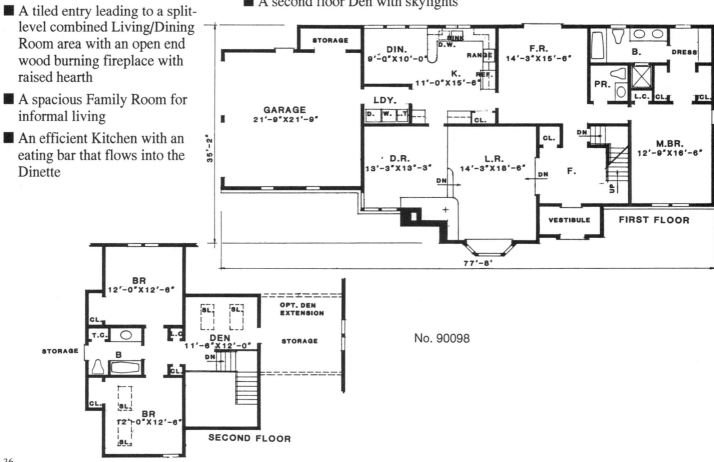

No. 90098

No. 90127

Spiral Stairs Lead to Loft

■ This plan features:

— Four bedrooms

— Two full baths

■ A large eat-in Kitchen easily serving the formal Dining Room or Great Room

■ A cathedral ceiling and cozy fireplace in the Great Room with sliding glass doors leading to patio

■ A Master Bedroom with a large Master Bath and two walk-in closets

■ Three additional bedrooms sharing a full hall bath

■ An optional basement or crawl space foundation — please specify when ordering

FIRST FLOOR — 2,093 SQ. FT.
LOFT AREA — 326 SQ. FT.

TOTAL LIVING AREA: 2,419 SQ. FT.

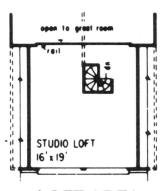

LOFT AREA

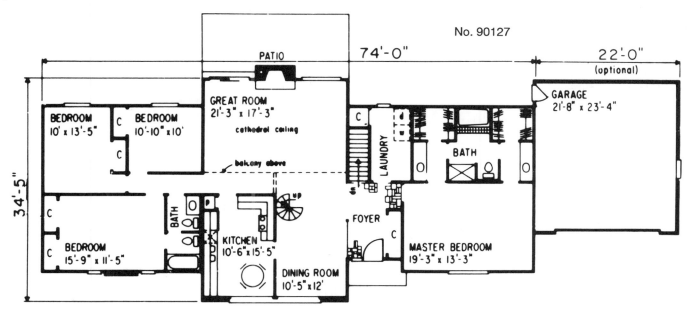

FIRST FLOOR WITH BASEMENT

No. 90390

Small Scale, Lots of Space

■ This plan features:

— Two bedrooms with possible third bedroom/den

— Two full baths

■ Vaulted ceilings and corner windows

■ A Living Room enhanced by cozy corner fireplace

■ A Master Suite featuring interesting angles and corner window treatments

FIRST FLOOR — 1,231 SQ. FT.

TOTAL LIVING AREA:
1,231 SQ. FT.

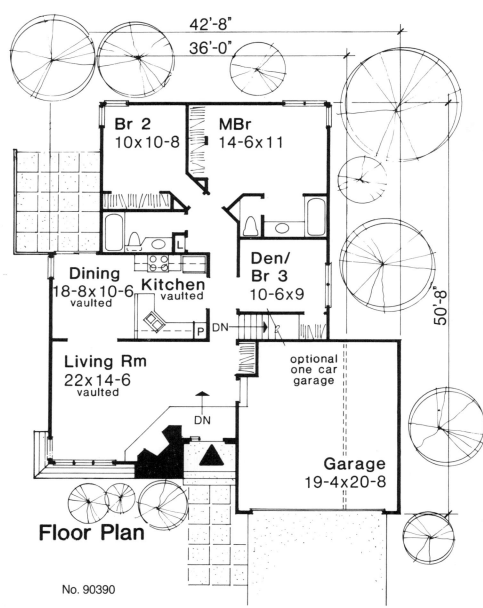

42'-8"

36'-0"

Br 2
10x10-8

MBr
14-6x11

Dining
18-8x10-6
vaulted

Kitchen
vaulted

Den/
Br 3
10-6x9

DN

Living Rm
22x14-6
vaulted

P

50'-8"

optional
one car
garage

DN

Garage
19-4x20-8

Floor Plan

No. 90390

No. 90990

Comfort and Style

■ This plan features:

— Two bedrooms (with possible third bedroom/den)

— Two full baths

■ Unfinished daylight basement providing possible space for family recreation

■ A Master Suite complete with private bath and skylight

■ A large Kitchen including an eating nook

■ A sundeck easily accessible from Master Suite, Nook and Living/Dining area

FIRST FLOOR — 1,423 SQ. FT.
BASEMENT — 1,423 SQ. FT.
GARAGE — 399 SQ. FT.
WIDTH — 46'-0"
DEPTH — 52'-0"

TOTAL LIVING AREA:
1,423 SQ. FT.

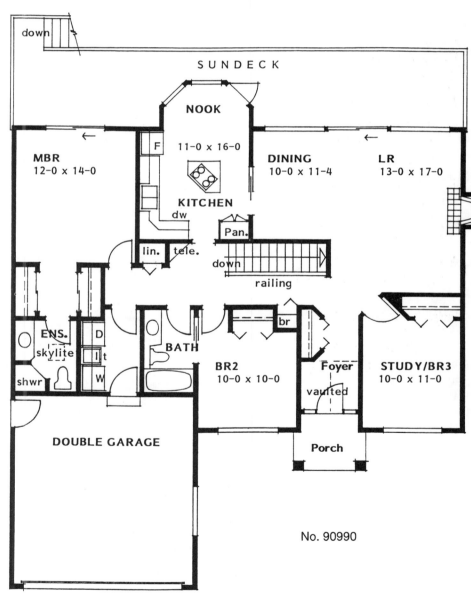

No. 90990

No. 90942
Built In Beauty

■ This plan features:

— Three bedrooms

— Three full baths

■ A huge, sunken Living Room with vaulted ceilings

■ A formal Dining Room overlooking the backyard

■ An open railing and a single stair separate the nook and the fire-placed Family Room

■ "Built Ins" throughout the house

■ An expansive Master Suite with private dressing room, walk-in closet, and double vanitied bath with step-in shower

FIRST FLOOR — 1,175 SQ. FT.
SECOND FLOOR — 776 SQ. FT.
BASEMENT — 1,165 SQ. FT.
GARAGE — 410 SQ. F.T

TOTAL LIVING AREA:
1,951 SQ. FT.

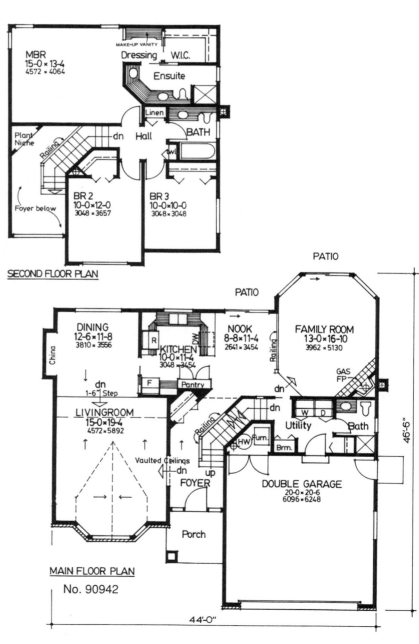

SECOND FLOOR PLAN

MBR
15-0 × 13-4
4572 × 4064

MAKE-UP VANITY
Dressing   W.I.C.
Ensuite
Linen
Plant Niche
Railing
dn   Hall
BATH
Foyer below
BR 2
10-0 ×12-0
3048 × 3657
BR 3
10-0 ×10-0
3048 × 3048

MAIN FLOOR PLAN
No. 90942

PATIO
PATIO
DINING
12-6 × 11-8
3810 × 3556
China
KITCHEN
10-0 ×11-4
3048 ×3454
R
DW
NOOK
8-8 ×11-4
2641 ×3454
FAMILY ROOM
13-0 ×16-10
3962 ×5130
GAS FP
Railing
F
Pantry
dn
1-6" Step
LIVINGROOM
15-0 ×19-4
4572 ×5892
Railing
dn
HW
Furn.
dn
W   D
Utility   Bath
Brm.
Vaulted Ceilings
FOYER
up
DOUBLE GARAGE
20-0 20-6
6096 ×6248
Porch
46-6"
44'-0"

No. 91448
An Elegant One Story Design

■ This plan features:

— Three bedrooms

— Two full baths

■ A barrel vaulted foyer opening into the vaulted Great Room

■ An open Kitchen/Nook featuring an optional pass through, a walk-in pantry, and an eating bar

■ A vaulted Master Suite with private bath, large walk-in closet, and covered patio

■ A Garage with storage/shop area with access to the home through the utility room

FIRST FLOOR — 1,800 SQ. FT.
BASEMENT — 1,800 SQ. FT.
GARAGE — 370 SQ. FT.

TOTAL LIVING AREA:
1,800 SQ. FT.

No. 91448

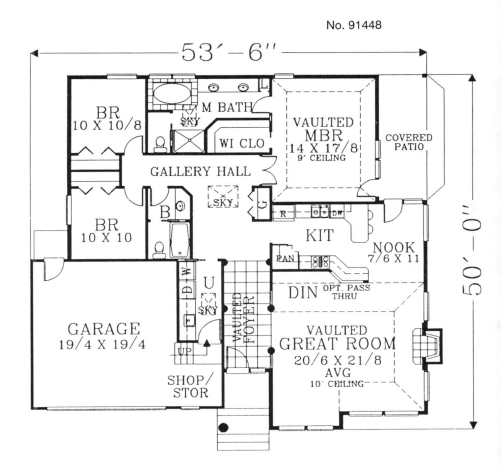

53'-6"

50'-0"

BR 10 X 10/8

M BATH

SKY

WI CLO

VAULTED MBR 14 X 17/8
9' CEILING

COVERED PATIO

GALLERY HALL

BR 10 X 10

B

SKY

SKY

R   DW

KIT

NOOK 7/6 X 11

GARAGE 19/4 X 19/4

D W

U

SKY

PAN

VAULTED FOYER

DIN   OPT. PASS THRU

UP

SHOP/ STOR

VAULTED GREAT ROOM 20/6 X 21/8 AVG
10' CEILING

No. 99626

A Traditional Farmhouse

■ This plan features:

— Four bedrooms

— Two full and one half baths

■ A decorative circular stairway enhancing the foyer

■ A heat-circulating fireplace in both the Family Room and the formal Living Room

■ An efficient, well-appointed Kitchen with a built-in pantry, double sinks and ample cabinet and counter space

■ A Master Suite equipped with a walk-in closet, and a large Master Bath

■ Three additional bedrooms that share a full hall bath

FIRST FLOOR — 1,183 SQ. FT.
SECOND FLOOR — 1,103 SQ. FT.
BASEMENT — 1,116 SQ. FT.
GARAGE & STORAGE — 467 SQ. FT.
PORCHES — 283 SQ. FT.

TOTAL LIVING AREA: 2,286 SQ. FT.

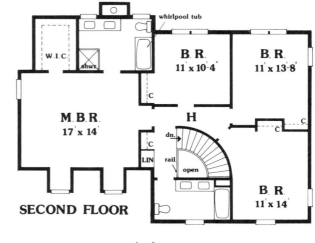

SECOND FLOOR

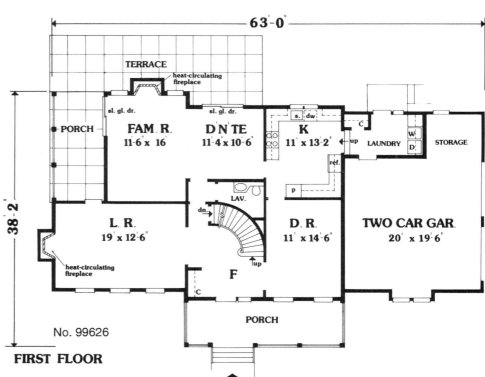

No. 99626

FIRST FLOOR

No. 90622

Two-Sink Baths Ease Rush

■ This plan features:

— Four bedrooms

— Two full and one half baths

■ A wood beam ceiling in the spacious Family Room

■ An efficient, island Kitchen with a sunny bay windowed dinette

■ A formal Living Room with a heat-circulating fireplace

■ A large Master Suite with a walk-in closet and a private Master Bath

■ Three additional bedrooms sharing a full hall bath

FIRST FLOOR — 983 SQ. FT.
SECOND FLOOR — 1,013 SQ. FT.
MUDROOM — 99 SQ. FT.
GARAGE — 481 SQ. FT.

TOTAL LIVING AREA: 2,095 SQ. FT.

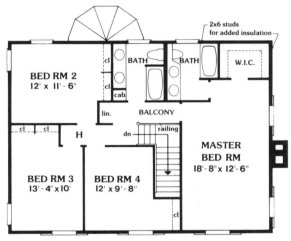

SECOND FLOOR PLAN

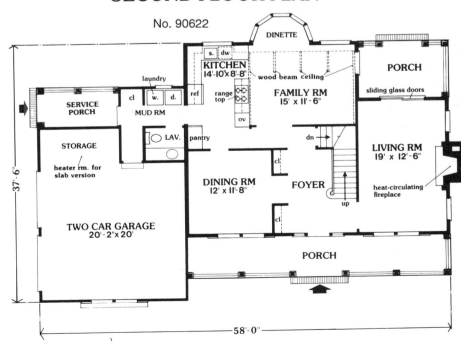

No. 90622

FIRST FLOOR PLAN

No. 90368

Lots of Living Space in Compact Design

■ This plan features:

— Two bedrooms with optional third bedroom/ den

— Two full baths

■ Flowing living spaces and yard views

■ A Master Suite including full bath and ample closet space

■ A Living and Dining Room combination enhanced by corner fireplace

FIRST FLOOR — 1,081 SQ. FT.

TOTAL LIVING AREA: 1,081 SQ. FT.

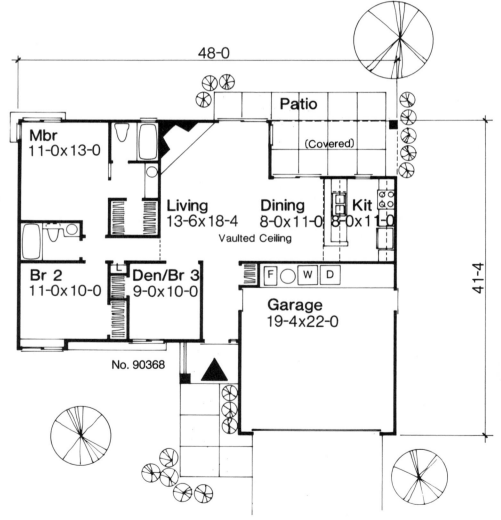

48-0

41-4

Patio

(Covered)

Mbr
11-0x13-0

Living
13-6x18-4

Vaulted Ceiling

Dining
8-0x11-0

Kit
8-0x11-0

Br 2
11-0x10-0

Den/Br 3
9-0x10-0

F ○ W D

Garage
19-4x22-0

No. 90368

No. 90436
Country Living in Any Neighborhood

■ This plan features:

— Three bedrooms

— Two full baths and two half baths

■ An expansive Family Room with fireplace

■ A Dining Room and Breakfast Nook lit by flowing natural light from bay windows

■ A first floor Master Suite with a double vanitied bath that wraps around his and her closets

■ An optional basement, slab or crawl space foundation — please specify when ordering

FIRST FLOOR — 1,477 SQ. FT.
SECOND FLOOR — 704 SQ. FT.
BASEMENT — 1,374 SQ. FT.

TOTAL LIVING AREA:
2,181 SQ. FT.

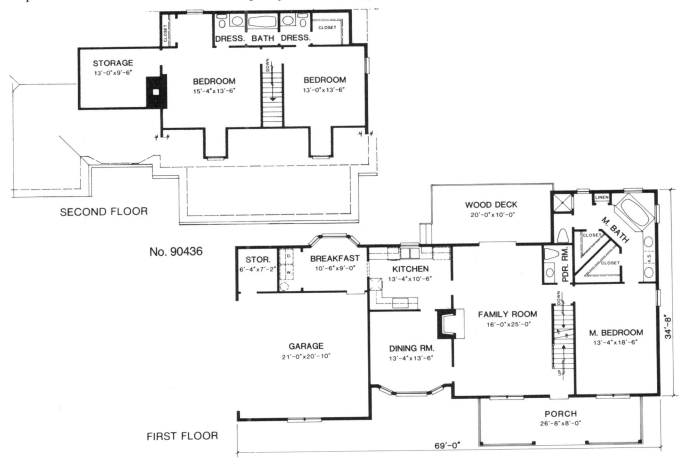

No. 90909

A Hint of Victorian Nostalgia

■ This plan features:

— Three bedrooms

— Two and one half baths

■ A classic center stairwell

■ A Kitchen with full bay window and built-in eating table

■ A spacious Master Suite including large walk-in closet and full bath

FIRST FLOOR — 1,206 SQ. FT.
SECOND FLOOR — 969 SQ. FT.
GARAGE — 471 SQ. FT.
BASEMENT — 1,206 SQ. FT.
WIDTH — 61'-0"
DEPTH — 44'-0"

TOTAL LIVING AREA:
2,175 SQ. FT.

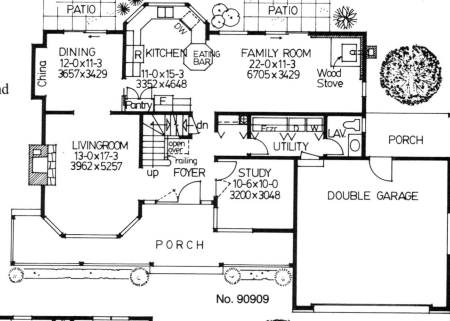

PATIO

PATIO

DINING
12-0×11-3
3657×3429

China

KITCHEN
11-0×15-3
3352×4648

EATING BAR

DW

FAMILY ROOM
22-0×11-3
6705×3429

Wood Stove

Pantry   F

LIVINGROOM
13-0×17-3
3962×5257

open over
railing

up   dn

FOYER

Frzr   D   W

UTILITY

LAV.

PORCH

STUDY
10-6×10-0
3200×3048

DOUBLE GARAGE

PORCH

No. 90909

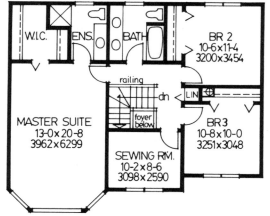

W.I.C.   ENS.   BATH

BR 2
10-6×11-4
3200×3454

railing

dn   LIN

MASTER SUITE
13-0×20-8
3962×6299

foyer below

BR 3
10-8×10-0
3251×3048

SEWING RM.
10-2×8-6
3098×2590

SECOND FLOOR

No. 90663

Circular Staircase Makes Stunning Impression

■ This plan features:

— Four bedrooms

— Two full baths

■ A sunny well-equipped Kitchen efficiently located near the Dinette and formal Dining Room

■ A spacious fireplaced Family Room

■ A bow window dressing up the Living Room and making it seem larger

■ A Master Suite with a walk-in closet and private Master Bath

FIRST FLOOR — 963 SQ. FT.
SECOND FLOOR — 892 SQ. FT.

TOTAL LIVING AREA: 1,855 SQ. FT.

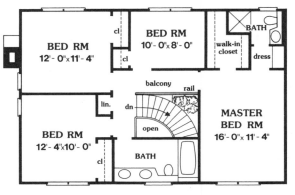

SECOND FLOOR PLAN

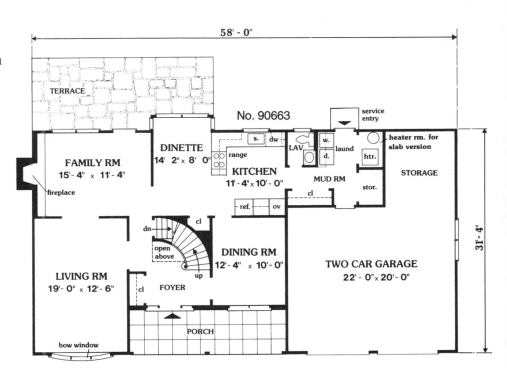

FIRST FLOOR PLAN

No. 99321
Nostalgia Returns

■ This plan features:

— Three bedrooms

— Two full baths

■ A half-round transom window with quarter-round detail and a vaulted ceiling in the Great Room

■ A cozy corner fireplace which brings warmth to the Great Room

■ A vaulted ceiling in the Kitchen/Breakfast area

■ A Master Suite with a walk-in closet and a private Master Bath

■ Two additional bedrooms which share a full hall bath

FIRST FLOOR — 1,368 SQ. FT.

TOTAL LIVING AREA: 1,368 SQ. FT.

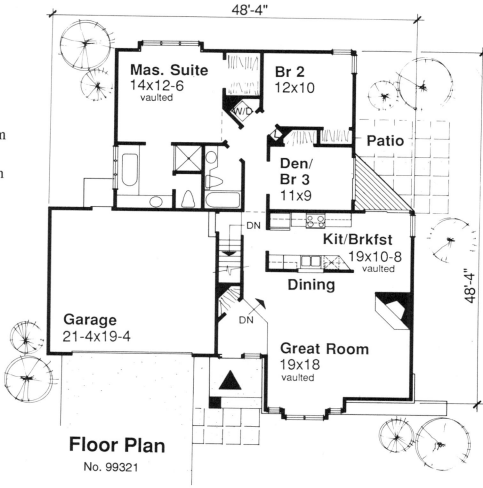

48'-4"

48'-4"

Mas. Suite
14x12-6
vaulted

Br 2
12x10

W/D

Patio

Den/
Br 3
11x9

DN

Kit/Brkfst
19x10-8
vaulted

Dining

Garage
21-4x19-4

DN

Great Room
19x18
vaulted

Floor Plan
No. 99321

No. 90329
Luxurious Master Suite

■ This plan features:

— Three bedrooms

— Two full and one half baths

■ A roomy Master Suite with an oversized corner tub, a shower, a walk-in closet, and a skylight

■ Two additional bedrooms that share a full hall bath

■ A Great Room with a vaulted ceiling, fireplace and a corner comprised of windows

■ A Dining Room with a wetbar and direct access to the large, eat-in Kitchen

■ A spacious Family Room with sliding glass doors to the deck

FIRST FLOOR — 904 SQ. FT.
SECOND FLOOR — 797 SQ. FT.
BASEMENT — 904 SQ. FT.
GARAGE — 405 SQ. FT.

TOTAL LIVING AREA:
1,701 SQ. FT.

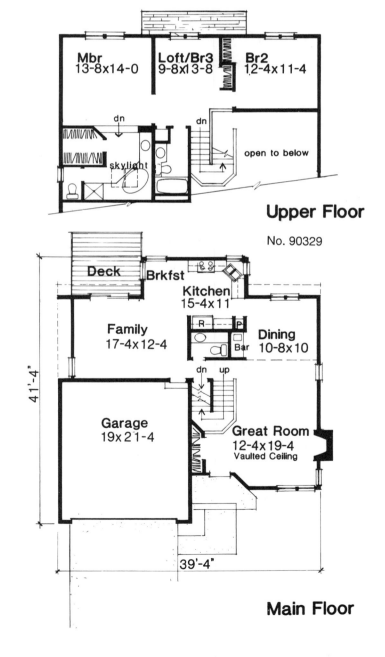

Upper Floor

No. 90329

Mbr
13-8x14-0

Loft/Br3
9-8x13-8

Br2
12-4x11-4

dn

dn

open to below

skylight

Deck

Brkfst

Kitchen
15-4x11

Family
17-4x12-4

R   P
Bar

Dining
10-8x10

dn up

Garage
19x21-4

Great Room
12-4x19-4
Vaulted Ceiling

41'-4"

39'-4"

Main Floor

No. 90387

Attractive and Affordable

■ This plan features:

— Three bedrooms

— One and a half baths

■ A country style Kitchen with a greenhouse window and pass-through convenience to the formal Dining Room

■ A fireplaced Living Room with vaulted ceiling

■ A full bath on the second floor with two-way access for convenience

FIRST FLOOR — 713 SQ. FT.
SECOND FLOOR — 691 SQ. FT.

TOTAL LIVING AREA: 1,404 SQ. FT.

No. 90387

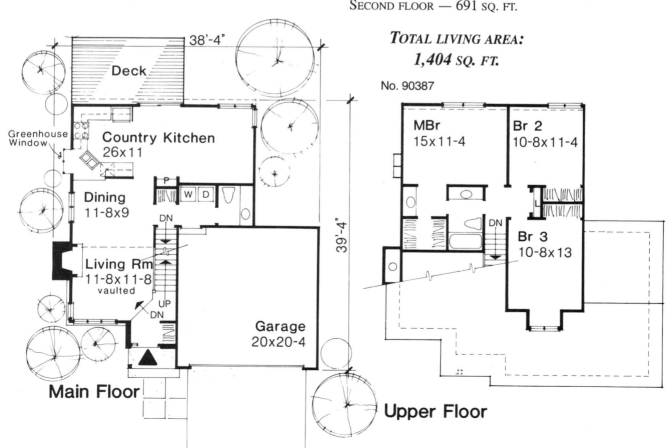

Greenhouse Window

Deck

38'-4"

Country Kitchen 26x11

Dining 11-8x9

P W D

DN

Living Rm 11-8x11-8 vaulted

UP
DN

Garage 20x20-4

39'-4"

Main Floor

MBr 15x11-4

Br 2 10-8x11-4

DN

Br 3 10-8x13

Upper Floor

No. 90360
Detailed Ranch Design

- **This plan features:**
  — Three bedrooms
  — Two full baths

- A breakfast area with a vaulted ceiling and access to the deck

- An efficient Kitchen with built-in pantry and appliances

- A Master bedroom with private bath and ample closet space

- A large Great Room with a vaulted ceiling and cozy fireplace

FIRST FLOOR — 1,283 SQ. FT.

TOTAL LIVING AREA:
1,283 SQ. FT.

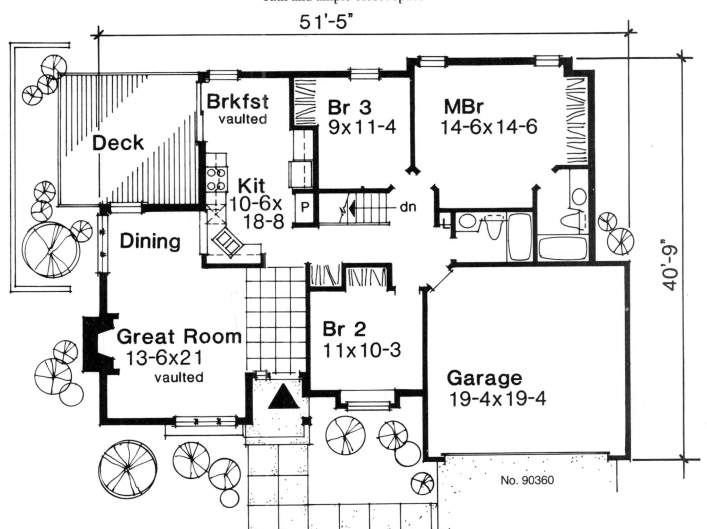

51'-5"

40'-9"

Deck

Brkfst
vaulted

Br 3
9x11-4

MBr
14-6x14-6

Kit
10-6x
18-8

P

dn

Dining

Great Room
13-6x21
vaulted

Br 2
11x10-3

Garage
19-4x19-4

No. 90360

No. 99327

Tradition Combined with Contemporary

■ This plan features:

— Three bedrooms

— Two full baths

■ A vaulted ceiling in the entry

■ A formal Living Room with a fireplace and a half-round transom

■ A Dining Room with sliders to the deck and easy access to the Kitchen

■ A main floor Master Suite with corner windows, walk-in closet and private bath access

■ Two additional bedrooms that share a full hall bath

FIRST FLOOR — 858 SQ. FT.
SECOND FLOOR — 431 SQ. FT.
BASEMENT — 858 SQ. FT.

TOTAL LIVING AREA: 1,289 SQ. FT.

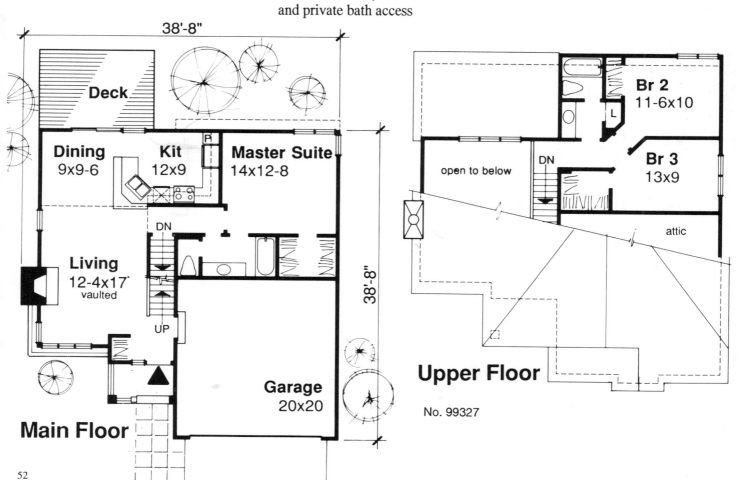

Main Floor

38'-8"

Deck

Dining 9x9-6

Kit 12x9

Master Suite 14x12-8

DN

Living 12-4x17 vaulted

UP

Garage 20x20

38'-8"

Upper Floor

Br 2 11-6x10

open to below

DN

Br 3 13x9

attic

No. 99327

No. 91418
Carefree Comfort

■ This plan features:

— Three bedrooms

— Two full baths

■ A dramatic vaulted foyer

■ A range top island Kitchen with a sunny eating Nook surrounded by a built-in planter

■ A vaulted ceiling in the Great Room with a built-in bar and corner fireplace

■ A bayed Dining Room that combines with the Great Room for a spacious feeling

■ A Master Bedroom with a private reading nook, vaulted ceiling, walk-in closet, and a well-appointed private bath

■ Two additional bedrooms sharing a full hall bath

FIRST FLOOR — 1,665 SQ. FT.
GARAGE — 2-CAR

TOTAL LIVING AREA:
1,665 SQ. FT.

ALTERNATE BASEMENT PLAN

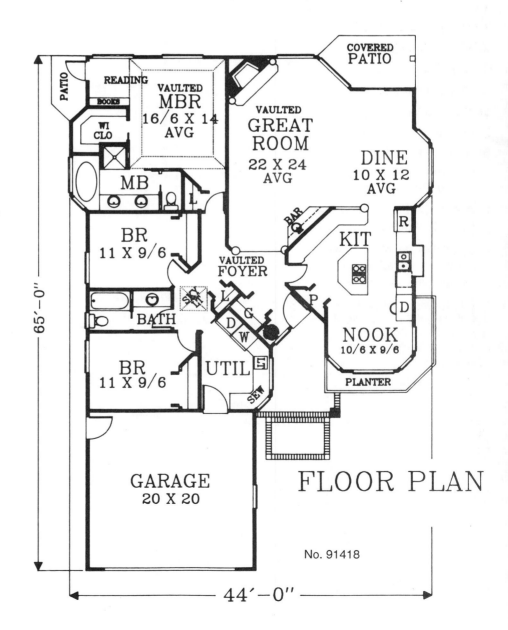

COVERED PATIO

PATIO

READING

BOOKS

VAULTED
MBR
16/6 X 14
AVG

WI CLO

MB

BR
11 X 9/6

VAULTED
GREAT
ROOM
22 X 24
AVG

DINE
10 X 12
AVG

BAR

KIT

R

VAULTED
FOYER

BATH

L

G

D W

P

NOOK
10/6 X 9/6

D

BR
11 X 9/6

UTIL

SEW

PLANTER

GARAGE
20 X 20

FLOOR PLAN

No. 91418

65' – 0"

44' – 0"

No. 90901

Great Traffic Pattern Highlights Home

■ This plan features:

— Three bedrooms

— Two full and one half baths

■ A sheltered entry leading to the two-story foyer

■ An island Kitchen with a convenient pass-through to the formal Dining Room

■ A cozy Living Room brightened by a bay window

■ A lovely Master Suite with a sitting area, walk-in closet and private bath

FIRST FLOOR — 940 SQ. FT.
SECOND FLOOR — 823 SQ. FT.
BASEMENT — 940 SQ. FT.
GARAGE — 440 SQ. FT.
WIDTH — 54'-0"
DEPTH — 33'-0"

TOTAL LIVING AREA:
1,763 SQ. FT.

SECOND FLOOR

No. 90901

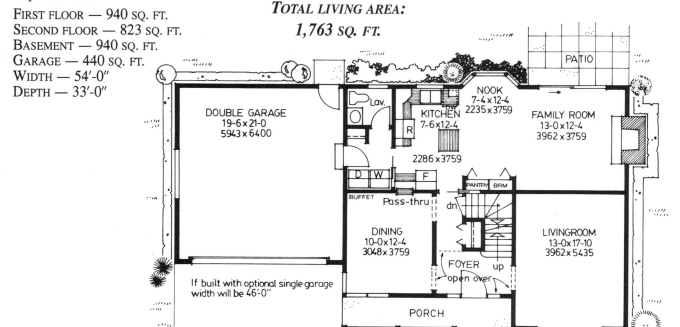

No. 90629

A Home For All Seasons

■ This plan features:

— Three bedrooms

— Three full and one half baths

■ All rooms with outdoor decks

■ A Living Room with a heat-circulating fireplace

■ A Kitchen with ample counter and cabinet space and easy access to Dining Room and outdoor dining area

■ A Master Bedroom with a heat-circulating fireplace, plush Master Bath and a walk-in closet

■ A basement foundation only

FIRST FLOOR — 1,001 SQ. FT.
SECOND FLOOR — 712 SQ. FT.
LOWER FLOOR — 463 SQ. FT.

TOTAL LIVING AREA: 2,176 SQ. FT.

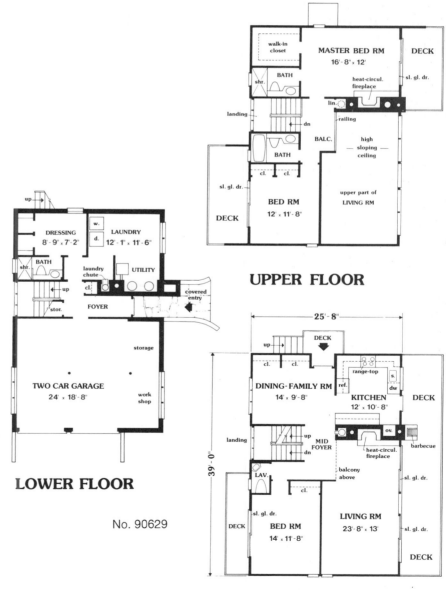

UPPER FLOOR

LOWER FLOOR

No. 90629

MAIN FLOOR

No. 90202

Multi-Level Home Includes a View from Every Room

■ This plan features:

— Four bedrooms

— Two full and one half baths

■ An L-shaped Living Room and Dining Room arrangement with a fireplace in the Living Room and sliders to the terrace in the Dining Room

■ A well-equipped Kitchen adjoining a sunny Nook which overlooks the backyard

■ Steps down to a Family Room with rustic exposed beams and a fireplace

■ A Master Bedroom equipped with a dressing room, walk-in closet, a private full bath and a balcony

FIRST FLOOR — 728 SQ. FT.
SECOND FLOOR — 874 SQ. FT.
LOWER LEVEL — 310 SQ. FT.

TOTAL LIVING AREA: 1,912 SQ. FT.

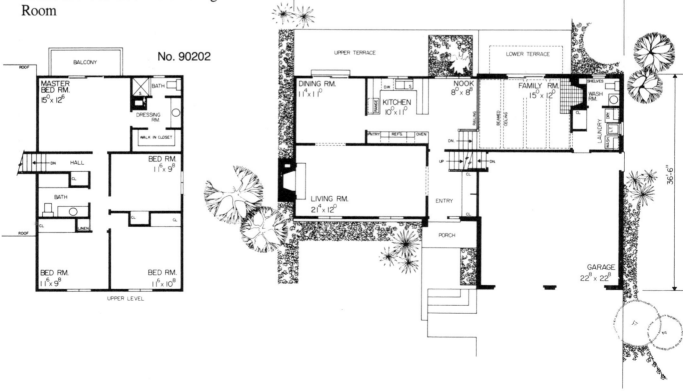

No. 90134

Extra Large Family Kitchen in Cozy Three Bedroom

■ This plan features:

— Three bedrooms

— One full and one half baths

■ A sheltered porch providing a protected entrance

■ An extra large Kitchen with a galley-style food preparation area separated from the rest of the room by an eating bar

■ Three bedrooms clustered around the full bath

■ A large outdoor storage area built-into the back of the carport

■ An optional basement, slab or crawl space foundation — please specify when ordering

FIRST FLOOR — 1,120 SQ. FT.

TOTAL LIVING AREA: *1,120 SQ. FT.*

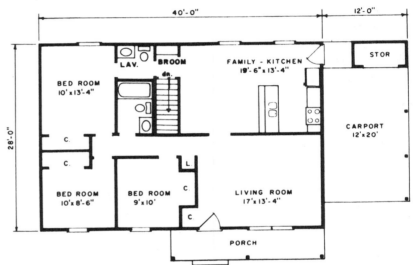

No. 90134

WITH BASEMENT

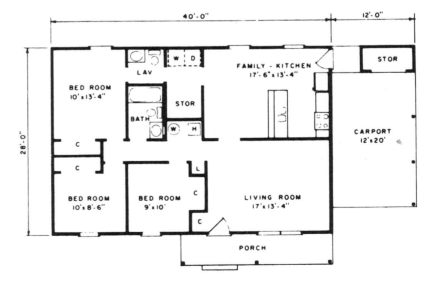

WITHOUT BASEMENT

No. 90357
High Impact Angles

■ This plan features:

— Three bedrooms

— Two full baths

■ Soaring ceilings to give the house a spacious, contemporary feeling

■ A fireplaced Great Room adjoining a convenient Kitchen with sunny Breakfast Nook

■ Sliding glass doors opening onto an angular deck

■ A Master Suite with vaulted ceilings and private bath

FIRST FLOOR — 1,368 SQ. FT.

TOTAL LIVING AREA:
1,368 SQ. FT.

48'-0"

48'-0"

Mbr
14x12-6
Vaulted Ceiling

Br2
12x10

L

Patio

Den/Br3
11x9

Dn

Kitchen/Brkfst
19x10-8

P

Dining

Garage
21-4x19-4

Dn

Great Room
19x18
Vaulted Ceiling

No. 90357

Main Floor Plan

No. 90378

Lots of Space in this Small Package

■ This plan features:

— Two bedrooms with possible third bedroom/den

— Two full baths

■ A Living Room with dynamic, soaring angles and fireplace

■ A first floor Master Suite with full bath and walk in-closet

■ Walk-in closets in all bedrooms

FIRST FLOOR — 878 SQ. FT.
SECOND FLOOR — 405 SQ. FT.

TOTAL LIVING AREA:
1,283 SQ. FT.

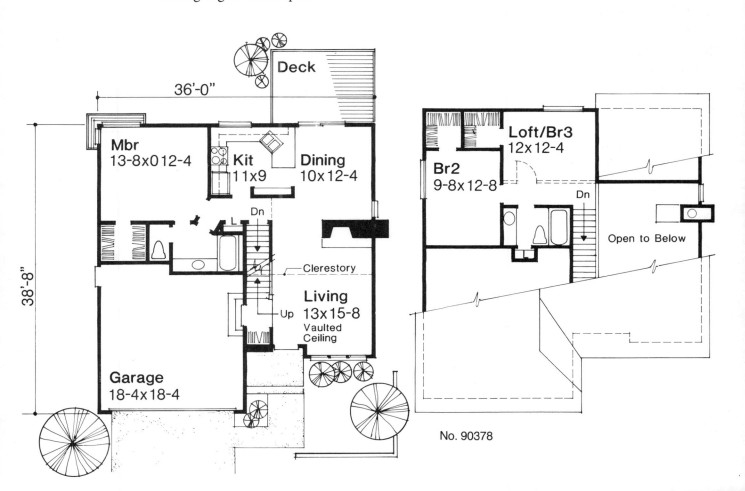

Deck

36'-0"

38'-8"

Mbr
13-8x012-4

Kit
11x9

Dining
10x12-4

Dn

Clerestory

Living
13x15-8
Vaulted Ceiling

Up

Garage
18-4x18-4

Loft/Br3
12x12-4

Br2
9-8x12-8

Dn

Open to Below

No. 90378

No. 90324

Flexible Plan Creates Many Options

■ This plan features:

— Two bedrooms with optional third bedroom/den

— Two full baths

■ A Great Room featuring vaulted ceiling, fireplace, and built-in bookcase

■ An eat-in Kitchen opening onto a partially enclosed deck through sliding doors

■ An L-shaped design of the Kitchen providing for easy meal preparation

■ A Master Bedroom with private bath, large walk-in closet, and window seat

FIRST FLOOR — 1,016 SQ. FT.

TOTAL LIVING AREA: 1,016 SQ. FT.

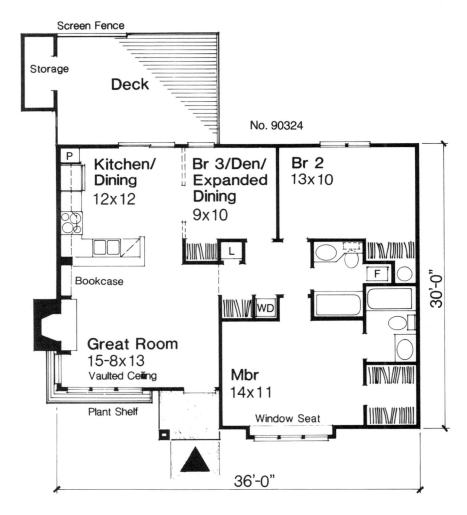

Screen Fence

Storage

Deck

No. 90324

P

Kitchen/ Dining
12x12

Br 3/Den/ Expanded Dining
9x10

Br 2
13x10

L

Bookcase

WD

F

Great Room
15-8x13
Vaulted Ceiling

Mbr
14x11

Plant Shelf

Window Seat

30'-0"

36'-0"

No. 90328

Open Plan Features Great Room and Exterior Options

■ This plan features:

— Three bedrooms

— Two full baths

■ A Great Room highlighted by a skylight and vaulted ceiling

■ An eat-in Kitchen with an efficient U-shaped work area

■ A Master Bedroom combining bath and dressing area

FIRST FLOOR — 1,400 SQ. FT.
BASEMENT — 1,350 SQ. FT.
GARAGE — 374 SQ. FT.

TOTAL LIVING AREA:
1,400 SQ. FT.

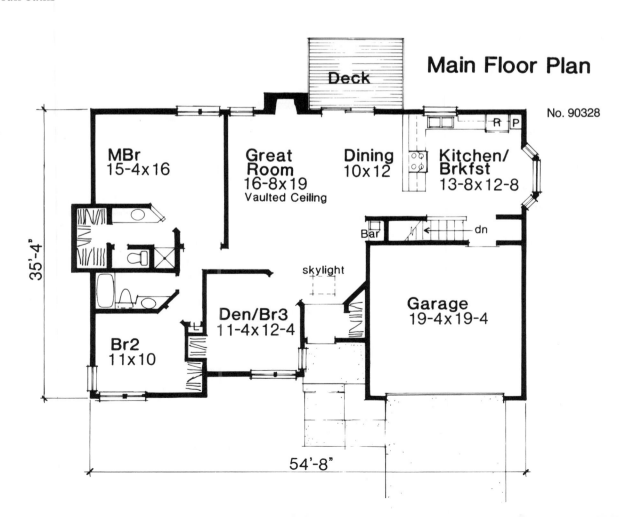

Main Floor Plan

No. 90328

Deck

MBr
15-4 x 16

Great Room
16-8 x 19
Vaulted Ceiling

Dining
10 x 12

Kitchen/ Brkfst
13-8 x 12-8

R P

Bar

dn

Br2
11 x 10

Den/Br3
11-4 x 12-4

skylight

Garage
19-4 x 19-4

35'-4"

54'-8"

No. 99216
Easy one floor living

■ This plan features:

— Three bedrooms

— Two full baths

■ Living areas conveniently grouped in the right half of the home for everyday activities

■ A Living Room with vaulted ceiling and fireplace

■ A Kitchen designed for easy cooking with a closet pantry, plenty of counter space, and cupboards

■ A third bedroom making a perfect home office or study

FIRST FLOOR — 1,521 SQ. FT.
BASEMENT — 1,521 SQ. FT.

TOTAL LIVING AREA: 1,521 SQ. FT.

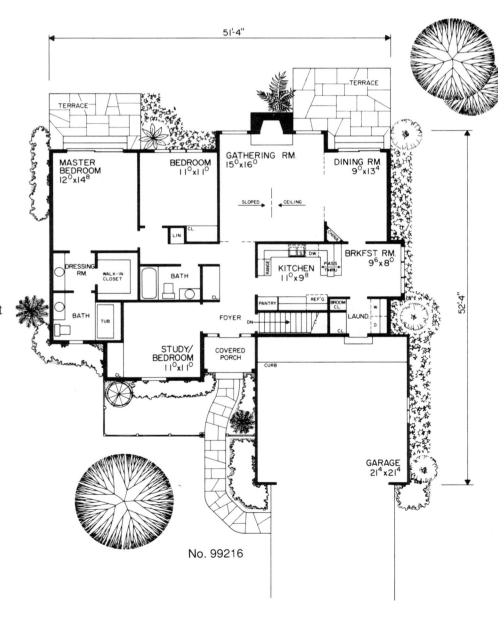

No. 99216

No. 90105
Great Room Features Fireplace

■ This plan features:

— Three bedrooms

— Two full baths

■ A spacious Great Room with a cozy fireplace

■ A Kitchen with a pass through serving for convenience

■ A combination Mud Room/Laundry to make cleaning up a breeze

■ An optional basement, slab or crawl space foundation — please specify when ordering

First floor — 1,345 sq. ft.

*TOTAL LIVING AREA:
1,345 SQ. FT.*

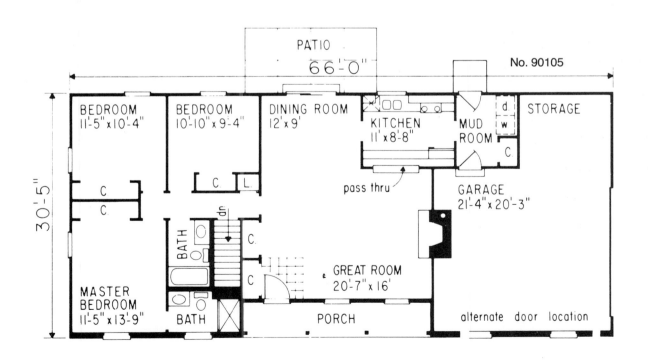

No. 91430
Open Concept Plan

■ This plan features:

— Three bedrooms

— Two full and one half baths

■ A vaulted ceiling in the Great Room with an overhead balcony

■ An island Kitchen efficiently flowing into the Breakfast Room

■ A Master Suite with a walk-in closet, private deck and a Master Bath

■ An additional bedroom on the second floor also with access to a private deck

■ A third bedroom off the Library with a bay window

FIRST FLOOR — 2,030 SQ. FT.
SECOND FLOOR — 1,409 SQ. FT.

TOTAL LIVING AREA:
3,439 SQ. FT.

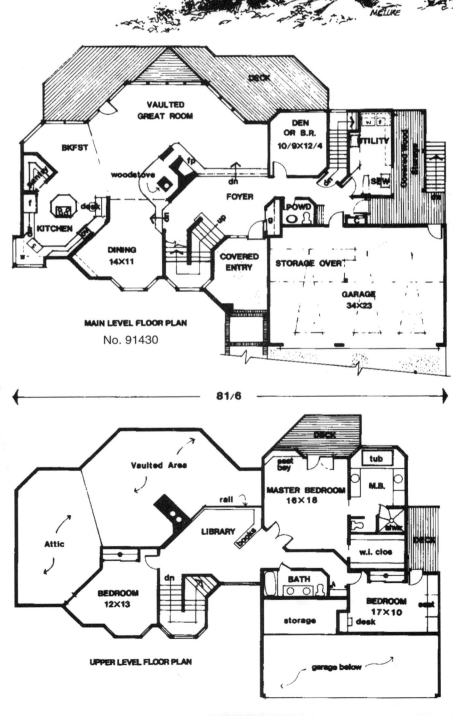

MAIN LEVEL FLOOR PLAN
No. 91430

UPPER LEVEL FLOOR PLAN

No. 91640

Gable and Glass Grace Facade

■ This plan features:

— Four bedrooms

— Two full and one half baths

■ A Sun Room that opens directly into the Family Room

■ A modern wrap-around Kitchen with a central island

■ A large front window in the formal Living Room which flows directly into the formal Dining Room

■ A spacious Master Suite with a huge walk-in closet and private Master Bath

■ Three additional bedrooms served by full hall bath

FIRST FLOOR — 1,540 SQ. FT.
SECOND FLOOR — 1,178 SQ. FT.
BONUS ROOM — 222 SQ. FT.

TOTAL LIVING AREA: 2,718 SQ. FT.

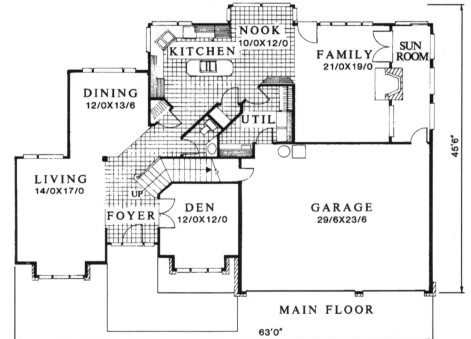

No. 91640

KITCHEN
NOOK 10/0X12/0
FAMILY 21/0X19/0
SUN ROOM
DINING 12/0X13/6
UTIL
LIVING 14/0X17/0
UP
FOYER
DEN 12/0X12/0
GARAGE 29/6X23/6
45'6"
63'0"
MAIN FLOOR

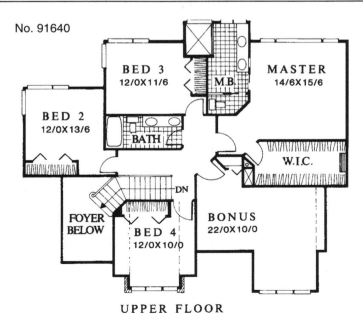

BED 3 12/0X11/6
M.B.
MASTER 14/6X15/6
BED 2 12/0X13/6
BATH
W.I.C.
DN
FOYER BELOW
BED 4 12/0X10/0
BONUS 22/0X10/0

UPPER FLOOR

No. 90840

Eye-Catching Elevation

■ This plan features:

— Four bedrooms

— Three full baths

■ A cozy Family Room with a fireplace and sunny bayed window

■ A Living Room enhanced by a fireplace and bay window

■ A U-shaped Kitchen efficiently located just steps away from the Dining Room and Nook

■ A Master Suite with an ample double closet and a private Master Bath

■ Each additional bedroom located next to a full hall bath

FIRST FLOOR — 1,510 SQ. FT.
LOWER FLOOR — 1,253 SQ. FT.

TOTAL LIVING AREA: 2,763 SQ. FT.

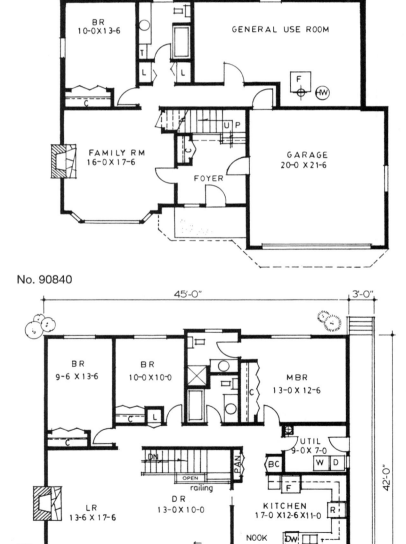

No. 90840

No. 90838
Room to Grow

■ This plan features:

— Three bedrooms

— Three full baths

■ A corner gas fireplace in the spacious Living Room

■ A Master Suite including a private bath with a whirlpool tub, separate shower and double vanity

■ An island Kitchen that is well-equipped to efficiently serve both formal Dining Room and informal Nook

■ Two additional bedrooms sharing a full bath on the second floor

FIRST FLOOR — 1,778 SQ. FT.
SECOND FLOOR — 799 SQ. FT.

TOTAL LIVING AREA: 2,577 SQ. FT.

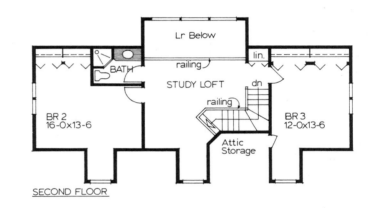

SECOND FLOOR

Lr Below

BATH

railing

STUDY LOFT

lin.

dn

railing

BR 2
16-0x13-6

Attic
Storage

BR 3
12-0x13-6

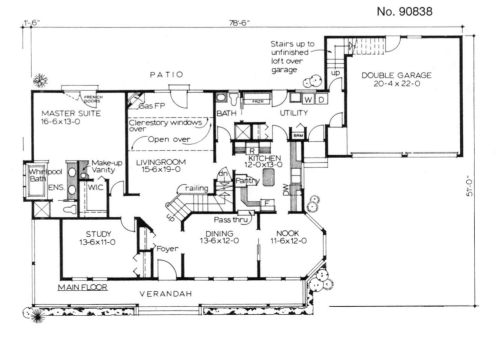

No. 90838

1'-6"

78'-6"

PATIO

Stairs up to
unfinished
loft over
garage

up

DOUBLE GARAGE
20-4 x 22-0

FRENCH
DOORS

Gas FP

BATH

FRZR

W D

UTILITY

MASTER SUITE
16-6 x 13-0

Clerestory windows
over

Open over

BRM

51'-0"

Whirlpool
Bath

ENS.

Make-up
Vanity

WIC

LIVINGROOM
15-6 x 19-0

dn

railing

R

KITCHEN
12-0x13-0

Pantry

DW

F

Pass thru

STUDY
13-6x11-0

Foyer

DINING
13-6x12-0

NOOK
11-6x12-0

MAIN FLOOR

VERANDAH

No. 90678

Cozy Home Keeps Budget in Check

■ This plan features:

— Three bedrooms

— Two full baths

■ A natural cedar and stone exterior

■ A roomy, well appointed Kitchen

■ A Master Suite enjoying the luxury of a private bath and double closets

FIRST FLOOR — 1,183 SQ. FT.

TOTAL LIVING AREA: 1,183 SQ. FT.

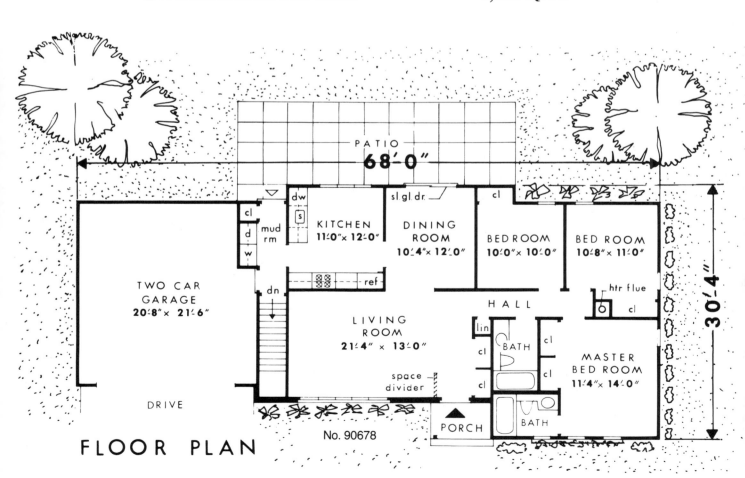

PATIO

68'-0"

30'-4"

cl

dw
s

KITCHEN
11'-0" x 12'-0"

sl. gl. dr.

DINING ROOM
10'-4" x 12'-0"

cl

BED ROOM
10'-0" x 10'-0"

BED ROOM
10'-8" x 11'-0"

cl

mud rm

d
w

ref

dn

TWO CAR GARAGE
20'-8" x 21'-6"

LIVING ROOM
21'-4" x 13'-0"

htr flue

cl

HALL

lin

cl

cl

BATH

cl

cl

MASTER BED ROOM
11'-4" x 14'-0"

space divider

cl

BATH

DRIVE

PORCH

BATH

FLOOR PLAN

No. 90678

No. 90264

Good Things Come in Small Packages

■ This plan features:

— Three bedrooms

— Two and one half baths

■ A bonus space over the Garage

■ An entry opening to a fireplaced Living Room

■ A Dining Room overlooking the backyard

■ A Kitchen spacious enough for informal family meals

FIRST FLOOR — 624 SQ. FT.
SECOND FLOOR — 624 SQ. FT.

TOTAL LIVING AREA:
1,248 SQ. FT.

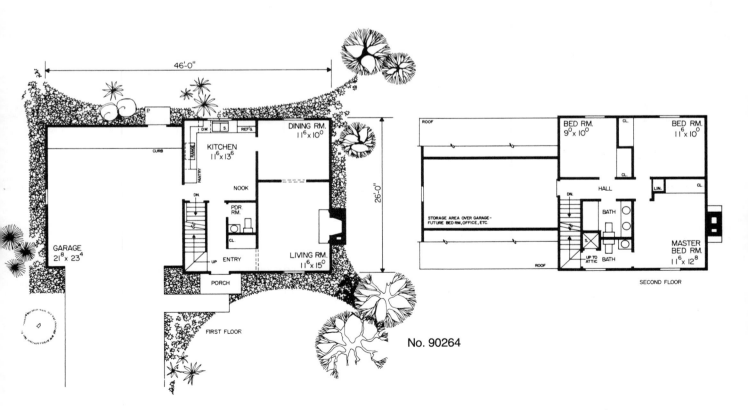

No. 90264

No. 91002
Above Reproach

■ This plan features:

— Three bedrooms

— One and one half baths

■ Firedrum fireplace warming both entryway and Living Room

■ Dining and Living Rooms opening onto deck that surrounds the house on three sides

■ A crawl space foundation

FIRST FLOOR — 744 SQ. FT.
SECOND FLOOR — 288 SQ. FT.

TOTAL LIVING AREA:
1,032 SQ. FT.

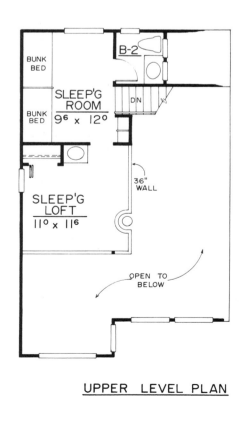

UPPER LEVEL PLAN

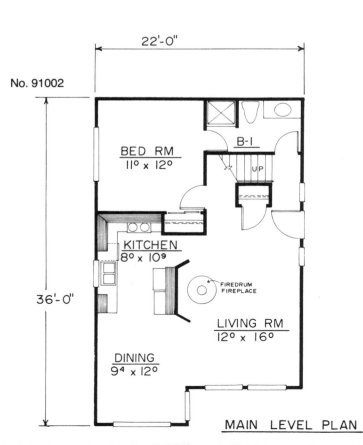

MAIN LEVEL PLAN

No. 91731
Country Style Charm

■ This plan features:

— Three bedrooms

— Two full baths

■ Brick accents, front facing gable, and railed wrap-around covered porch

■ A built-in range and oven in a dog-leg shaped Kitchen

■ A Nook with Garage access for convenient unloading of groceries and other supplies

■ A bay window wrapping around the front of the formal Living Room

■ A Master Suite with French doors opening to the deck

FIRST FLOOR — 1,775 SQ. FT.
GARAGE — 681 SQ. FT.

TOTAL LIVING AREA: 1,775 SQ. FT.

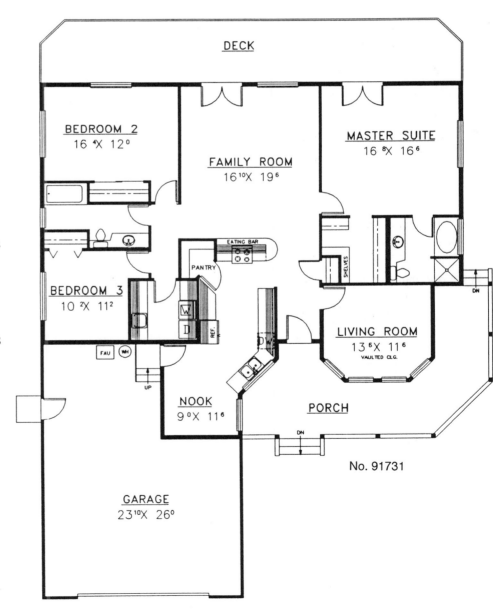

DECK

BEDROOM 2
16⁴X 12⁰

FAMILY ROOM
16¹⁰X 19⁶

MASTER SUITE
16⁸X 16⁶

EATING BAR

PANTRY

BEDROOM 3
10²X 11²

SHELVES

LIVING ROOM
13⁵X 11⁶
VAULTED CLG.

REF.

FAU   WH

UP

DN

NOOK
9⁰X 11⁶

PORCH

DN

No. 91731

GARAGE
23¹⁰X 26⁰

No. 90613
Year Round Retreat

■ This plan features:

— Three bedrooms

— Two full baths

■ A Living Room with a dramatic sloping ceiling and a wood burning stove

■ A Kitchen and Living Room opening onto the rear deck

■ A Master Suite with a full bath, linen closet and ample closet space

■ An optional slab foundation

FIRST FLOOR — 960 SQ. FT.
SECOND FLOOR — 465 SQ. FT.

TOTAL LIVING AREA:
1,425 SQ. FT.

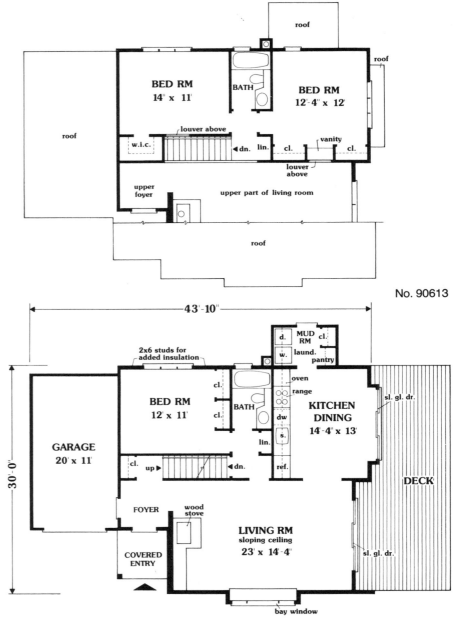

No. 90613

No. 90980

Compact Country Charmer

■ This plan features:

— Four bedrooms

— Two full baths

■ The option of being a vacation home or permanent residence

■ A covered upper deck and lower patio

■ Large windows in the open Kitchen, Dining and Living Rooms

■ A finished basement including two bedrooms and a Family Room

FIRST FLOOR — 884 SQ. FT.
BASEMENT — 884 SQ. FT.
WIDTH — 34'-0"
DEPTH — 31'-0"

TOTAL LIVING AREA: 1,768 SQ. FT.

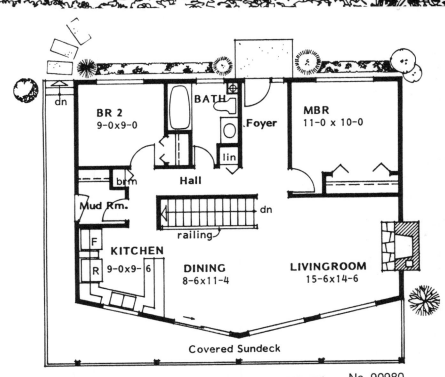

No. 90980

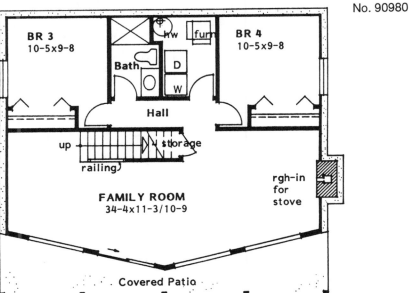

No. 99360

Empty-Nester Plan

- This plan features:

— Three bedrooms

— Two full and one half baths

- A spacious Family Room with a fireplace

- A well-appointed Kitchen with step-in pantry, corner double sinks and a sunny Breakfast bay

- A Master Suite with a vaulted ceiling, walk-in closet and private Master Bath

- A Living Room/Dining Room combination with vaulted ceiling and corner fireplace

- Two additional bedrooms having ample closet space and sharing use of a full bath

FIRST FLOOR — 1,538 SQ. FT.
SECOND FLOOR — 465 SQ. FT.

TOTAL LIVING AREA:
2,003 SQ. FT.

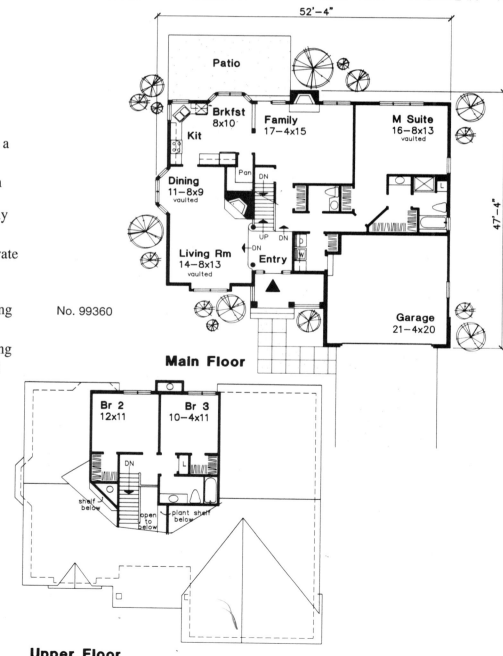

No. 99360

Main Floor

Upper Floor

No. 99349
For the Growing Family

■ This plan features:

— Three bedrooms

— Two full baths

■ A split-entry

■ A Kitchen with peninsula counter, corner double sink, built-in pantry and sunny Breakfast area

■ A formal Dining Room in close proximity to the Kitchen

■ A formal Living Room with a fireplace and access to the patio through sliders

■ A Master Suite with a vaulted ceiling, walk-in closet, and private Master Bath

■ Two additional bedrooms that share a full hall bath

FIRST FLOOR — 1,549 SQ. FT.
BASEMENT — 700 SQ. FT.
GARAGE — 640 SQ. FT.

TOTAL LIVING AREA: 1,549 SQ. FT.

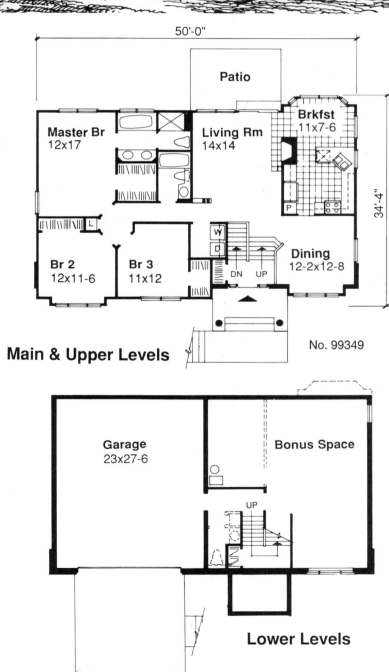

Patio

Master Br
12x17

Living Rm
14x14

Brkfst
11x7-6

P

Br 2
12x11-6

Br 3
11x12

W
D

DN UP

Dining
12-2x12-8

50'-0"

34'-4"

Main & Upper Levels

No. 99349

Garage
23x27-6

Bonus Space

UP

Lower Levels

No. 91407

Vertical Siding Adds Contemporary Appeal

■ This plan features:

— Three bedrooms

— Two and one half baths

■ An entry flanked by dramatic vaulted Living Room

■ Informal areas at the rear of house commanding an expansive view of backyard

■ A unique, open arrangement of the rangetop island Kitchen

■ U-shaped stairs, just across from the handy powder room leading to a balcony

FIRST FLOOR — 1,153 SQ. FT.
SECOND FLOOR — 787 SQ. FT.
GARAGE — 537 SQ. FT.

TOTAL LIVING AREA:
1,940 SQ. FT.

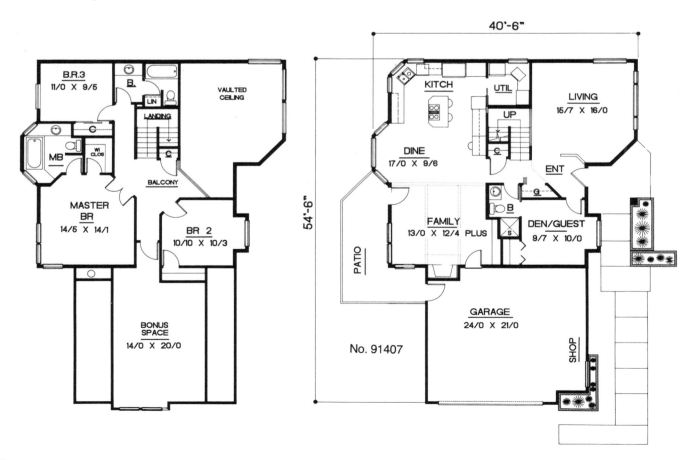

No. 91312
Small but Spacious

■ This plan features:

— Three bedrooms

— Two and one half baths

■ A spacious entry dominated by an open staircase

■ A fireplaced Family Room adjoining a bay windowed Breakfast Nook off the Kitchen

■ A sunken Living Room featuring a corner window arrangement

■ A compact Kitchen at the rear of the house convenient to both eating areas

FIRST FLOOR — 879 SQ. FT.
SECOND FLOOR — 746 SQ. FT.

TOTAL LIVING AREA:
1,625 SQ. FT.

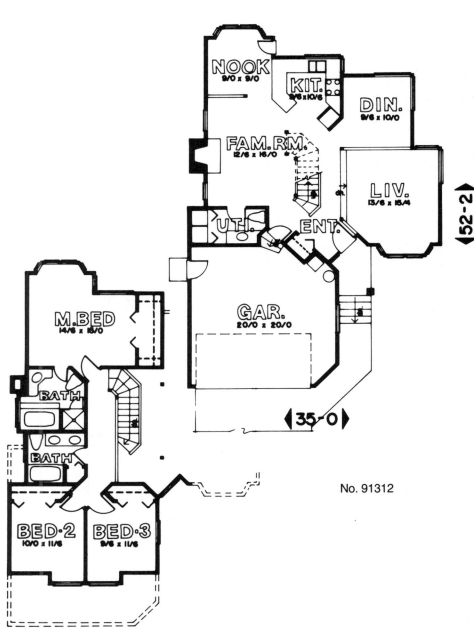

No. 91312

No. 99605

A Country Estate

■ This plan features:

— Four bedrooms

— Two full and one half baths

■ A decorative circular stair and curved corners in the foyer

■ A sunken Living Room with a heat-circulating fireplace and a tray ceiling

■ A Family Room with a heat-circulating fireplace

■ A fully equipped Kitchen with a built-in pantry and ample counter space

■ A formal Dining Room and a Dinette eating area

■ A Master Suite with a private study, walk-in closet and lavish Master Bath

■ Three additional bedrooms that share a full hall bath

FIRST FLOOR — 1,273 SQ. FT.
SECOND FLOOR — 1,416 SQ. FT.

TOTAL LIVING AREA: 2,689 SQ. FT.

SECOND FLOOR

No. 99605

FIRST FLOOR

No. 90608
New England Tradition

■ This plan features:

— Three bedrooms

— Three full baths

■ A Dining and Living Room that flow into each other for easy entertaining

■ A U-shaped Kitchen with an efficient layout, peninsula counter, and easy access to both formal and informal areas

■ A Master Suite with a walk-in closet and private, plush Master Bath

■ Two additional bedrooms that share a full hall bath

FIRST FLOOR — 1,195 SQ. FT.
SECOND FLOOR — 840 SQ. FT.

TOTAL LIVING AREA: 2,035 SQ. FT.

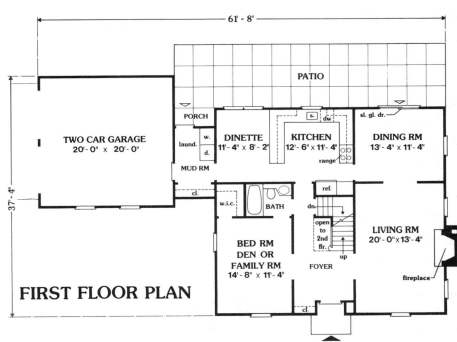

FIRST FLOOR PLAN

61' - 8"

37' - 4"

TWO CAR GARAGE
20' - 0" x 20' - 0"

PATIO

PORCH

DINETTE
11' - 4" x 8' - 2"

KITCHEN
12' - 6" x 11' - 4"

DINING RM
13' - 4" x 11' - 4"

laund.

MUD RM

range

BATH

w.i.c.

BED RM
DEN OR
FAMILY RM
14' - 8" x 11' - 4"

ref.

open to 2nd flr.

dn.

up

FOYER

LIVING RM
20' - 0" x 13' - 4"

fireplace

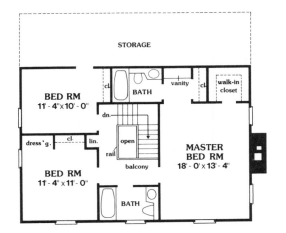

SECOND FLOOR PLAN

No. 90608

STORAGE

BED RM
11' - 4" x 10' - 0"

cl.

BATH

vanity

cl.

walk-in closet

dn.

dress'g.

cl.

lin.

open

rail

balcony

BED RM
11' - 4" x 11' - 0"

BATH

MASTER
BED RM
18' - 0" x 13' - 4"

No. 91404

Master Suite Features Private Deck

■ This plan features:

— Four bedrooms

— Three full baths

■ A curving stairway surrounded by a two-story bay window

■ A sunken Great Room united with the outdoors by three magnificent window walls

■ A bayed formal Dining Room located efficiently close to the Kitchen

■ A well-appointed Kitchen that flows into a sunny eating Nook

■ A Master Bedroom with a private deck, walk-in closet, and a lavish Master Bath

FIRST FLOOR — 1,550 SQ. FT.
SECOND FLOOR — 1,001 SQ. FT.
GARAGE — 750 SQ. FT.

TOTAL LIVING AREA: 2,551 SQ. FT.

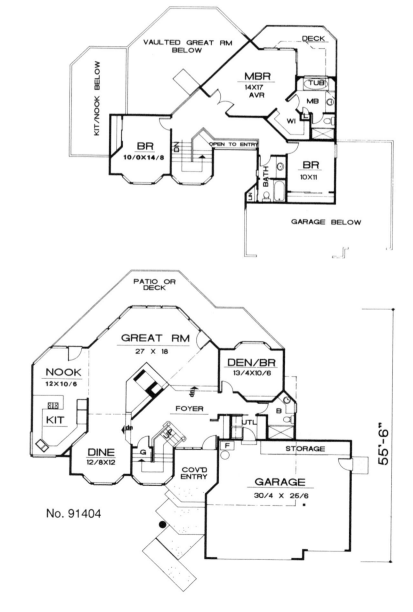

No. 91404

No. 91402

Contemporary Energy-Saver

■ This plan features:

— Three bedrooms

— Two full baths

■ A dramatic Living Room dominated by a huge arched window

■ A sky-lit Kitchen that opens to the Family/Dining Room

■ A wood stove between the Living and Family Rooms

■ A Master Bedroom with a private Master Bath

FIRST FLOOR — 1,154 SQ. FT.
SECOND FLOOR — 585 SQ. FT.
GARAGE — 516 SQ. FT.

TOTAL LIVING AREA: 1,739 SQ. FT.

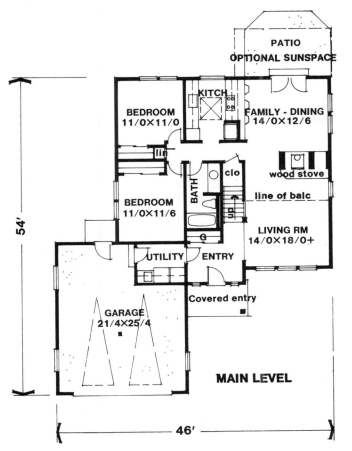

PATIO
OPTIONAL SUNSPACE

KITCH

BEDROOM
11/0×11/0

FAMILY - DINING
14/0×12/6

lin

BATH

clo

wood stove

line of balc

BEDROOM
11/0×11/6

up

LIVING RM
14/0×18/0+

UTILITY

ENTRY

Covered entry

GARAGE
21/4×25/4

54'

46'

MAIN LEVEL

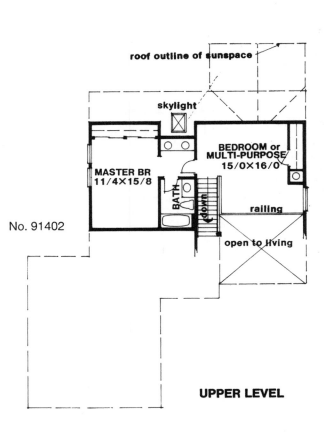

roof outline of sunspace

skylight

No. 91402

MASTER BR
11/4×15/8

BATH

down

BEDROOM or
MULTI-PURPOSE
15/0×16/0

railing

open to living

UPPER LEVEL

No. 90418

House with a View

■ This plan features:

— Three bedrooms

— Two full baths

■ A large, open Living Room accented by a fireplace and open stairs to the second floor

■ Access to the Garage through the Utility Room which adjoins Kitchen

■ A large Master Bedroom with a private bath and dressing area, one wall of closets, and access to a private patio

■ An optional basement, slab or crawl space foundation — please specify when ordering

FIRST FLOOR — 1,304 SQ. FT.
SECOND FLOOR — 303 SQ. FT.

TOTAL LIVING AREA: 1,607 SQ. FT.

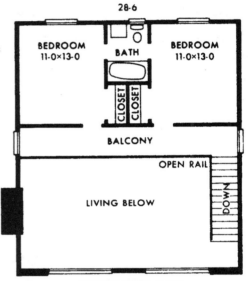

SECOND FLOOR

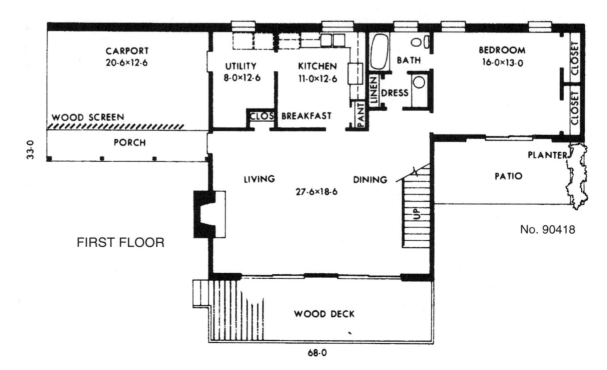

FIRST FLOOR

No. 90418

No. 90171
Versatile Chalet

■ This plan features:

— Three bedrooms

— One full bath

■ A rustic, shingled exterior giving a deep woods charm

■ A large Living Room, with a stone fireplace, joining the deck through sliding doors

■ An efficient Kitchen keeping cleanup to a minimum

■ An optional basement, crawl space or pier/beam foundation — please specify when ordering

FIRST FLOOR — 780 SQ. FT.
SECOND FLOOR — 500 SQ. FT.
BASEMENT — 780 SQ. FT.

TOTAL LIVING AREA:
1,280 SQ. FT.

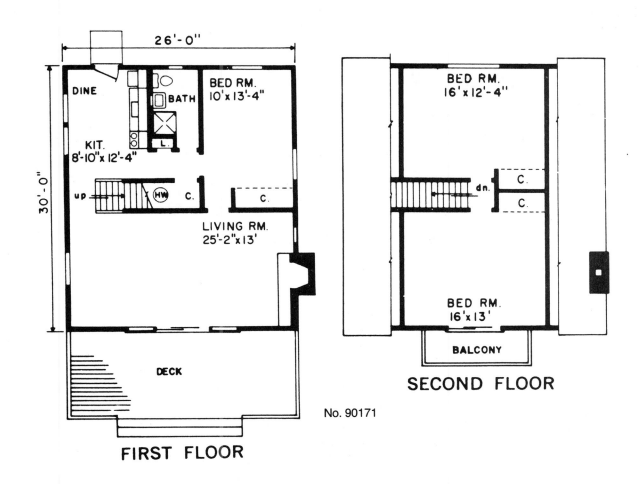

26'-0"

30'-0"

DINE

KIT.
8'-10" x 12'-4"

BATH

BED RM.
10' x 13'-4"

up

HW

C.

C.

L.

LIVING RM.
25'-2" x 13'

DECK

FIRST FLOOR

BED RM.
16' x 12'-4"

dn.

C.

C.

BED RM.
16' x 13'

BALCONY

SECOND FLOOR

No. 90171

No. 90125

Open Floor Plan Enhanced by Sloped Ceilings

■ This plan features:

— Three bedrooms

— Two full baths

■ A step down into the tiled entrance area

■ An open Great Room and Living Room enhanced by sloping ceilings, cozy fireplace, and sliding doors to back patio

■ An L shaped Kitchen sharing snack bar with Dining Room

■ An optional basement or crawlspace foundation — please specify when ordering

FIRST FLOOR — 1,440 SQ. FT.

TOTAL LIVING AREA: 1,440 SQ. FT.

No. 90125

No. 90131

Impressive Use of Space

■ This plan features:

— Three bedrooms

— Two full baths

■ A Great Room with sloped ceilings rising two stories

■ A Master Bedroom with a balcony, double closets and private bath

■ An L-shaped Kitchen located conveniently between Dining Area and Garage

■ A Kitchen also including built-in grill and sliding doors to patio

■ An optional basement, slab or crawl space foundation — please specify when ordering

FIRST FLOOR — 1,320 SQ. FT.
SECOND FLOOR — 444 SQ. FT.

**TOTAL LIVING AREA:
1,764 SQ. FT.**

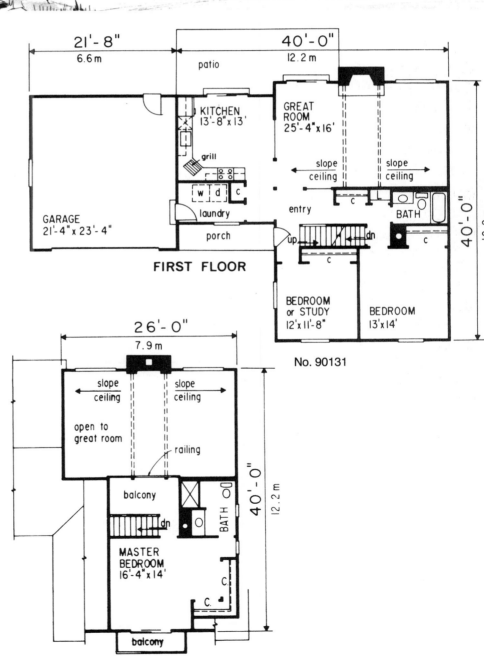

FIRST FLOOR

No. 90131

No. 90158

Compact Plan Allows for Gracious Living

■ This plan features:

— Three bedrooms

— Two full baths

■ A Great Room accessible from foyer offering cathedral ceilings, exposed beams, and brick fireplace

■ A Kitchen with a center island and cathedral ceiling accented by round top window

■ A Master Bedroom with full bath and walk-in closet

■ An optional basement, slab or crawl space foundation — please specify when ordering

FIRST FLOOR — 1,540 SQ. FT.
BASEMENT — 1,540 SQ. FT.

*TOTAL LIVING AREA:
1,540 SQ. FT.*

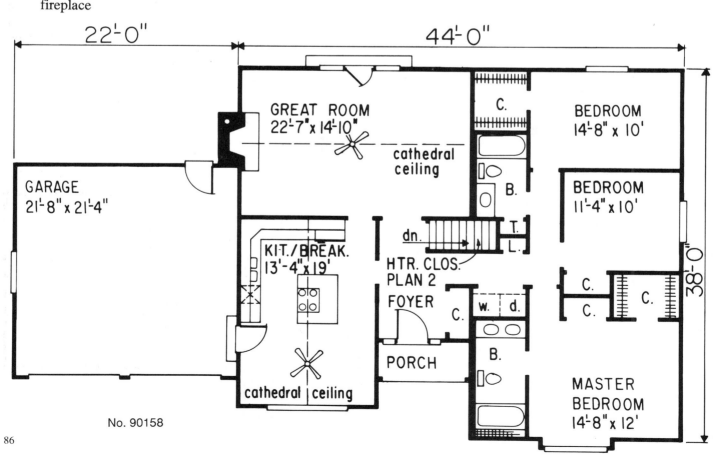

No. 90158

No. 91766

Design for a Slope that Falls Off to the Back

■ This plan features:

— Three bedrooms

— Two and one half baths

■ A design made for a sloping lot

■ A main floor including Garage, Master Suite, and family living areas

■ A wide window bay, brightening the formal Dining area of the combined Living/Dining area

■ Eating areas designed to take full advantage of back yard views

FIRST FLOOR — 1,125 SQ. FT.
LOWER FLOOR — 918 SQ. FT.
GARAGE — 588 SQ. FT.

TOTAL LIVING AREA: 2,043 SQ. FT.

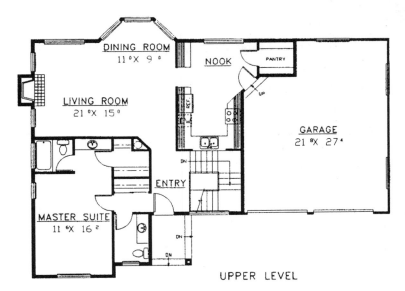

UPPER LEVEL

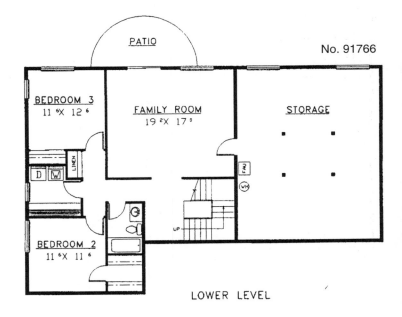

No. 91766

LOWER LEVEL

No. 90353

Living Room Features Vaulted Ceiling

■ This plan features:

— Three bedrooms

— Two full baths

■ A vaulted ceiling in the Living Room and the Dining Room with a clerestory above

■ A Master Bedroom with a walk-in closet and private full bath

■ An efficient Kitchen with a corner double sink and peninsula counter

■ A Dining Room with sliding doors to the deck

■ A Living Room with a fireplace to add warmth to open areas

■ Two additional bedrooms that share a full hall bath

FIRST FLOOR — 846 SQ. FT.
SECOND FLOOR — 400 SQ. FT.

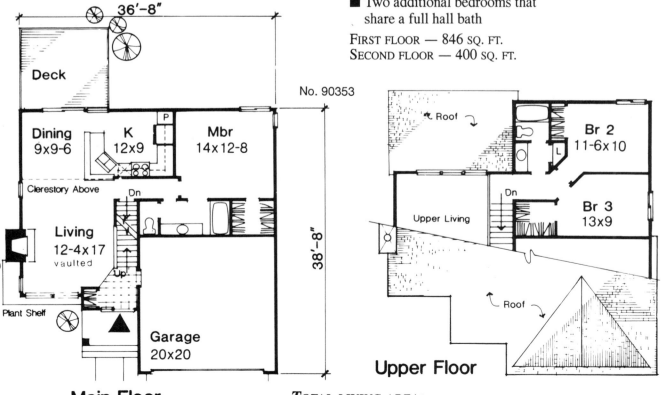

36'-8"

Deck

Dining
9x9-6

K
12x9

P

Mbr
14x12-8

Clerestory Above

Dn

Living
12-4x17
vaulted

Up

Plant Shelf

Garage
20x20

38'-8"

Main Floor

No. 90353

Roof

Br 2
11-6x10

Dn

Upper Living

Br 3
13x9

Roof

Upper Floor

TOTAL LIVING AREA:
1,246 SQ. FT.

No. 99315

Lattice Trim Adds Nostalgic Charm

■ This plan features:

— Three bedrooms

— Two and one half baths

■ Wood and fieldstone exterior

■ A vaulted Living Room with balcony view and floor to ceiling corner window treatment

■ A Master Suite with private bath and dressing area

■ A two car Garage with access to Kitchen

FIRST FLOOR — 668 SQ. FT.
SECOND FLOOR — 691 SQ. FT.

**TOTAL LIVING AREA:
1,359 SQ. FT.**

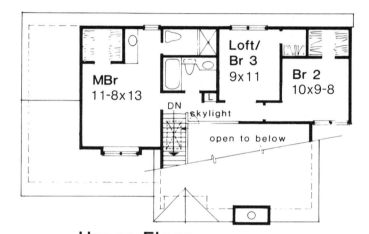

Upper Floor

No. 99315

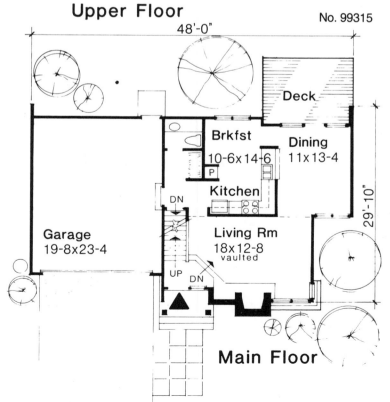

Main Floor

No. 90601
Varied Roof Heights Create Interesting Lines

■ This plan features:

— Three bedrooms

— Two full baths

■ A spacious Family Room with a heat-circulating fireplace which is visible from the Foyer

■ A large Kitchen with a cook top island opens into the dinette bay

■ A Master Suite with his and her closets and a private Master Bath

■ Two additional bedrooms which share a full hall bath

■ Formal Dining and Living Rooms flowing into each other for easy entertaining

FIRST FLOOR — 1,613 SQ. FT.

TOTAL LIVING AREA: 1,613 SQ. FT.

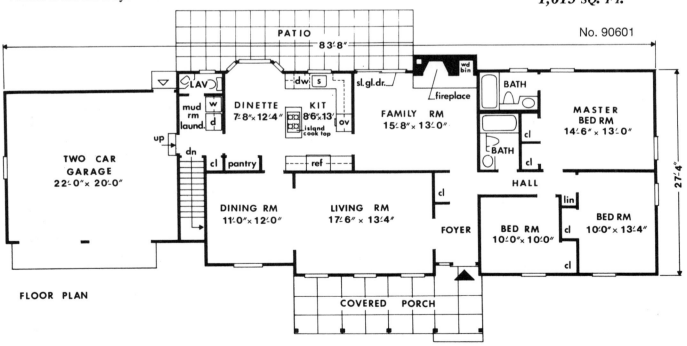

FLOOR PLAN

No. 90610
Zoned for Comfort

■ This plan features:

— Three bedrooms

— Two full baths

■ A spacious Kitchen with a built-in pantry, ample cabinet and counter space and a sunny Breakfast area

■ A large Family Room with a fireplace and sliding doors to a covered porch

■ A Master Suite with a walk-in closet and a private Bath

■ Two additional bedrooms with ample closet space and access to the full hall bath

■ A Dining and Living Room laid out for ease in entertaining

FIRST FLOOR — 1,771 SQ. FT.

TOTAL LIVING AREA:
1,771 SQ. FT.

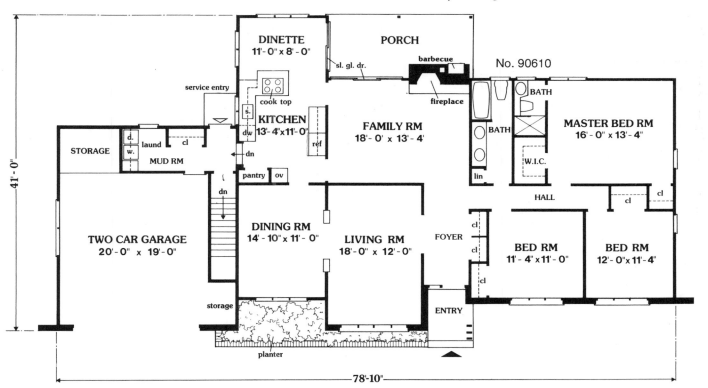

No. 99303

Captivating Sun-Catcher

■ This plan features:

— Two bedrooms

— Two full baths

■ A glass-walled Breakfast Room adjoining the vaulted-ceiling Kitchen

■ A fireplaced, vaulted ceiling Living Room that flows from the Dining Room

■ A greenhouse window over the tub in the luxurious Master Bath

■ Two walk-in closets and glass sliders in the Master Bedroom

FIRST FLOOR — 1,421 SQ. FT.

TOTAL LIVING AREA: 1,421 SQ. FT.

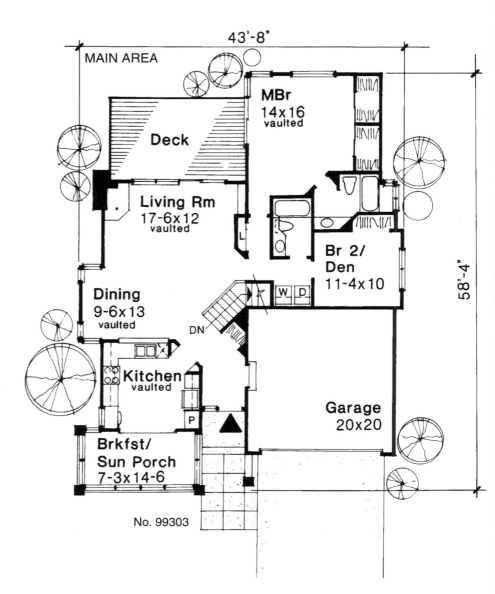

MAIN AREA

43'-8"

58'-4"

MBr
14x16
vaulted

Deck

Living Rm
17-6x12
vaulted

Br 2/
Den
11-4x10

Dining
9-6x13
vaulted

DN

W D

Kitchen
vaulted

P

Garage
20x20

Brkfst/
Sun Porch
7-3x14-6

No. 99303

No. 99354

Inviting Columned Entranceway

■ This plan features:

— Three bedrooms

— Two and one half baths

■ A vaulted ceiling Living Room with a fireplace that flows into the formal Dining Room, also with vaulted ceiling

■ A Master Suite with a walk-in closet and private Master Bath

■ Two additional upstairs bedrooms that share a full bath

FIRST FLOOR — 1,112 SQ. FT.
SECOND FLOOR — 490 SQ. FT.
BASEMENT — 1,112 SQ. FT.
GARAGE — 387 SQ. FT.

TOTAL LIVING AREA: 1,602 SQ. FT.

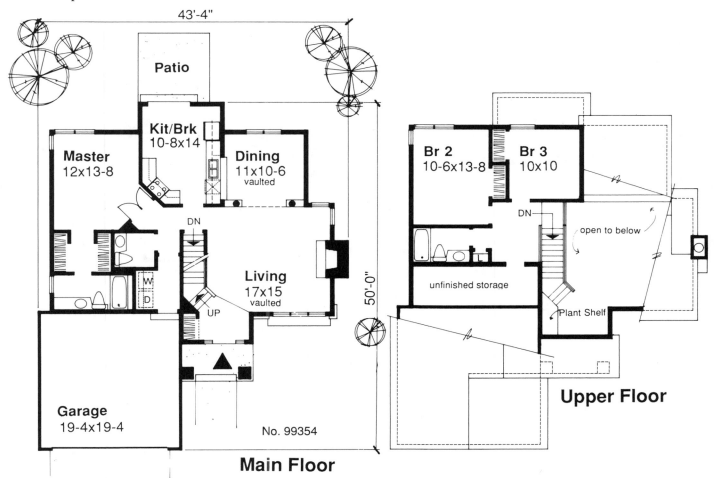

Main Floor

43'-4"

Patio

Kit/Brk
10-8x14

Master
12x13-8

Dining
11x10-6
vaulted

DN

Living
17x15
vaulted

UP

W
D

Garage
19-4x19-4

50'-0"

No. 99354

Upper Floor

Br 2
10-6x13-8

Br 3
10x10

DN

open to below

unfinished storage

Plant Shelf

No. 90558

Twin Fireplaces Add Traditional Warmth

■ This plan features:

— Three bedrooms

— Three full baths

■ A vaulted ceiling in the entry, Living Room and Dining Room

■ A range-top island Kitchen with sunny eating Nook and a built-in pantry

■ A Family Room with the cozy warmth of a wood stove

■ Sky-lit baths with double vanities

■ A Master Suite having a private sitting nook as well as a walk-in closet and a private bath

FIRST FLOOR — 1,460 SQ. FT.
SECOND FLOOR — 1,005 SQ. FT.

TOTAL LIVING AREA: 2,465 SQ. FT.

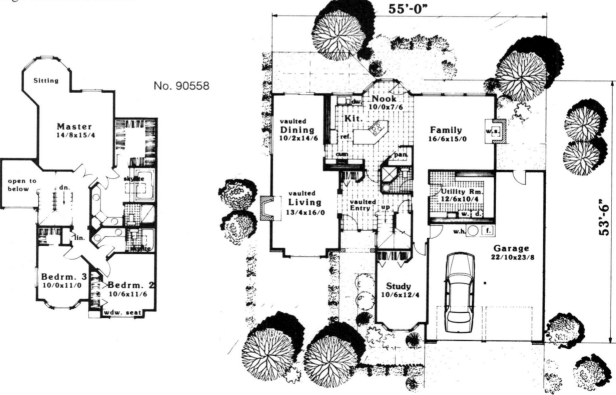

No. 90558

No. 90334

Contemporary Offers Sunken Living Room

■ This plan features:

— Four bedrooms

— Two full and one half baths

■ A built-in Greenhouse

■ A sunken Living Room with a vaulted ceiling and masonry fireplace

■ An efficient Kitchen with a connecting Breakfast Room appearing larger because of the vaulted ceiling

■ A wetbar and wood burning fireplace in the Family Room

■ A Master Bedroom with his/hers walk-in closets, a whirlpool bath surrounded by tile and a cathedral ceiling with circle-top windows

FIRST FLOOR — 1,382 SQ. FT.
SECOND FLOOR — 1,328 SQ. FT.

TOTAL LIVING AREA: 2,710 SQ. FT.

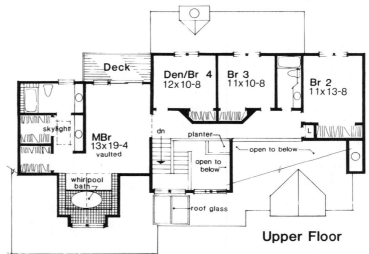

Upper Floor

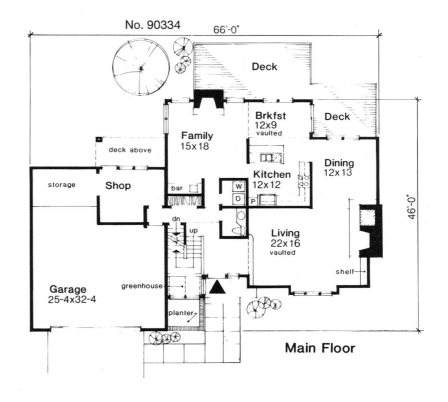

Main Floor

No. 90557

Soaring Entry Opens Family Plan

■ This plan features:

— Three bedrooms

— Two full and one half baths

■ A sunny, island Kitchen with a Breakfast nook opening to the Family Room

■ A Family Room accentuated by a lovely fireplace

■ A Living and Dining Room having vaulted ceilings enhancing spacious feeling

■ A Master Suite with a private Master Bath and a walk-in closet

■ Two additional bedrooms sharing a full hall bath

FIRST FLOOR — 1,475 SQ. FT.
SECOND FLOOR — 1,060 SQ. FT.

TOTAL LIVING AREA:
2,535 SQ. FT.

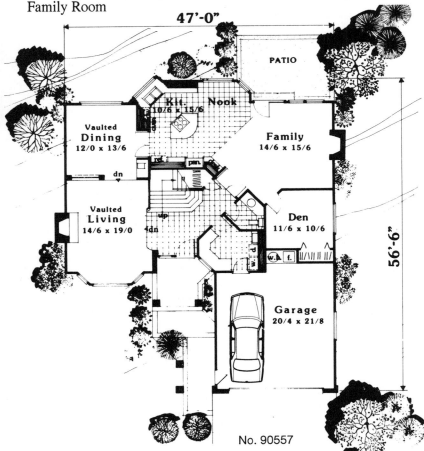

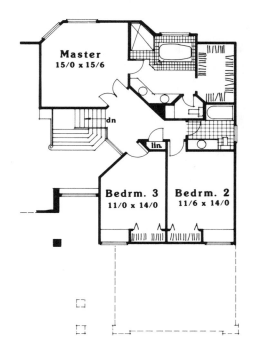

No. 90557

No. 90541

Hillside Excitement

■ This plan features:

— Three bedrooms

— Two full baths

■ An expansive island Kitchen with a sunny Breakfast Bay

■ An elegant formal Dining Room right off the Kitchen for ease in serving

■ A comfortable Family Room with a cozy fireplace

■ A Living Room enhanced by sunny bay windows and a fireplace

■ A luxurious Master Suite with a compartmentalized bath including a raised tub and step-in shower

FIRST FLOOR — 2,174 SQ. FT.

TOTAL LIVING AREA: 2,174 SQ. FT.

crawlspace

Garage
23/0x29/6

No. 90541

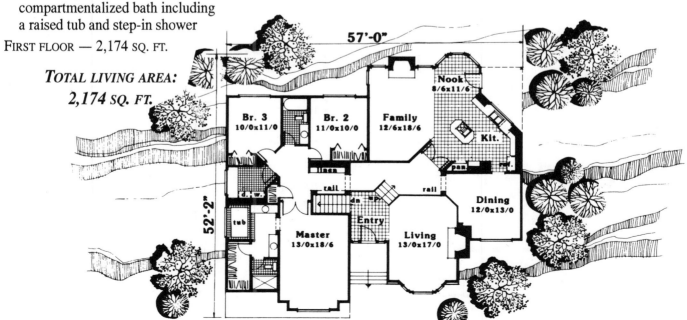

57'-0"

52'-2"

Nook
8/6x11/6

Br. 3
10/0x11/0

Br. 2
11/0x10/0

Family
12/6x18/6

Kit.

Master
13/0x18/6

Entry

Living
13/0x17/0

Dining
12/0x13/0

No. 90682

Inviting Porch Adorns Affordable Home

■ This plan features:

— Three bedrooms

— Two full baths

■ A large and spacious Living Room that adjoins the Dining Room for ease in entertaining

■ A private bedroom wing offering a quiet atmosphere

■ A Master Bedroom with his and her closets and a private bath

■ An efficient Kitchen with a walk-in pantry

FIRST FLOOR — 1,160 SQ. FT.
LAUNDRY/MUDROOM — 83 SQ. FT.

TOTAL LIVING AREA:
1,243 SQ. FT.

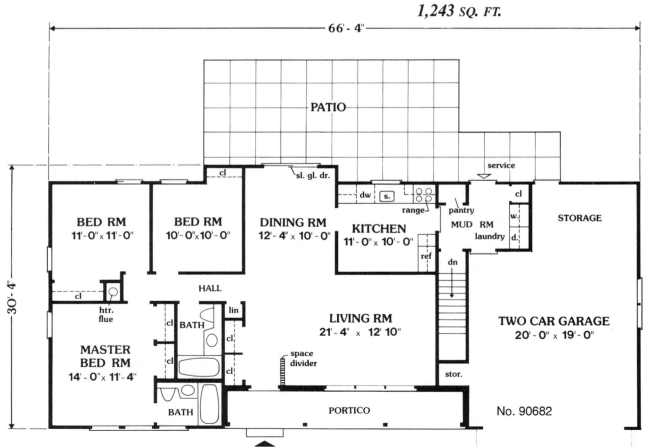

No. 90420
Isolated Master Suite

■ This plan features:

— Three bedrooms

— Two full and one half baths

■ A spacious, sunken Living Room with a cathedral ceiling

■ An isolated Master Suite with a private bath and walk-in closet

■ Two additional bedrooms with a unique bath-and-a-half and ample storage space

■ An efficient U-shaped Kitchen with a double sink, ample cabinets, counter space and a Breakfast area

■ A second floor Studio overlooking the Living Room

■ An optional basement, slab or crawl space foundation — please specify when ordering

FIRST FLOOR — 2,213 SQ. FT.
SECOND FLOOR — 260 SQ. FT.
BASEMENT — 2,213 SQ. FT.
GARAGE — 422 SQ. FT.

TOTAL LIVING AREA: 2,473 SQ. FT.

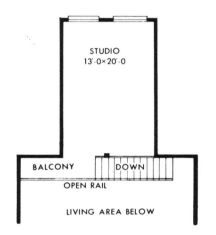

No. 90409
Rocking Chair Living

- This plan features:
- — Three bedrooms
- — Two full baths

- A massive fireplace separating Living and Dining Rooms
- An isolated Master Suite with a walk-in closet and compartmentalized bath
- A galley type Kitchen between the Breakfast Room and Dining Room

- An optional basement, slab or crawl space foundation — please specify when ordering

FIRST FLOOR — 1,670 SQ. FT.

TOTAL LIVING AREA: 1,670 SQ. FT.

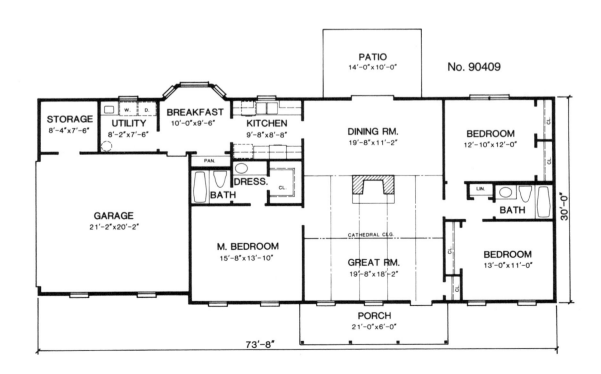

No. 90409

PATIO
14'-0" x 10'-0"

STORAGE
8'-4" x 7'-6"

UTILITY
8'-2" x 7'-6"

W. D.

BREAKFAST
10'-0" x 9'-6"

KITCHEN
9'-8" x 8'-8"

DINING RM.
19'-8" x 11'-2"

BEDROOM
12'-10" x 12'-0"

CL.

PAN.

DRESS.

CL.

BATH

LIN.

CL.

BATH

GARAGE
21'-2" x 20'-2"

M. BEDROOM
15'-8" x 13'-10"

CATHEDRAL CLG.

GREAT RM.
19'-8" x 18'-2"

CL.

CL.

BEDROOM
13'-0" x 11'-0"

30'-0"

PORCH
21'-0" x 6'-0"

73'-8"

No. 90217

Porch Adds Shelter and Classic Appeal

■ This plan features:

— Three or four bedroom plan

— Two and one half baths

■ Main living areas opening off the central entry dominated by a handsome staircase

■ A formal Living Room and Dining Rooms flowing together in an L-shaped design

■ A Family Room area off the Kitchen having the same sunny ambiance as the Breakfast Nook

■ A Breakfast Nook overlooking the sunken fireplaced Family Room with rustic ceiling and sliders to the terrace

FIRST FLOOR — 990 SQ. FT.
SECOND FLOOR — 728 SQ. FT.

TOTAL LIVING AREA:
1,718 SQ. FT.

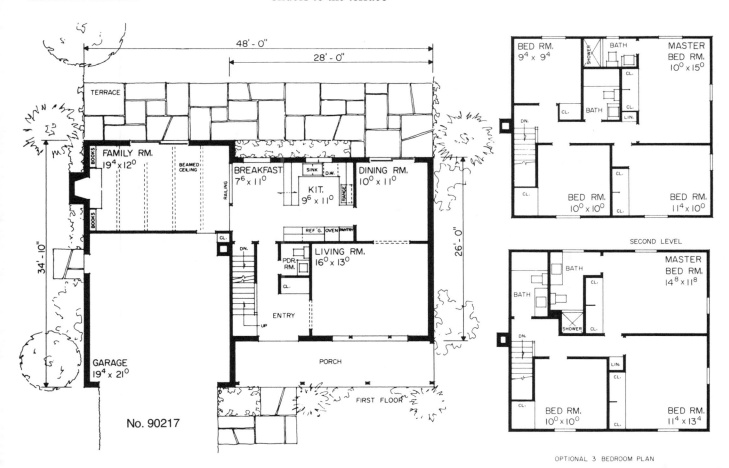

No. 90924

French Doors Lead to Study

■ This plan features:

— Three bedrooms

— Two and one half baths

■ An angular, vaulted ceiling Living Room and a Dining Room with private covered Sundeck

■ A spacious Kitchen overlooking the sunken Family Room with a fireplace

■ A Master Suite with a walk-in closet and private Master Bath

FIRST FLOOR — 1,211 SQ. FT.
SECOND FLOOR — 734 SQ. FT.
GARAGE — 452 SQ. FT.
WIDTH — 46'-0"
DEPTH — 44'-0"

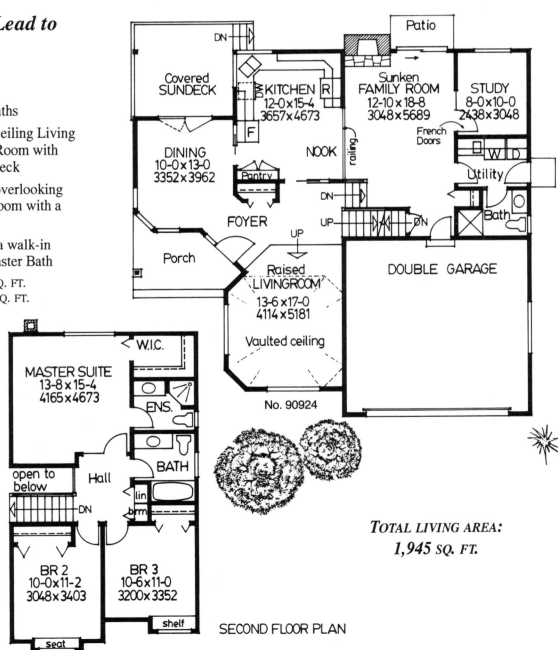

Covered SUNDECK

KITCHEN
12-0 x 15-4
3657 x 4673

Sunken FAMILY ROOM
12-10 x 18-8
3048 x 5689

STUDY
8-0 x 10-0
2438 x 3048

Patio

DINING
10-0 x 13-0
3352 x 3962

NOOK

French Doors

Pantry

Utility

FOYER

Bath

Porch

Raised LIVINGROOM
13-6 x 17-0
4114 x 5181

Vaulted ceiling

DOUBLE GARAGE

No. 90924

MASTER SUITE
13-8 x 15-4
4165 x 4673

W.I.C.

ENS.

open to below

Hall

BATH

lin

brm

BR 2
10-0 x 11-2
3048 x 3403

BR 3
10-6 x 11-0
3200 x 3352

shelf

seat

SECOND FLOOR PLAN

TOTAL LIVING AREA:
1,945 SQ. FT.

No. 90556

An Asset to Any Neighborhood

■ This plan features:

— Four bedrooms

— Two and one half baths

■ A built-in desk in the back bedroom

■ "Built-Ins" in the Family Room and a pantry tucked under the stairs for convenience

■ A Master Suite having an exceptional amount of closet space, double vanities, and spa tub

FIRST FLOOR — 1,055 SQ. FT.
SECOND FLOOR — 1,030 SQ. FT.

TOTAL LIVING AREA:
2,085 SQ. FT.

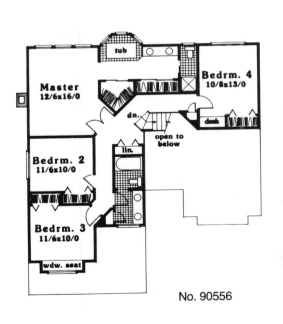

No. 90556

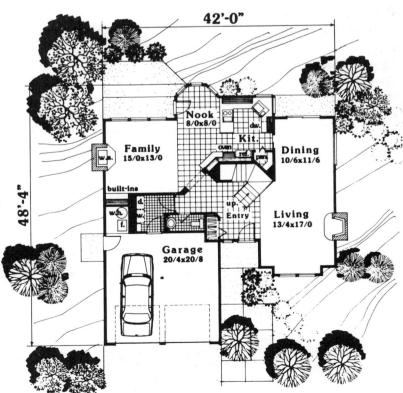

No. 90687
Country Comforts

■ This plan features:

— Four bedrooms

— Two and one half baths

■ A covered porch, window boxes, and two chimneys

■ Cozy Living and Dining Rooms

■ Cabinets and greenhouse bay separate the Kitchen, dinette, and Family Room overlooking the backyard

■ A covered porch just off the fire-placed Family Room

FIRST FLOOR — 1,065 SQ. FT.
SECOND FLOOR — 1,007 SQ. FT.
LAUNDRY/MUDROOM — 88 SQ. FT.
GARAGE — 428 SQ. FT.

TOTAL LIVING AREA:
2,160 SQ. FT.

SECOND FLOOR PLAN

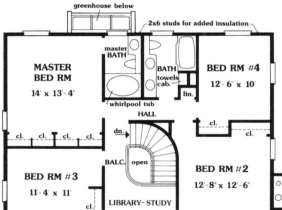

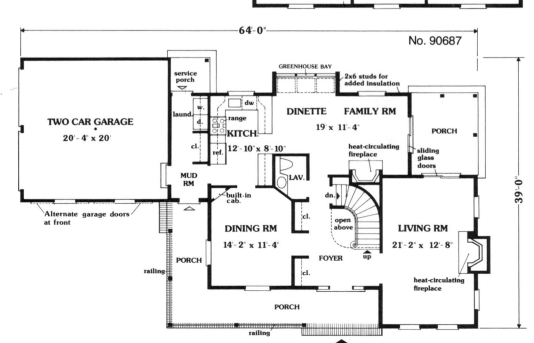

No. 90606

Traditional Elements Combine in Friendly Colonial

■ This plan features:

— Four bedrooms

— Two and one half baths

■ A beautiful circular stair ascending from the central foyer and flanked by the formal Living Room and Dining Room

■ Exposed beams, wood paneling, and a brick fireplace wall in the Family Room

■ A separate dinette opening to an efficient Kitchen

■ An optional slab foundation

FIRST FLOOR — 1,099 SQ. FT.
SECOND FLOOR — 932 SQ. FT.

TOTAL LIVING AREA: 2,031 SQ. FT.

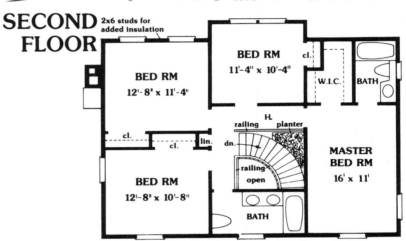

SECOND FLOOR 2x6 studs for added insulation

BED RM
11'-4" x 10'-4"

cl.

W.I.C.

BATH

BED RM
12'-8" x 11'-4"

cl.

cl.

lin.

dn.

railing

H.

planter

MASTER BED RM
16' x 11'

BED RM
12'-8" x 10'-8"

railing

open

BATH

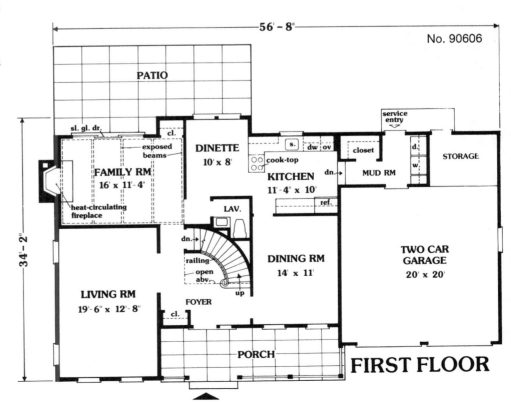

56'-8"

No. 90606

PATIO

34'-2"

sl. gl. dr.

cl.

exposed beams

DINETTE
10' x 8'

s.

cook-top

dw ov

closet

service entry

d.

w.

STORAGE

FAMILY RM
16' x 11'-4"

KITCHEN
11'-4" x 10'

dn.

MUD RM

heat-circulating fireplace

LAV.

ref.

dn.

railing

open abv.

DINING RM
14' x 11'

TWO CAR GARAGE
20' x 20'

LIVING RM
19'-6" x 12'-8"

up

FOYER

cl.

PORCH

FIRST FLOOR

No. 90118

Windows Highlight This Spacious Traditional Home

■ This plan features:

— Four or five bedrooms

— Two and one half baths

■ Double windows in the Living Room and the formal Dining Room

■ A bay window off the Kitchen's dining area

■ A fireplace with built-in bookshelves in the spacious Family Room

■ A Master Suite with a private Master Bath and his and her closets

■ A mudroom entrance with a half bath

■ A basement foundation only

FIRST FLOOR — 1,392 SQ. FT.
SECOND FLOOR — 1,282 SQ. FT.

TOTAL LIVING AREA: 2,674 SQ. FT.

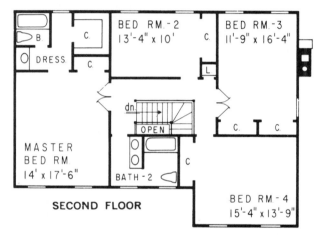

SECOND FLOOR

No. 90118

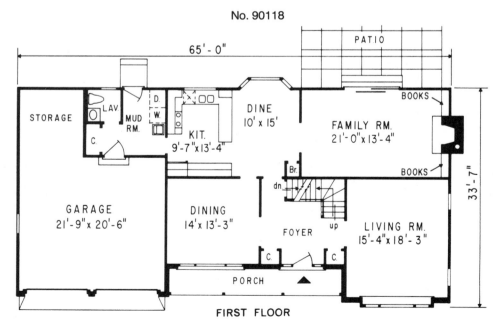

FIRST FLOOR

No. 90115
Cozy Cape Cod

■ This plan features:

— Four bedrooms

— Two full baths

■ A Living Room with a focal point fireplace adding to the atmosphere

■ A Family Room that opens into the efficient eat-in Kitchen

■ A huge Master Bedroom with private dressing area and full bath

■ A back service entrance, mudroom and Laundry convenient to the Kitchen

■ Two additional bedrooms sharing a full hall bath

■ An optional basement, slab or crawl space foundation — please specify when ordering

FIRST FLOOR — 1,068 SQ. FT.
SECOND FLOOR — 804 SQ. FT.

TOTAL LIVING AREA: 1,872 SQ. FT.

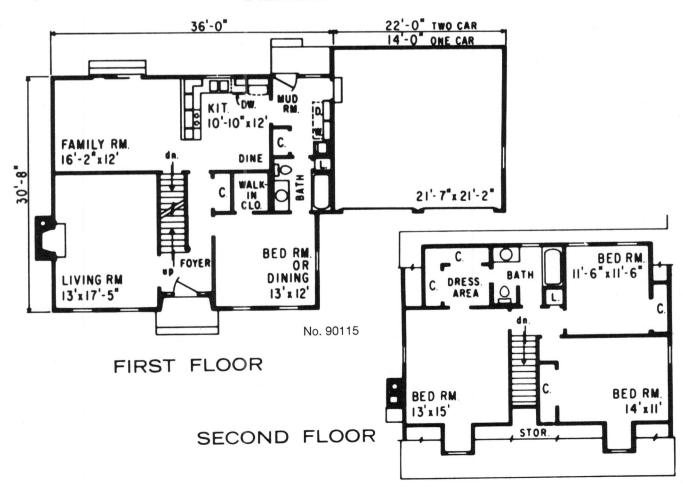

FIRST FLOOR

No. 90115

SECOND FLOOR

No. 90270

Soaring Ceilings, Multiple Levels Add Contemporary Flair

■ This plan features:

— Three bedrooms

— Two full and one half baths

■ A Master Suite with a raised tub, step-in shower, and private terrace entrance

■ An efficient island Kitchen adjoining an informal eating Nook and convenient to the formal Dining area

■ Railings separating the massive Gathering/Dining Room

■ A fireplace in Family Room that adds warmth to the rest of the house

FIRST FLOOR — 2,652 SQ. FT.

TOTAL LIVING AREA: 2,652 SQ. FT.

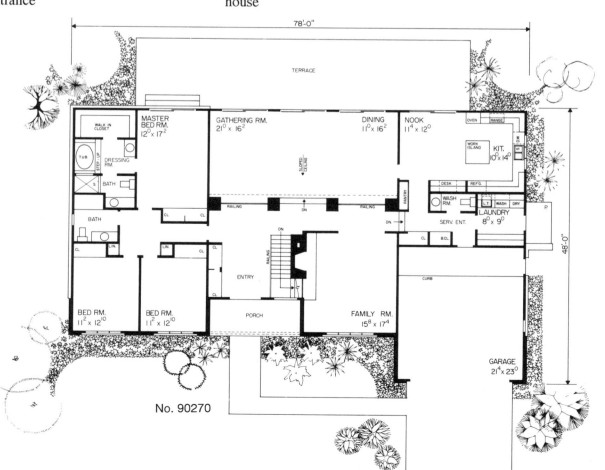

No. 90270

No. 99244

A Ranch Lover's Dream

■ This plan features:

— Three bedrooms

— Two full and one half baths

■ An open layout between the Family Room, Kitchen and Dining Room

■ A Master Bedroom with a walk-in closet and private Master Bath

■ An inviting Living Room with cozy fireplace and a row of windows looking out over the covered front porch

■ Two additional bedrooms with walk-in closets served by a full hall bath

FIRST FLOOR — 1,949 SQ. FT.
BASEMENT — 1,949 SQ. FT.

**TOTAL LIVING AREA:
1,949 SQ. FT.**

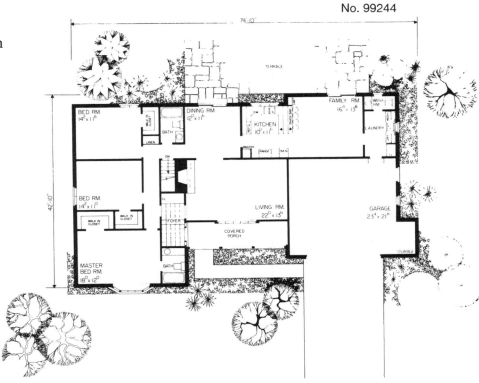

No. 91772
Compact and Economical Starter

■ This plan features:

— Three bedrooms

—Two full baths

■ A Master Suite with custom-shaped Sitting Nook, double walk-in closet, and Master Bath

■ A spacious Kitchen with generous storage and counter space including an eating bar for informal meals

■ A Dining Room with sliding glass doors opening out to a deck

FIRST FLOOR —1, 589 SQ. FT.
GARAGE — 624 SQ. FT.

TOTAL LIVING AREA:
1,589 SQ. FT.

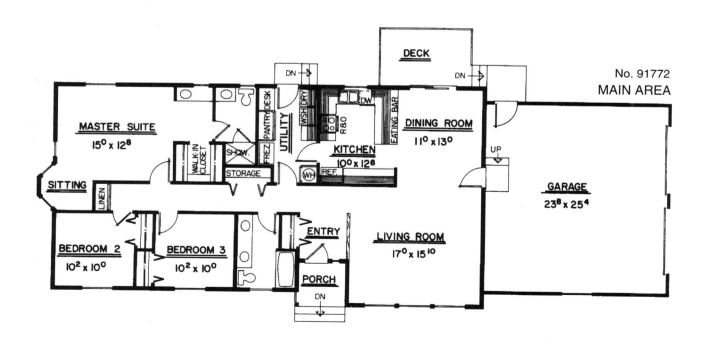

No. 91772
MAIN AREA

No. 90692
Carefree Comfort

■ This plan features:

— Three bedrooms

— Two full baths

■ Cedar shingle siding and flowerboxes

■ A heat-circulating fireplace

■ A central foyer separating active areas from the bedroom wing

■ A sunny Living Room with an arched window, fireplace, and soaring cathedral ceilings

■ A formal Dining Room adjoining the Living Room

FIRST FLOOR — 1,492 SQ. FT.

TOTAL LIVING AREA:
1,492 SQ. FT.

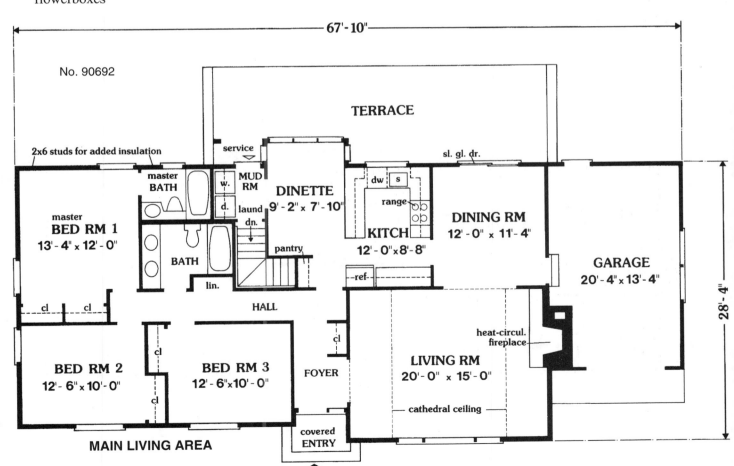

No. 92029

Designed with Care

- This plan features:
  — Three bedrooms
  — One full bath

- A large Living Room with attached open Dining area
- An L-shaped Kitchen with access to the large attached single car Garage

- A central hall with laundry closet
- An ample amount of closet space throughout the home

FIRST FLOOR — 1,008 SQ. FT.

TOTAL LIVING AREA: 1,008 SQ. FT.

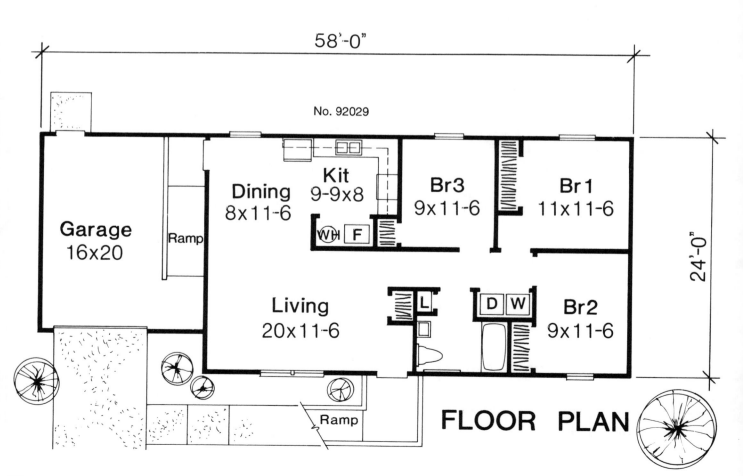

58'-0"

No. 92029

24'-0"

Garage 16x20 | Ramp | Dining 8x11-6 | Kit 9-9x8 | Br3 9x11-6 | Br 1 11x11-6

WH | F

Living 20x11-6 | L | D W | Br2 9x11-6

Ramp

FLOOR PLAN

No. 92044

Traditional Lines Enhance Plan

■ This plan features:

— Three bedrooms

— Two full baths

■ A formal entry with 10' ceilings

■ An L-shaped Kitchen with an island eating bar

■ A two car attached Garage to make carrying groceries easier

■ A Master Bedroom with a large walk-in closet and luxury bath

FIRST FLOOR — 1,753 SQ. FT.
GARAGE — 528 SQ. FT.

TOTAL LIVING AREA:
1,753 SQ. FT.

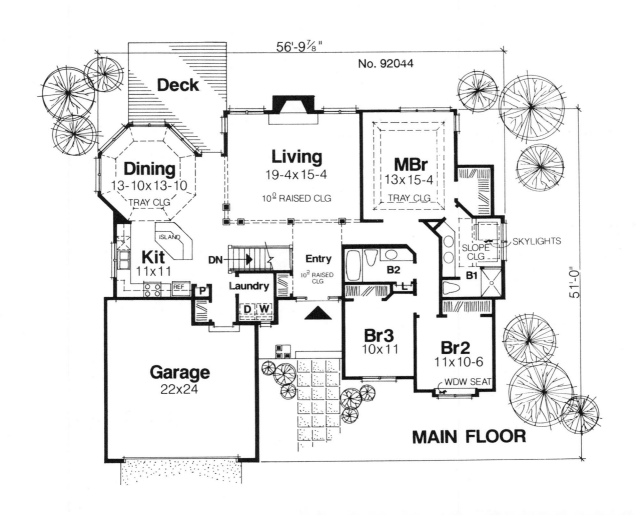

MAIN FLOOR

No. 90983
Attractive Roof Lines

■ This plan features:

— Three bedrooms

— Two full baths

■ An open floor plan shared by the sunken Living Room, Dining and Kitchen areas

■ An unfinished daylight Basement which will provide future bedrooms, bathroom and laundry facilities

■ A Master Suite with a big walk-in closet and a private bath featuring a double shower

FIRST FLOOR — 1,396 SQ. FT.
BASEMENT — 1,396 SQ. FT.
GARAGE — 389 SQ. FT.
WIDTH — 48'-0"
DEPTH — 55'-0"

TOTAL LIVING AREA:
1,396 SQ. FT.

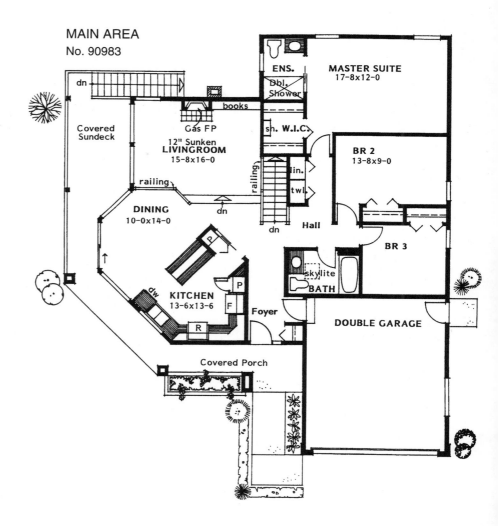

MAIN AREA
No. 90983

No. 91021

Inviting Porch Has Dual Function

■ This plan features:

— Three Bedrooms

— Two full Baths

■ An inviting wrap-around porch entry with sliding glass doors leading right into a bayed Dining Room

■ A Living Room with a cozy feeling enhanced by the fireplace

■ An efficient Kitchen opening to both Dining and Living Rooms

■ A Master Suite with a walk-in closet and private Master Bath

■ An optional basement, slab or crawl space foundation — please specify when ordering

FIRST FLOOR — 1,295 SQ. FT.

TOTAL LIVING AREA: 1,295 SQ. FT.

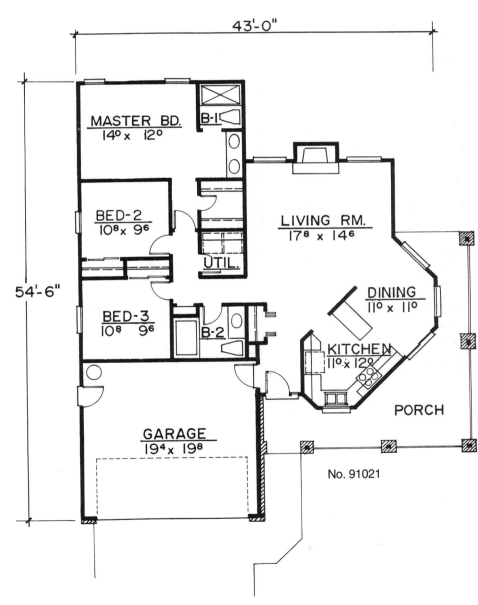

43'-0"

54'-6"

MASTER BD.
14⁰ x 12⁰

B-1

BED-2
10⁸ x 9⁶

UTIL.

LIVING RM.
17⁸ x 14⁶

BED-3
10⁸ 9⁶

B-2

DINING
11⁰ x 11⁰

KITCHEN
11⁰ x 12⁸

PORCH

GARAGE
19⁴ x 19⁸

No. 91021

No. 90121

Glass Captures Views & Sun in A-Frame

■ This plan features:

— Three bedrooms

— Two full baths

■ Large exterior exposed beams

■ A Family Room with sliders to the deck

■ Wooden seats railing the deck which flows into a dining patio on the left side

■ A Master Bedroom including a large fireplaced sitting area

■ An optional basement, slab or crawl space foundation — please specify when ordering

FIRST FLOOR — 1,126 SQ. FT.
SECOND FLOOR — 603 SQ. FT.

TOTAL LIVING AREA:
1,729 SQ. FT.

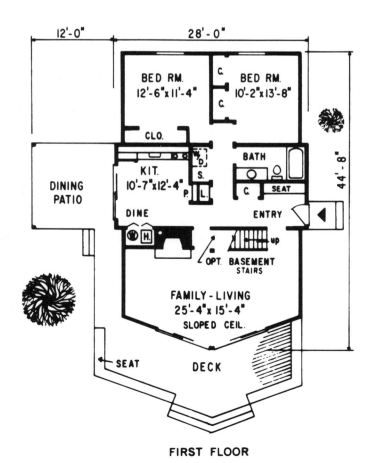

FIRST FLOOR

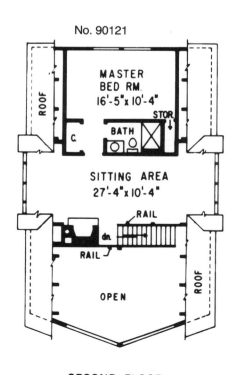

SECOND FLOOR

No. 90123

Old American Saltbox Design

■ This plan features:

— Three bedrooms

— One and one half baths

■ A sloping Living Room ceiling that lends to spaciousness

■ A centrally located fireplace

■ Laundry facilities conveniently located off Kitchen area

■ A slab foundation only

FIRST FLOOR — 840 SQ. FT.
SECOND FLOOR — 440 SQ. FT.

TOTAL LIVING AREA: 1,280 SQ. FT.

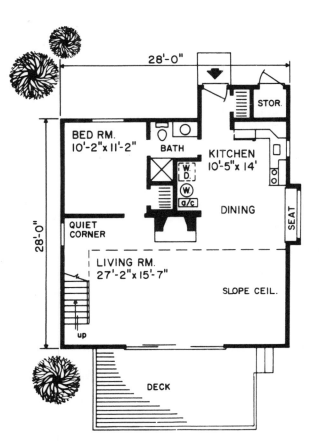

FIRST FLOOR

28'-0"

28'-0"

BED RM.
10'-2"x11'-2"

BATH

STOR.

KITCHEN
10'-5"x 14'

DINING

SEAT

QUIET CORNER

W. D.

W

g/c

LIVING RM.
27'-2"x15'-7"

SLOPE CEIL.

up

DECK

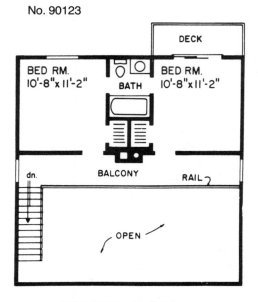

No. 90123

DECK

BED RM.
10'-8"x11'-2"

BATH

BED RM.
10'-8"x11'-2"

dn.

BALCONY

RAIL

OPEN

SECOND FLOOR

No. 90365

Special Features Enhance Plan

■ This plan features:

— Four bedrooms

— Two full and one half baths

■ A Living Room with a vaulted ceiling

■ A huge Family Room with a cozy fireplace

■ A garden Kitchen and Breakfast area that extend living area to the Deck outside

■ A Master Suite with an oval tub, double vanity and walk-in closet

■ Three additional bedrooms that share the full hall bath

FIRST FLOOR — 1,403 SQ. FT.
SECOND FLOOR — 957 SQ. FT.
GARAGE — 693 SQ. FT.

TOTAL LIVING AREA: 2,360 SQ. FT.

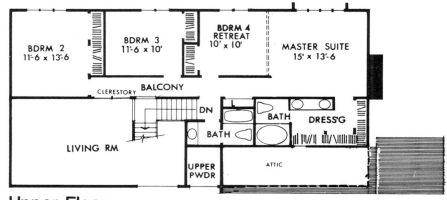

Upper Floor

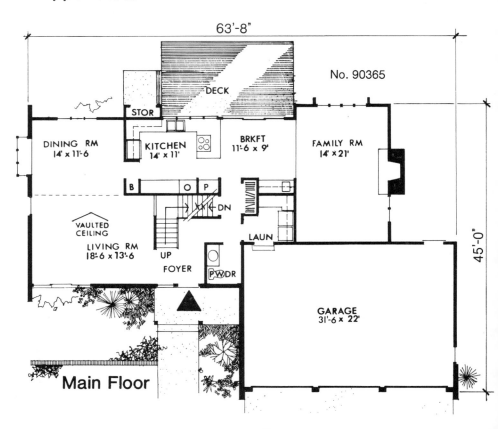

Main Floor

No. 91342
Easy Living Design

■ This plan features:

— Three bedrooms

— Two full baths

■ A handicapped Master Bath plan available

■ Vaulted Great Room, Dining Room and Kitchen areas

■ A Kitchen accented with angles and an abundance of cabinets for storage

■ A Master Bedroom with an ample sized wardrobe, large covered private deck, and private bath

FIRST FLOOR — 1,345 SQ. FT.

TOTAL LIVING AREA:
1,345 SQ. FT.

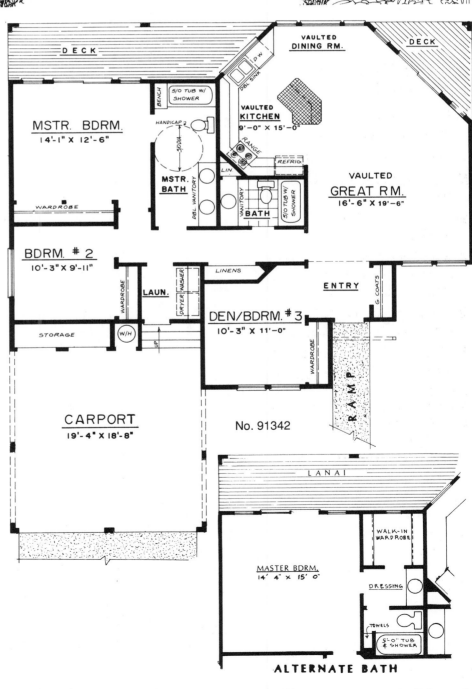

DECK

VAULTED DINING RM.

DECK

DBL SINK

MSTR. BDRM.
14'-1" X 12'-6"

BENCH

5/0 TUB W/ SHOWER

VAULTED KITCHEN
9'-0" X 15'-0"

HANDICAP 2

5/0 DIA

WARDROBE

MSTR. BATH

RANGE

LIN

REFRIG

VAULTED GREAT RM.
16'-6" X 19'-6"

DBL VANITORY

VANITORY

BATH

5/0 TUB W/ SHOWER

BDRM. # 2
10'-3" X 9'-11"

LINENS

ENTRY

G. COATS

WARDROBE

LAUN.

DRYER WASHER

DEN/BDRM. # 3
10'-3" X 11'-0"

STORAGE

W/H

UP

WARDROBE

RAMP

CARPORT
19'-4" X 18'-8"

No. 91342

LANAI

MASTER BDRM.
14' 4" X 15' 0"

WALK-IN WARDROBE

DRESSING

TOWELS

5'-0" TUB & SHOWER

ALTERNATE BATH

No. 90106
Graceful Porch Enhances Charm

- This plan features:
- — Three bedrooms
- — Two full baths
- A formal Living Room sheltered by a railed porch

- A hobby area including laundry facilities
- A Kitchen, Dining, and Family Room in a "three in one" design
- An optional basement, slab or crawl space foundation — please specify when ordering

FIRST FLOOR — 1,643 SQ. FT.

TOTAL LIVING AREA: 1,643 SQ. FT.

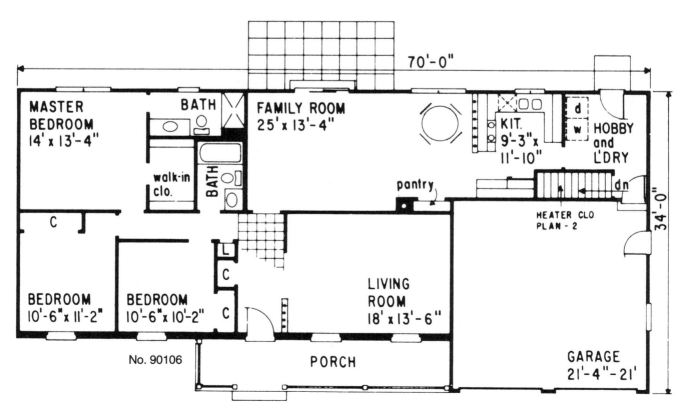

No. 90112

Appealing Multi-Level Home

■ This plan features:

— Three bedrooms

— Two full baths

■ A unified Kitchen and Dining area making set up and clean up easy

■ A large Master Bedroom with ample closet and a separate entry to the full Bath

■ Spacious bedrooms along the front of the house

■ A Family Room just steps down from the entry

■ A private den on the lower level

MAIN & UPPER LEVELS — 1,356 SQ. FT.
LOWER LEVEL — 720 SQ. FT.

TOTAL LIVING AREA:
2,076 SQ. FT.

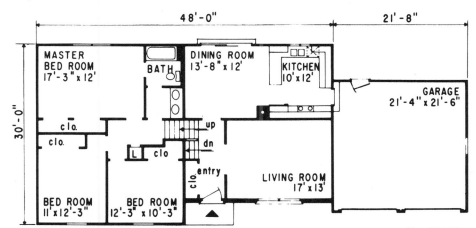

MAIN AND UPPER LEVEL

No. 90112

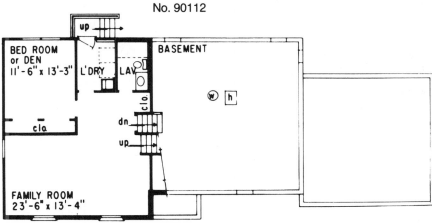

LOWER LEVEL

No. 90327

Contemporary Exteriors

■ This plan features:

— Three bedrooms

— Two full baths

■ A vaulted ceiling and front corner windows enhancing the Living Room

■ A clerestory accenting the open design of the Dining Room and Kitchen

■ A U-shaped Kitchen with a corner double sink and peninsula counter, plus all the amenities

■ A secluded Master Bedroom with a walk-in closet and a large, compartmented bath

■ Two additional bedrooms that share the full hall bath

FIRST FLOOR — 846 SQ. FT.
SECOND FLOOR — 400 SQ. FT.
BASEMENT — 846 SQ. FT.
GARAGE — 400 SQ. FT.

TOTAL LIVING AREA:
1,246 SQ. FT.

Upper Floor

Main Floor

No. 90325

Designed for Informal Life Styles

■ This plan features:

— Two bedrooms

— One full bath

■ A Great Room and Kitchen accented by vaulted ceilings

■ A conveniently arranged L-shaped food preparation center

■ A Dining Room overlooking a deck through sliding doors

■ A Great Room highlighted by a corner fireplace

■ A Master Bedroom including a separate vanity and dressing area

FIRST FLOOR — 988 SQ. FT.
BASEMENT — 988 SQ. FT.
GARAGE — 400 SQ. FT.

TOTAL LIVING AREA:
988 SQ. FT.

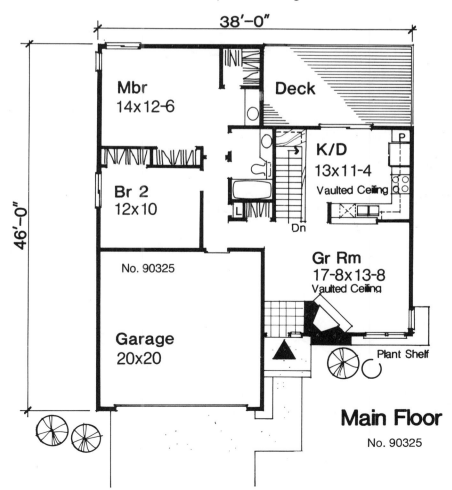

Main Floor

No. 90325

No. 92016
Appeal Everyone Wants

■ This plan features:

— Three bedrooms

— Two and one half baths

■ Repeating front gables, shuttered windows, and wrap-around front porch

■ A large Family/Kitchen opening to a screened porch and private side deck

■ A Master Bedroom with private bath and one wall of closet space

■ Second floor laundry facilities

FIRST FLOOR — 760 SQ. FT.
SECOND FLOOR — 728 SQ. FT.
BASEMENT — 768 SQ. FT.

TOTAL LIVING AREA:
1,488 SQ. FT.

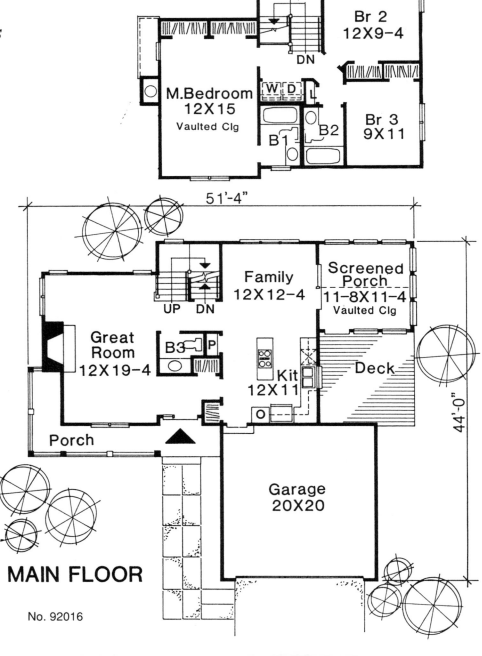

M.Bedroom
12X15
Vaulted Clg

Br 2
12X9-4

DN

W D

B1 B2

Br 3
9X11

51'-4"

Family
12X12-4

Screened Porch
11-8X11-4
Vaulted Clg

UP DN

Great Room
12X19-4

B3 P

Kit
12X11

Deck

44'-0"

Porch

Garage
20X20

MAIN FLOOR

No. 92016

No. 90245
Compact Dream House

■ This plan features:

— Three bedrooms

— Two and one half baths

■ A central entry flanked by a cozy Study and sunny formal Living Room

■ Two fireplaces to help with heating bills

■ A Kitchen featuring a triple window with built-in seating and a beamed ceiling

FIRST FLOOR — 1,020 SQ. FT.
SECOND FLOOR — 777 SQ. FT.

TOTAL LIVING AREA:
1,797 SQ. FT.

No. 90245

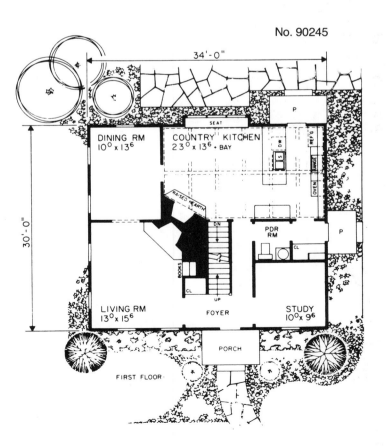

FIRST FLOOR

SECOND FLOOR

No. 99362
Affordable Charm

■ This plan features:

— Three bedrooms

— Two and one half baths

■ An eat-in Kitchen leading out onto patio

■ A Living Room which can be expanded behind the Garage

■ A Master Suite with vaulted ceilings and a walk-in closet

■ A two car Garage

FIRST FLOOR — 669 SQ. FT.
SECOND FLOOR — 727 SQ. FT.

TOTAL LIVING AREA:
1,396 SQ. FT.

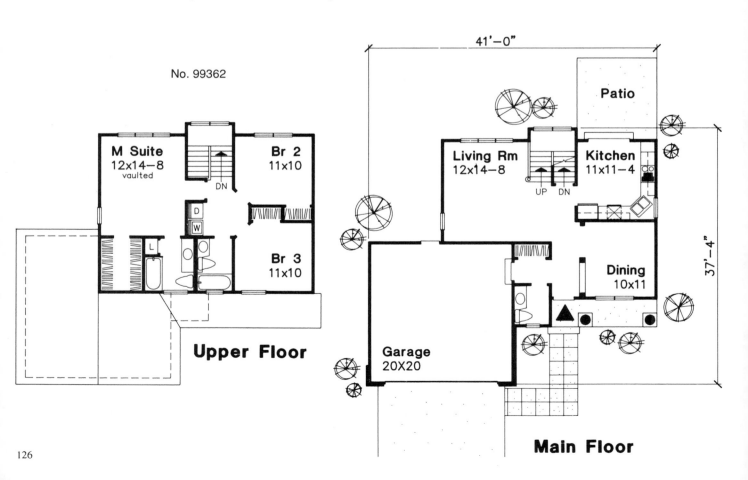

No. 99362

Upper Floor

M Suite
12x14—8
vaulted

Br 2
11x10

Br 3
11x10

DN

D
W
L

Main Floor

41'—0"

37'—4"

Patio

Living Rm
12x14—8

Kitchen
11x11—4

UP   DN

Dining
10x11

Garage
20X20

No. 99365
Country Charm

■ This plan features:

— Three bedrooms

— Two full baths and opt. half bath

■ 10-foot high ceilings in Living Room, Family Room, and Dinette area

■ A heat-circulating fireplace

■ A Master Bath with separate stall shower and whirlpool tub

■ A Two car Garage with access through a mud room

UPPER LEVEL — 1,203 SQ. FT.
GARAGE — 491 SQ. FT.

TOTAL LIVING AREA:
1,203 SQ. FT.

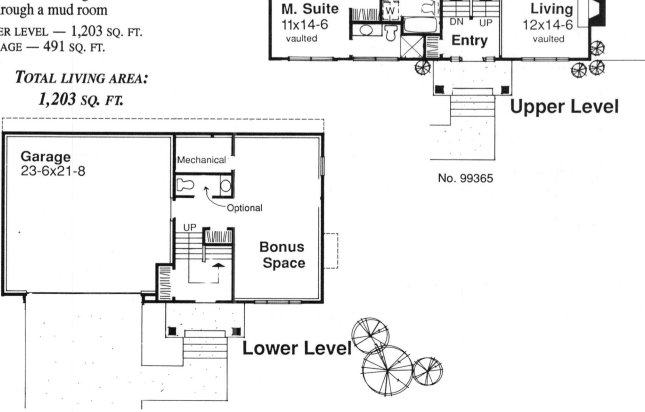

45'-0"

Deck

| Br 2 11x10 | Br 3 10x10 | Dining 10x10 | Kit 10-6 x11 |

M. Suite 11x14-6 vaulted

DN UP

Living 12x14-6 vaulted

Entry

26'-8"

Upper Level

No. 99365

Garage 23-6x21-8

Mechanical

Optional

UP

Bonus Space

Lower Level

No. 90685

Farmhouse Flavor

■ This plan features:

— Three bedrooms

— Two full baths

■ An octagonal stair tower

■ A Foyer opening to a Living and Dining Room combination enhanced by a striking glass wall

■ A heat circulating fireplace adding welcome warmth

■ A galley style Kitchen including a large pantry, snack bar, and laundry area

■ A Master Suite with a private deck overlooking backyard

FIRST FLOOR — 1,073 SQ. FT.
SECOND FLOOR — 604 SQ. FT.
RETREAT TOWER — 93 SQ. FT.
GARAGE — 428 SQ. FT.

*TOTAL LIVING AREA:
1,770 SQ. FT.*

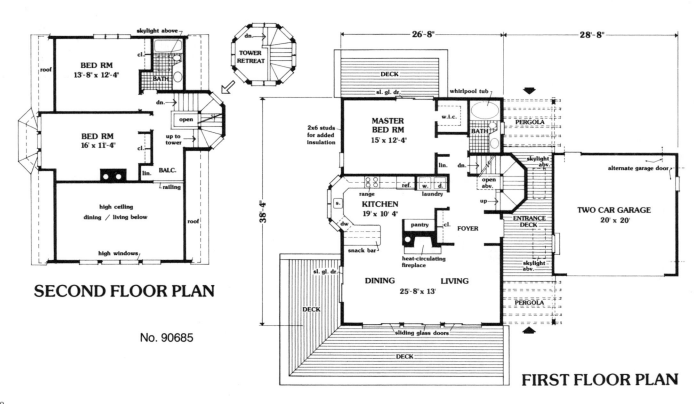

SECOND FLOOR PLAN

No. 90685

FIRST FLOOR PLAN

No. 90688

Vista Viewpoint

■ This plan features:

— Four bedrooms

— Two full and one half baths

■ Glass-walled active areas

■ A heat circulating fireplace in the Family Room

■ A galley type Kitchen centrally located for easy convenience to Dinette area and Dining Room

■ A second heat circulating fireplace in spacious Living Room

FIRST FLOOR — 1,100 SQ. FT.
SECOND FLOOR — 898 SQ. FT.
GARAGE AND LAUNDRY — 507 SQ. FT.

TOTAL LIVING AREA:
1,998 SQ. FT.

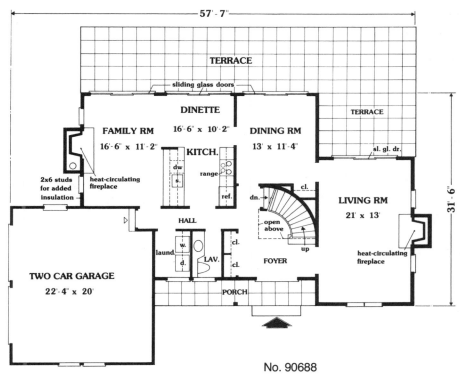

No. 90688

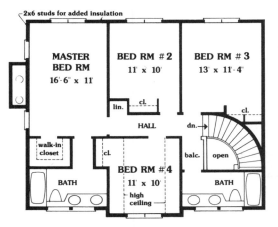

SECOND FLOOR

No. 90937

One-Level Budget Booster

■ This plan features:

— Three bedrooms

— Two full baths

■ A Master Suite with a walk-in closet and private Master Bath

■ A sunken, fireplaced Living Room easily accessible from the elegant bay windowed Dining Room

■ A well-equipped Kitchen with an adjoining Eating Nook area

FIRST FLOOR — 1,238 SQ. FT.
GARAGE — 399 SQ. FT.
WIDTH — 38'-0"
DEPTH — 52'-0"

TOTAL LIVING AREA:
1,238 SQ. FT.

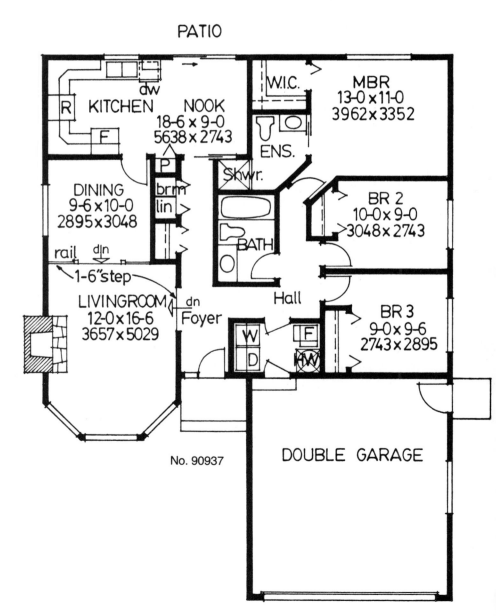

PATIO

KITCHEN

NOOK
18-6 x 9-0
5638 x 2743

W.I.C.

MBR
13-0 x 11-0
3962 x 3352

ENS.

DINING
9-6 x 10-0
2895 x 3048

Shwr.

BATH

BR 2
10-0 x 9-0
3048 x 2743

rail   dn

1-6" step

LIVINGROOM
12-0 x 16-6
3657 x 5029

dn
Foyer

Hall

BR 3
9-0 x 9-6
2743 x 2895

No. 90937

DOUBLE GARAGE

No. 91008
Bright and Beautiful

■ This plan features:

— Three bedrooms

— Two and a half baths

■ A fireplaced Living Room that flows into the Dining Room for easy entertaining

■ A Master Suite with a private Master Bath and walk-in closet

■ A bay windowed Kitchen with an informal Nook eating area

■ An optional basement or crawl space foundation — please specify when ordering

FIRST FLOOR — 1,153 SQ. FT.
SECOND FLOOR — 493 SQ. FT.

TOTAL LIVING AREA:
1,646 SQ. FT.

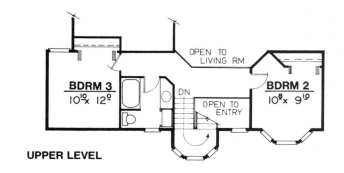

UPPER LEVEL

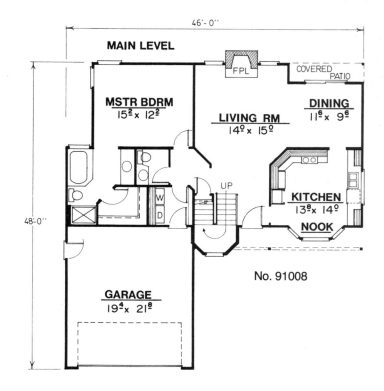

No. 91427
Columns Adorn Entry

■ This plan features:

— Three bedrooms

— Two full baths

■ A centrally located staircase that is open to the vaulted ceiling Living Room, complete with fireplace and built-in bar

■ A secluded Master Bedroom Suite that has a custom bath, walk-in closet and a spiral staircase to the sunspace below

■ Two additional bedrooms flanking a full bath

No. 91427

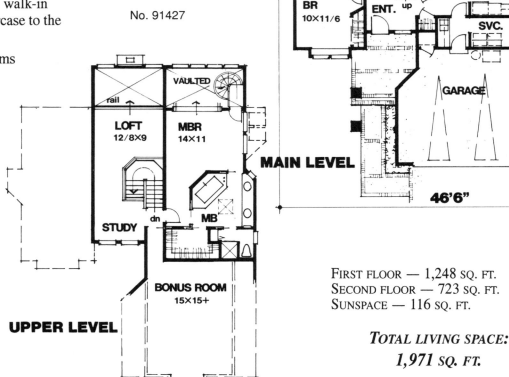

MAIN LEVEL

46'6"

57'

PATIO

SUNSPACE

VAULTED LIVING
12×16/6

FAM/DINE
18×10/6

BR
10×10/8

B

BR
10×11/6

bar under rail

KITC.
13×10/6

ENT.   up

SVC.

GARAGE

UPPER LEVEL

LOFT
12/8×9

MBR
14×11

VAULTED

rail

STUDY   dn   MB

BONUS ROOM
15×15+

FIRST FLOOR — 1,248 SQ. FT.
SECOND FLOOR — 723 SQ. FT.
SUNSPACE — 116 SQ. FT.

TOTAL LIVING SPACE:
1,971 SQ. FT.

No. 99310
Abundant Windows Add Outdoor Feeling

■ This plan features:

— Three bedrooms

— Two and one half baths

■ A traditional front porch

■ A breakfast bay overlooking the patio

■ A built-in bar in the Dining Room

■ An efficient Kitchen with range top island, built-in planning desk, and pantry

■ A Living Room with fireplace, vaulted ceilings, and windows on three sides

■ A Master Suite with a private, double vanity bath

FIRST FLOOR — 1,160 SQ. FT.
SECOND FLOOR — 797 SQ. FT.

*TOTAL LIVING AREA:
1,957 SQ. FT.*

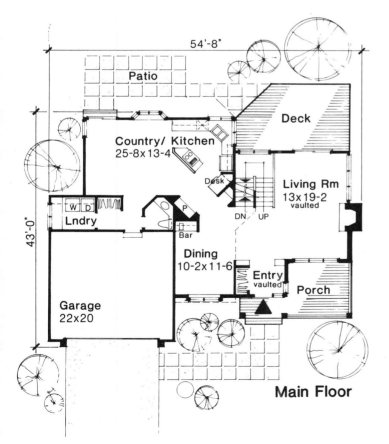

54'-8"

43'-0"

Patio

Deck

Country/ Kitchen
25-8x13-4

Desk

Living Rm
13x19-2
vaulted

W D

Lndry

P

Bar

DN UP

Dining
10-2x11-6

Entry
vaulted

Porch

Garage
22x20

Main Floor

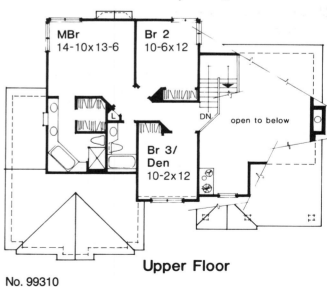

MBr
14-10x13-6

Br 2
10-6x12

L

DN

open to below

Br 3/
Den
10-2x12

No. 99310

Upper Floor

No. 91506

Privacy Zones

■ This plan features:

— Three bedrooms

— Two full baths

■ A sun-catching bay window accentuating the Living/Dining combination

■ A fireplace in the Family Room that spreads its warmth through the angular, efficient Kitchen and Nook

■ Sliding glass doors in the Nook leading to a rear patio

■ A Master Suite with a private bath equipped with a step-in shower

■ Two additional bedrooms that share a full hall bath

FIRST FLOOR — 1,546 SQ. FT.

**TOTAL LIVING AREA:
1,546 SQ. FT.**

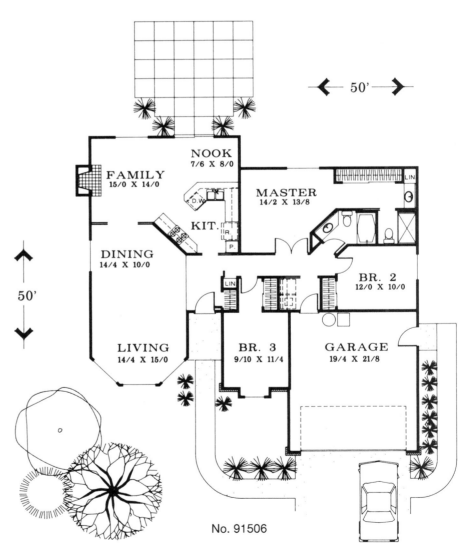

No. 91506

Bryden

No. 90652
Tudor Accents for a Modern Plan

■ This plan features:

— Three bedrooms

— Two full baths

■ A strategically located galley Kitchen for maximum efficiency

■ A heat-circulating fireplace separating the Living and Dining Rooms without compromising their open atmosphere

■ Sliding glass doors from the Living Room and Dining Room to the patio

■ A Master Suite with his and her closets and a private bath

■ Two additional bedrooms that share a full hall bath

FIRST FLOOR — 1,588 SQ. FT.

TOTAL LIVING AREA: 1,588 SQ. FT.

74'-8"

49'-7"

cl

MASTER BED RM
15'-0" x 13'-4"

alcove

cl

PATIO

up

BATH

cl

lin

BATH

HALL

sl.gl.drs

sl.gl.dr.

stor.

LIVING
20'-2" x 13'-4"

DINING
11'-0" x 12'-0"

cl

TWO CAR GARAGE
20'-0" x 20'-0"

Heat circulating fireplace

BED RM
12'-0" x 10'-6"

dn

MUD RM
LAUND.

ov

w

cl cl cl cl

FOYER

KIT
10'-10" x 9'-8"

cook-top

FAMILY RM
11'-0" x 12'-6"

d

ref

s

dw

cl

ENTRANCE PLATFORM

BED RM
13'-0" x 11'-0"

Flower box

No. 90652

FLOOR PLAN

No. 90361

Great Room has Vaulted Ceiling

■ This plan features:

— Three bedrooms

— Two full and one half baths

■ A bay window Breakfast area flowing into the charming Kitchen with ample cabinet and counter space

■ A vaulted ceiling in the Great Room with a cozy fireplace

■ A Master Bedroom with vaulted ceiling and luxurious Master Bath enhanced by platform tub, stall shower, and an oversized walk-in closet

■ Two additional bedrooms that share a full hall bath

FIRST FLOOR — 1,105 SQ. FT.
SECOND FLOOR — 460 SQ. FT.

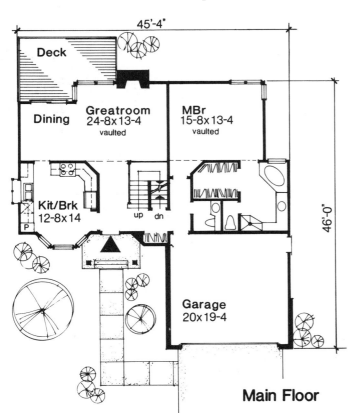

Main Floor

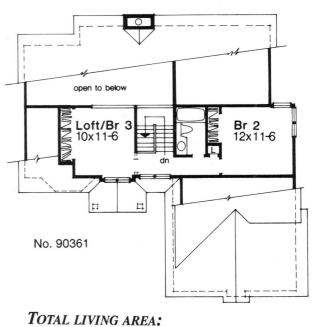

No. 90361

TOTAL LIVING AREA:
1,565 SQ. FT.

Upper Floor

No. 90335
Efficient Single Level Design

■ This plan features:

— Two bedrooms

— Two full baths

■ A large Kitchen with a center island and direct access to the Dining Room and Breakfast Room

■ A Great Room distinguished by a vaulted ceiling and corner fireplace

■ A Dining Room with a built-in wetbar

■ A Master Bedroom set off by a large bath area with a skylight and access to the deck

FIRST FLOOR — 1,700 SQ. FT.

TOTAL LIVING AREA: 1,700 SQ. FT.

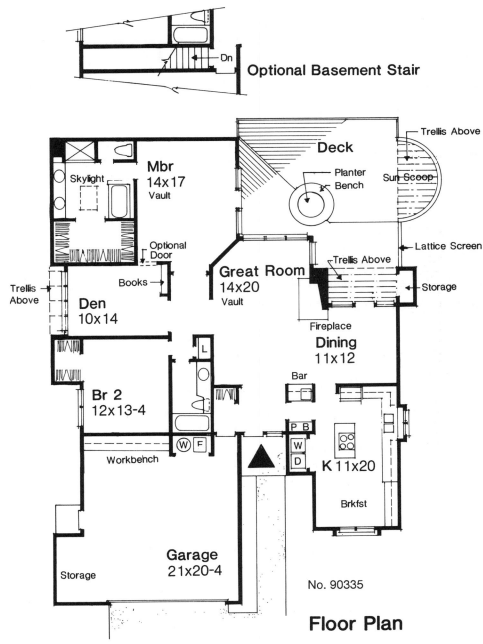

Optional Basement Stair

Mbr 14x17 Vault
Skylight
Optional Door
Books
Den 10x14
Trellis Above
Br 2 12x13-4
Workbehch
W F

Deck
Trellis Above
Planter Bench
Sun Scoop
Great Room 14x20 Vault
Trellis Above
Lattice Screen
Storage
Fireplace
Dining 11x12
Bar
P B
W
D
K 11x20
Brkfst

Garage 21x20-4
Storage

No. 90335

Floor Plan

No. 90410

Country Living in a Doll House

■ This plan features:

— Three bedrooms

— Two full and one half baths

■ An eat-in country Kitchen with an island counter and bay window

■ A spacious Great Room with a fireplace flowing easily into the Dining area

■ A first floor Master Suite including a walk-in closet and a private compartmentalized bath

■ Two additional bedrooms sharing a full bath with double vanity

■ An optional basement or crawl space foundation — please specify when ordering

FIRST FLOOR — 1,277 SQ. FT.
SECOND FLOOR — 720 SQ. FT.

TOTAL LIVING AREA: 1,997 SQ. FT.

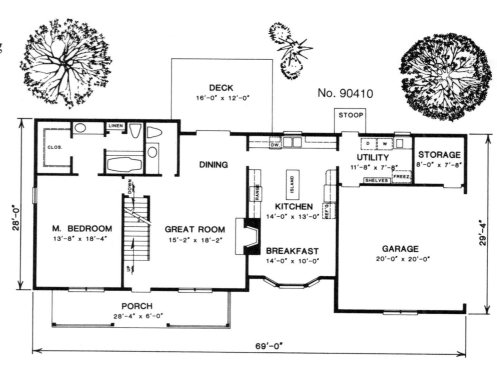

No. 91807

An Affordable Floor Plan

■ This plan features:

— Three bedrooms

— Two full baths

■ A covered porch entry

■ An old-fashioned hearth fireplace in the vaulted ceiling Living Room

■ An efficient Kitchen with U-shaped counter that is accessible from the Dining Room

■ A Master Bedroom with a large walk-in closet and private bath

FIRST FLOOR — 1,410 SQ. FT.
GARAGE — 484 SQ. FT.

TOTAL LIVING AREA: 1,410 SQ. FT.

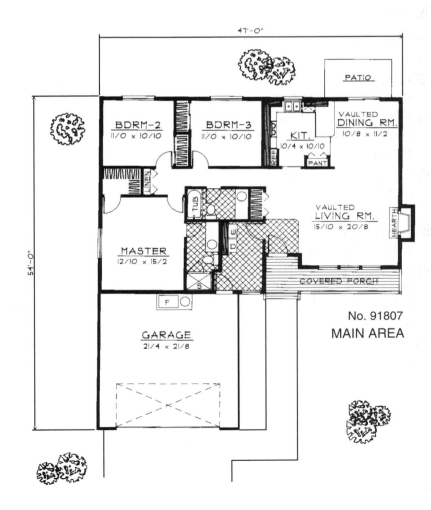

No. 91807
MAIN AREA

No. 91704

Secluded Vacation Retreat

■ This plan features:

— Two bedrooms

— Two full baths

■ A high vaulted ceiling in the Living Area with a large masonry fireplace and circular stairway

■ A wall of windows along the full cathedral height of the Living Area

■ A Kitchen with ample storage and counter space including a sink and a chopping block island

■ Private full baths for each of the bedrooms with 10 foot closets

■ A Loft with windowed doors opening to a deck

FIRST FLOOR — 1,448 SQ. FT.
LOFT — 389 SQ. FT.
CARPORT — 312 SQ. FT.

TOTAL LIVING AREA:
1,837 SQ. FT.

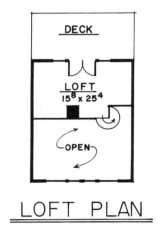

LOFT PLAN

No. 91704

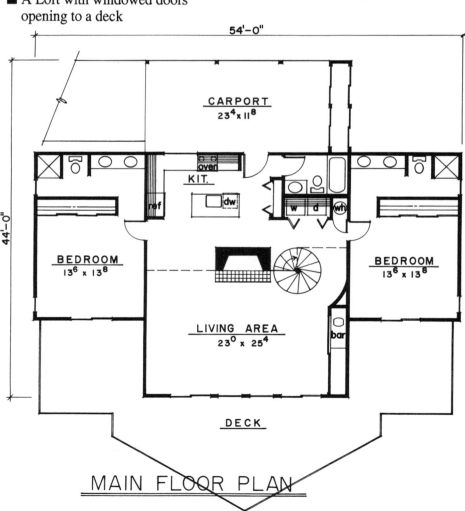

MAIN FLOOR PLAN

No. 90847
Versatile Chalet

■ This plan features:

— Two bedrooms

— Two full baths

■ A sunny and spacious Living Room/Dining Room with a cozy fireplace and sliding glass doors to the deck

■ An efficient Kitchen with a double sink and peninsula counter

■ A Master Bedroom with a Master Bath and sliding glass doors to a private deck

FIRST FLOOR — 864 SQ. FT.
SECOND FLOOR — 496 SQ. FT.
WIDTH — 27'-0"
DEPTH — 32'-0"

TOTAL LIVING AREA:
1,360 SQ. FT.

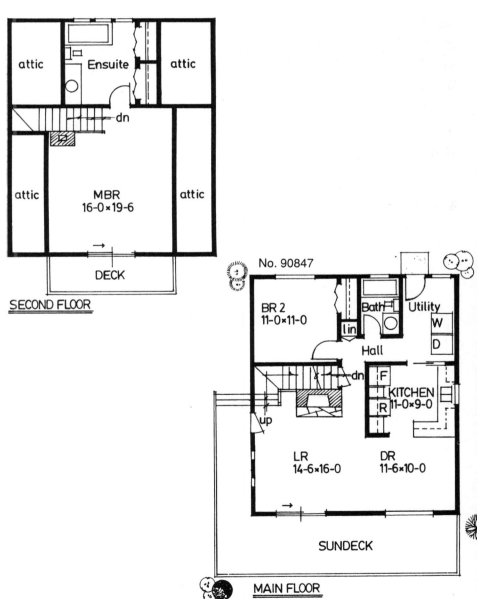

SECOND FLOOR

attic   Ensuite   attic

dn

attic   MBR
16-0×19-6   attic

DECK

No. 90847

BR 2
11-0×11-0   Bath   Utility

lin   W
D

Hall

dn   F

up   R   KITCHEN
11-0×9-0

LR
14-6×16-0   DR
11-6×10-0

SUNDECK

MAIN FLOOR

No. 91804

Contemporary Angles Add Exterior Appeal

- This plan features:
  — Four bedrooms
  — Three full baths
- A vaulted, two-story ceiling and an open stairway in the foyer
- An eleven foot high ceiling in the sunken Living Room, adding volume to the space
- An efficient, angular Kitchen that is open to the Nook and sunken Family Room

- A corner fireplace warming the Family Room
- A phenomenal Master Suite with a walk-in closet, spa tub, step-in shower, and a double vanity
- Two additional bedrooms that share a full hall bath

FIRST FLOOR — 1,396 SQ. FT.
SECOND FLOOR — 1,034 SQ. FT.

TOTAL LIVING AREA:
2,430 SQ. FT.

No. 91804

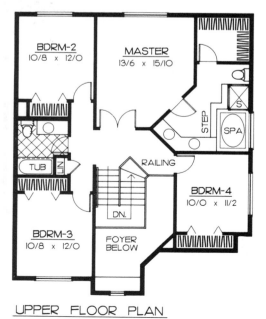

UPPER FLOOR PLAN

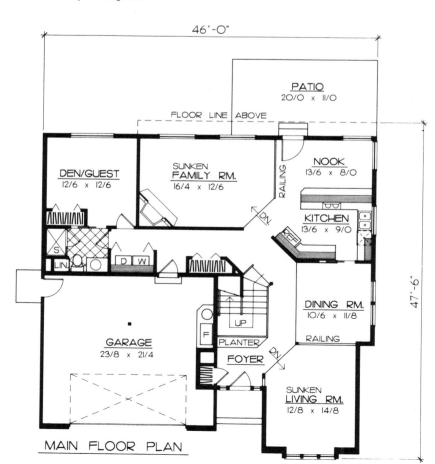

MAIN FLOOR PLAN

142

No. 90905

Compact Home is Surprisingly Spacious

■ This plan features:

— Three bedrooms

— Two full baths

■ A spacious Living Room warmed by a fireplace

■ A Dining Room flowing off the Living Room with sliding glass doors to the deck

■ An efficient, well-equipped Kitchen with snack bar, double sink, and ample cabinet and counter space

■ A Master Suite with a walk-in closet and private full bath

■ Two additional, roomy bedrooms with ample closet space and protection from street noise from the two-car Garage

FIRST FLOOR — 1,314 SQ. FT.
BASEMENT — 1,488 SQ. FT.
GARAGE — 484 SQ. FT.
WIDTH — 50'-0"
DEPTH — 54'-0"

TOTAL LIVING AREA:
1,314 SQ. FT.

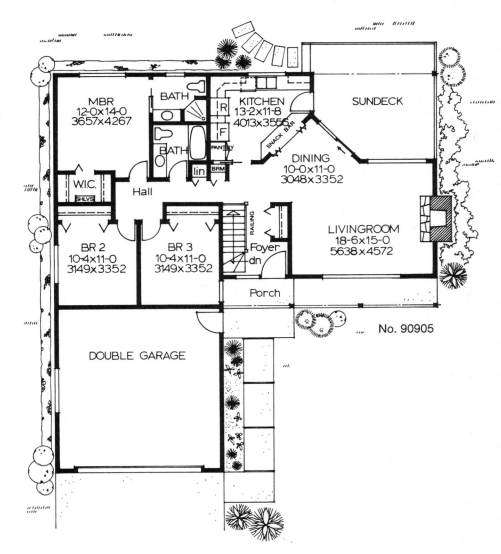

No. 90905

No. 90440
Rustic Warmth

■ This plan features:

— Three bedrooms

— Two full baths

■ A fireplaced Living Room with built-in bookshelves

■ A fully-equipped Kitchen with an island

■ A sunny Dining Room with glass sliders to wood deck

■ A first floor Master Suite with walk-in closet and lavish Master Bath

■ An optional basement or crawl space foundation — please specify when ordering

FIRST FLOOR — 1,100 SQ. FT.
SECOND FLOOR — 664 SQ. FT.
BASEMENT — 1,100 SQ. FT.

TOTAL LIVING AREA: 1,764 SQ. FT.

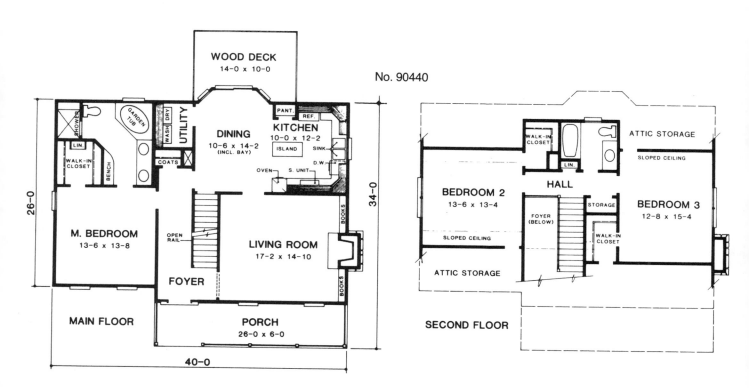

No. 99371

Cozy and Comfortable

■ This plan features:

— Three bedrooms

— Two and one half baths

■ A bayed window brightening the Breakfast area

■ A Master Bedroom with vaulted ceiling and large window area

■ A Living Room with a fireplace opening to the Dining Room

■ Access to the rear deck through the Breakfast area sliding doors

FIRST FLOOR — 842 SQ. FT.
SECOND FLOOR — 867 SQ. FT.

TOTAL LIVING AREA:
1,709 SQ. FT.

Upper Floor

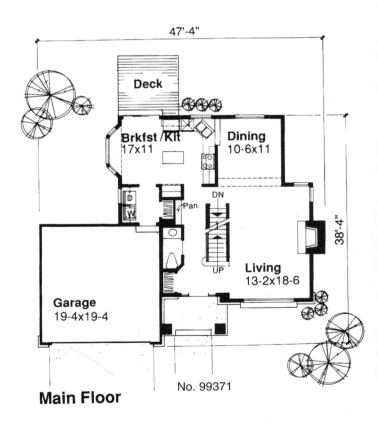

Main Floor

No. 99371

No. 90448
Classic Colonial

- This plan features:

— Three or five bedrooms

— Two to three full and one half baths

- An optional third floor with two additional bedrooms and a third full bath

- A Master Suite with a large walk-in closet, private bath with a corner tub, a full sized shower and double vanities

- A formal Dining Room with a tray ceiling to add elegance

- A spacious island Kitchen with all the amenities

- A sunny Breakfast bay for informal eating

- An expansive Great Room with a fireplace

- An optional basement or crawl space foundation — please specify when ordering

FIRST FLOOR — 1,098 SQ. FT.
SECOND FLOOR — 1,064 SQ. FT.
UNFINISHED THIRD FLOOR —
596 SQ. FT.
BASEMENT — 1,084 SQ. FT.

TOTAL LIVING AREA: 2,162 SQ. FT.

No. 90448

MATERIAL LIST AVAILABLE

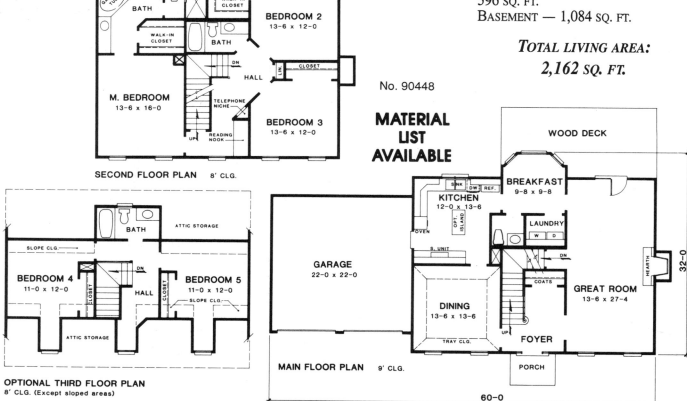

No. 90176
Flexible Cape Loaded with Amenities

■ This plan features:

— Three bedrooms

— Two full baths

■ A fireplace in the Living Room that gives the room a cozy glow

■ A formal Dining Room that could double as a fourth bedroom with a walk-in closet

■ A spacious Family Room with sliding glass doors to the patio

■ A Master Bedroom with a dressing area and private entrance to a full bath

■ An optional basement or crawl space foundation — please specify when ordering

FIRST FLOOR — 1,068 SQ. FT.

SECOND FLOOR — 804 SQ. FT.

TOTAL LIVING AREA: 1,872 SQ. FT.

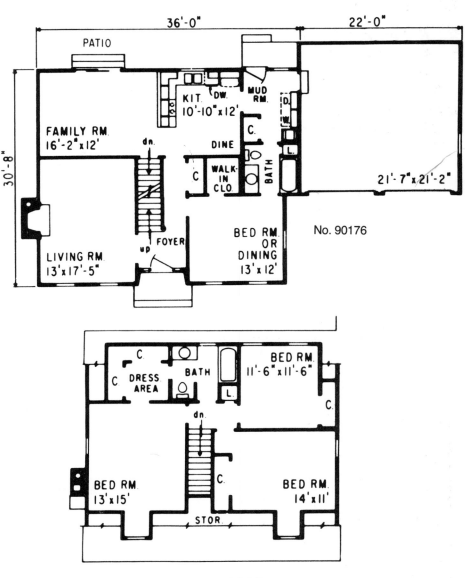

PATIO

36'-0" 22'-0"

30'-8"

FAMILY RM. 16'-2" x 12'

KIT. 10'-10" x 12'   DW   MUD RM.   D W

DINE   C   L

dn   C   WALK-IN CLO.   BATH

21'-7" x 21'-2"

No. 90176

LIVING RM. 13' x 17'-5"   up   FOYER   BED RM. OR DINING 13' x 12'

C   BATH   BED RM. 11'-6" x 11'-6"

C   DRESS AREA   L   C

dn

BED RM. 13' x 15'   C

BED RM. 14' x 11'

STOR.

SECOND FLOOR

No. 92111

Two-Story Daylight Basement Design

■ This plan features:

— Four bedrooms

— Four full and one half baths

■ A secluded Study with corner window

■ An exceptional Family Room with an elegant corner fireplace

■ An island Kitchen with a double sink, walk-in pantry, ample cabinet and cupboard space and an eating Nook area

■ A Master Suite with a private Master Bath and large walk-in closet

■ Two second floor bedrooms that share a full bath and a third bedroom with a private bath

■ A Recreation Room with a wetbar, private bath, luxurious hot tub and an angled vanity

FIRST FLOOR — 1,888 SQ. FT.
SECOND FLOOR — 1,613 SQ. FT.
FINISHED BASEMENT — 1,365 SQ. FT.
SHOP — 543 SQ. FT.
GARAGE — 955 SQ. FT.

TOTAL LIVING AREA:
4,866 SQ. FT.

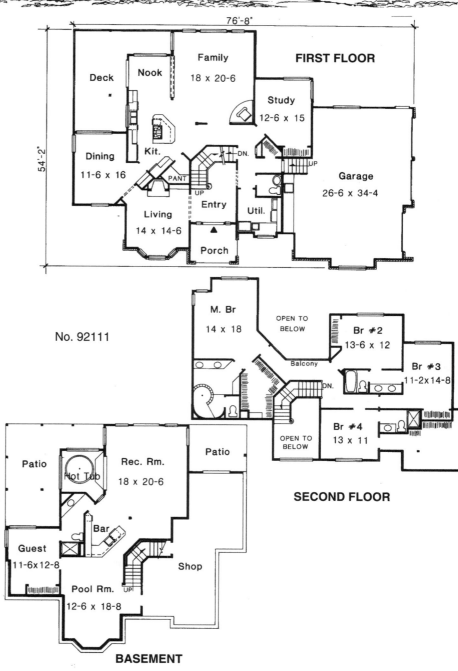

No. 92111

148

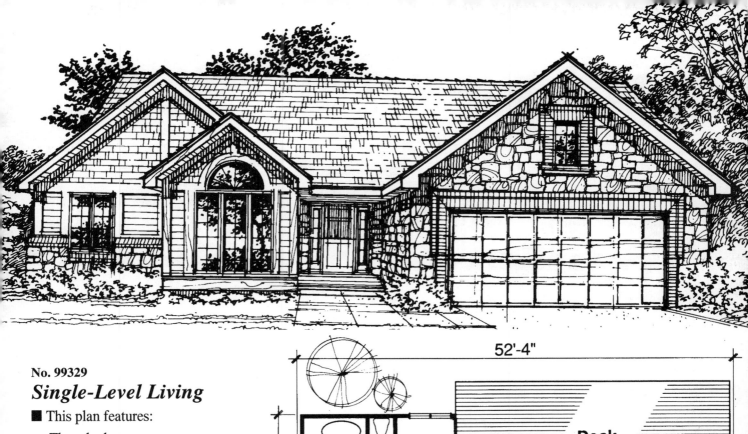

No. 99329

Single-Level Living

■ This plan features:

— Three bedrooms

— Two full baths

■ A fireplace which forms the focus of the Living Room

■ An angled Kitchen with a sunny Breakfast room, built-in pantry and ample storage and counter space

■ A vaulted ceiling in the Master Suite with a sky-lit bath and walk-in closet

■ Two additional bedrooms that are served by a full hall bath

FIRST FLOOR — 1,642 SQ. FT.

TOTAL LIVING AREA:
1,642 SQ. FT.

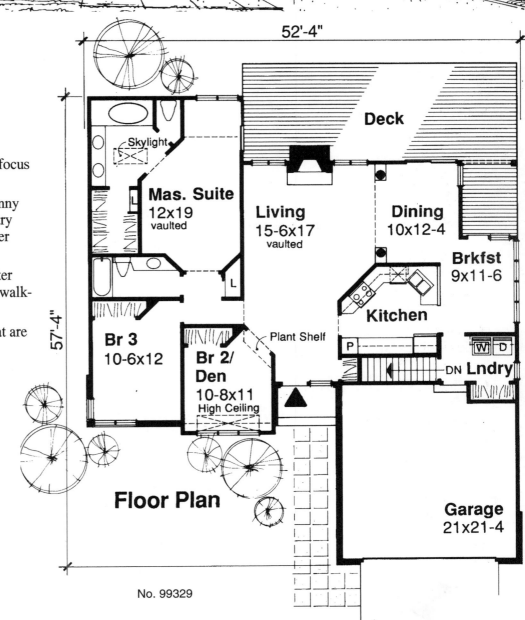

52'-4"

57'-4"

Skylight

Mas. Suite
12x19
vaulted

Living
15-6x17
vaulted

Deck

Dining
10x12-4

Brkfst
9x11-6

Kitchen

Plant Shelf

P

W D

DN **Lndry**

Br 3
10-6x12

**Br 2/
Den**
10-8x11
High Ceiling

Garage
21x21-4

Floor Plan

No. 99329

No. 90421
Ideal for Formal Entertaining

■ This plan features:

— Three bedrooms

— Two full baths

■ A lovely French Provincial design

■ A large Family Room with a raised hearth fireplace and double doors to the patio

■ An L-shaped, island Kitchen with a Breakfast Bay and open counter to the Family Room

■ A Master Suite including one double closet and a compartmentalized bath with walk-in closet, step-up garden tub, double vanity and linen closet

■ Two front bedrooms sharing a full hall bath with a linen closet

■ An optional basement, slab or crawl space foundation — please specify when ordering

FIRST FLOOR — 1,940 SQ. FT.

TOTAL LIVING AREA: 1,940 SQ. FT.

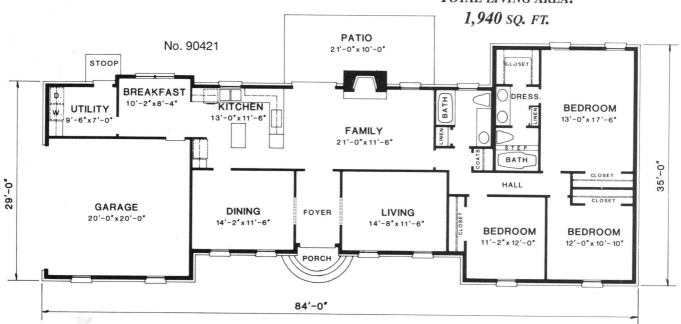

No. 90421

STOOP

BREAKFAST
10'-2" x 8'-4"

KITCHEN
13'-0" x 11'-6"

UTILITY
9'-6" x 7'-0"

D.W.

PATIO
21'-0" x 10'-0"

FAMILY
21'-0" x 11'-6"

BATH

LINEN

CLOSET

DRESS.

LINEN

BEDROOM
13'-0" x 17'-6"

COATS

STEP

BATH

GARAGE
20'-0" x 20'-0"

DINING
14'-2" x 11'-6"

FOYER

LIVING
14'-8" x 11'-6"

CLOSET

HALL

CLOSET

CLOSET

PORCH

BEDROOM
11'-2" x 12'-0"

BEDROOM
12'-0" x 10'-10"

29'-0"

35'-0"

84'-0"

No. 91340

Spanish Style Affordable Home

■ This plan features:

— Two bedrooms

— Two full baths

■ A large Master Suite with vaulted ceilings and handicap accessible private bath

■ Vaulted ceilings in Great Room

■ An open Kitchen area with an eating bar

FIRST FLOOR — 1,111 SQ. FT.

TOTAL LIVING AREA: 1,111 SQ. FT.

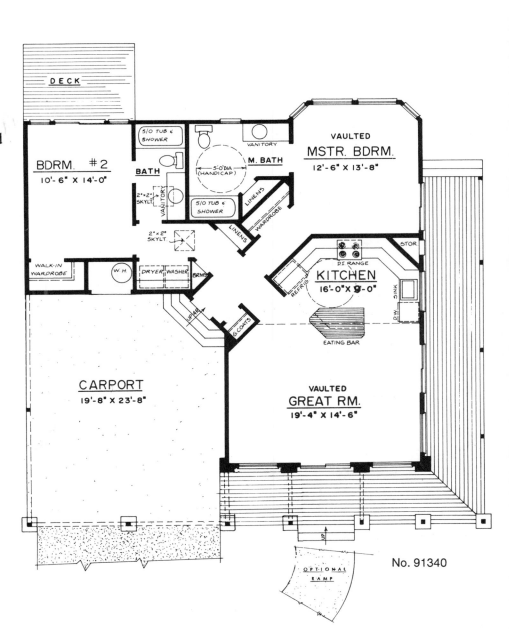

DECK

5/0 TUB & SHOWER

VANITORY

VAULTED MSTR. BDRM. 12'-6" X 13'-8"

BDRM. #2 10'-6" X 14'-0"

BATH

2'x2' SKYLT

VANITORY

5/0 TUB & SHOWER

M. BATH

5'-0" DIA (HANDICAP)

LINENS

WARDROBE

LINENS

STOR.

2'x2' SKYLT

WALK-IN WARDROBE

W. H.

DRYER WASHER

BR. M. S.

UP M.R.

COATS

REFRIG

DI RANGE

KITCHEN 16'-0" X 9'-0"

SINK

D.W.

EATING BAR

CARPORT 19'-8" X 23'-8"

VAULTED GREAT RM. 19'-4" X 14'-6"

UP

OPTIONAL RAMP

No. 91340

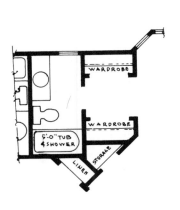

WARDROBE

WARDROBE

5'-0" TUB & SHOWER

STORAGE

LINEN

ALTERNATE BATH

No. 90968

Main Floor Study Sure to be a Hit

■ This plan features:

— Three bedrooms

— Two full and one half baths

■ A gas fireplace in the spacious Family Room

■ An island Kitchen efficiently flanked by the formal Dining Room and the informal Nook

■ A built-in china cabinet in the formal Dining Room

■ A bayed sitting area in the Master Suite that is equipped with a walk-in closet and a private Master Bath

■ A Bonus Room so that the home grows with your family

FIRST FLOOR — 1,268 SQ. FT.
SECOND FLOOR — 912 SQ. FT.
BONUS ROOM — 224 SQ. FT.
BASEMENT — 1,200 SQ. FT.
GARAGE — 421 SQ. FT.
WIDTH — 41'-0"
DEPTH — 52'-0"

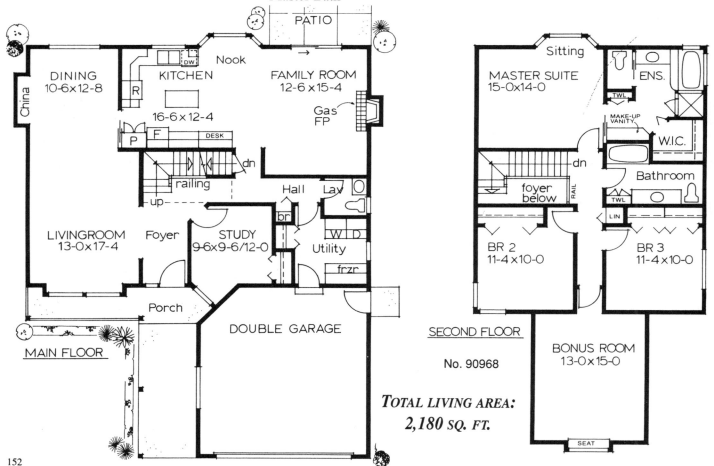

MAIN FLOOR

SECOND FLOOR

No. 90968

TOTAL LIVING AREA: 2,180 SQ. FT.

No. 90933

Tradition with a Twist

■ This plan features:

— Four bedrooms

— Two full and one half baths

■ A sky-lit foyer

■ A sunken Family Room warmed by a fireplace and separated by a railing from the Breakfast Nook

■ A well-appointed Kitchen which serves either the informal Breakfast Nook or the formal Dining Room with efficiency

■ A Master Suite with a walk-in closet, full bath and a private, hidden sun deck

FIRST FLOOR — 1,104 SQ. FT.
SECOND FLOOR — 845 SQ. FT.
GARAGE & WORKSHOP — 538 SQ. FT.
BASEMENT — 1,098 SQ. FT.
WIDTH — 55'-0"
DEPTH — 32'-0"

TOTAL LIVING AREA: 1,949 SQ. FT.

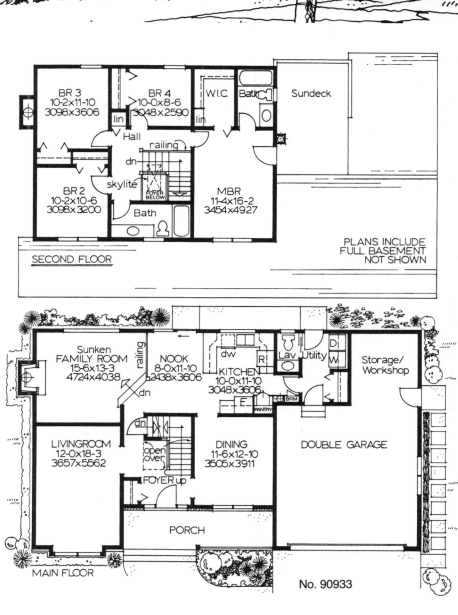

No. 99210

Country Colonial

■ This plan features:

— Three bedrooms

— Three full and one half baths

■ A dramatic cathedral ceiling entry with balcony overlook

■ A two-story Family Room with a divided window wall

■ A well-planned Kitchen that opens onto a sunny, "greenhouse" Breakfast Room

■ Separate his and her dressing/bath suites in the Master Bedroom

FIRST FLOOR — 2,116 SQ. FT.
SECOND FLOOR — 1,848 SQ. FT.
GARAGE — 667 SQ. FT.

TOTAL LIVING AREA: 3,964 SQ. FT.

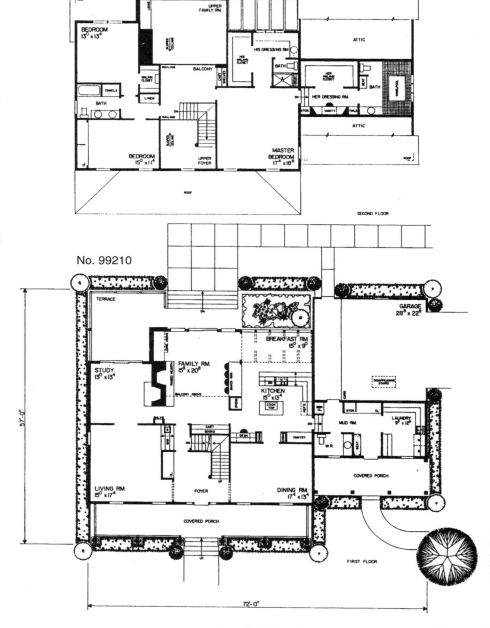

No. 99210

No. 99238

Economical Vacation Home Provides Viewing Deck

■ This plan features:

— Three bedrooms

— Two full baths

■ A large rectangular Living Room with a fireplace at one end and plenty of room for separate activities at the other end

■ A galley-style Kitchen with adjoining Dining area

■ A second-floor Master Bedroom with a children's dormitory across the hall

■ A second-floor deck outside the Master Bedroom

FIRST FLOOR — 784 SQ. FT.
SECOND FLOOR — 504 SQ. FT.

TOTAL LIVING AREA:
1,288 SQ. FT.

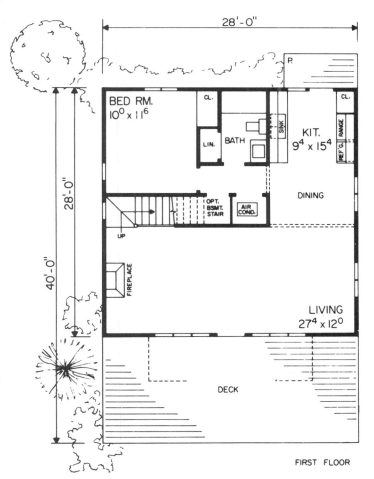

FIRST FLOOR

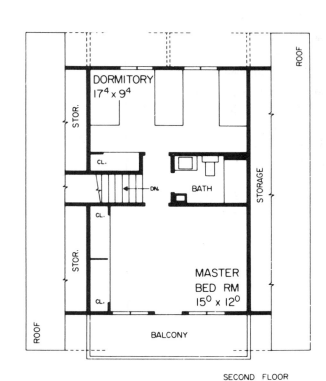

No. 99238

SECOND FLOOR

No. 91706

Master Suite is Home Away from Home

■ This plan features:

— Three bedrooms

— Two full and one half baths

■ A secluded, second floor Master Suite with sky-lit Master Bath, laundry chute, private study and a corner fireplace

■ A pre-fabricated Solarium, doubling the size of the bright Kitchen/Family Room

■ An elegant Living Room with a corner fireplace and large front windows

■ A formal Dining Room conveniently located next to the Kitchen

■ Two additional bedrooms that are served by a full hall bath

FIRST FLOOR — 1,856 SQ. FT.
SECOND FLOOR — 618 SQ. FT.
GARAGE — 704 SQ. FT.

TOTAL LIVING AREA: 2,474 SQ. FT.

No. 91706

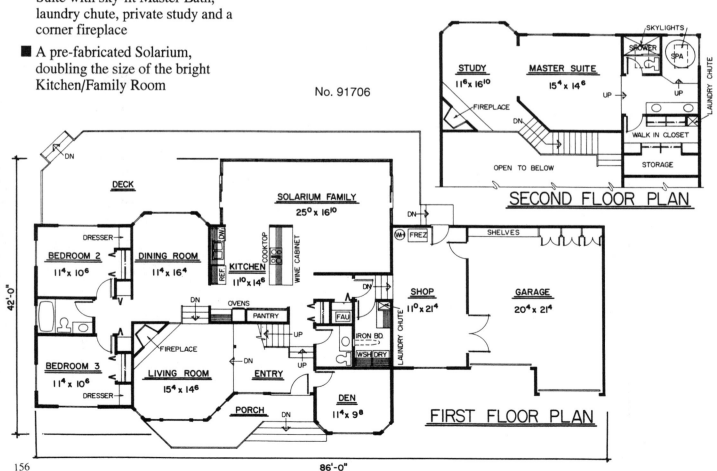

No. 90954

Rooms with a View

■ This plan features:

— Three bedrooms

— Two full and one half baths

■ A vaulted foyer offering access to every area of the house

■ A Kitchen featuring a built-in pantry and desk, and a bay Nook for informal meals

■ A Master Suite with private access to the sun deck

FIRST FLOOR — 1,617 SQ. FT.
BASEMENT — 1,617 SQ. FT.

TOTAL LIVING AREA:
1,617 SQ. FT.

No. 90954

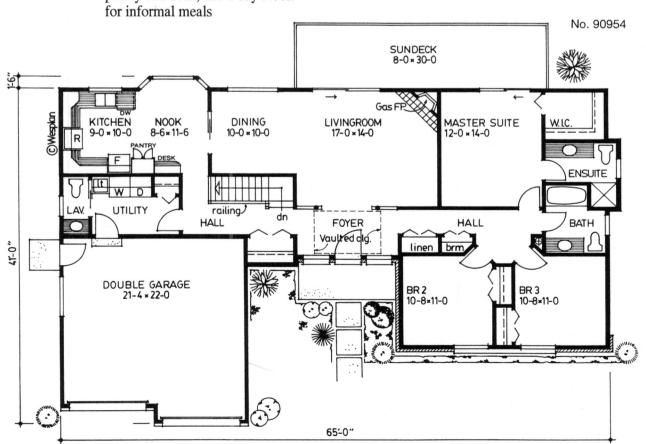

No. 90412

No Wasted Space

■ This plan features:

— Three bedrooms

— Two full baths

■ A centrally located Great Room with a cathedral ceiling, exposed wood beams, and large areas of fixed glass

■ The Living and Dining areas separated by a massive stone fireplace

■ A secluded Master Suite with a walk-in closet and private Master Bath

■ An efficient Kitchen with a convenient laundry area

■ An optional basement, slab or crawl space foundation — please specify when ordering

FIRST FLOOR — 1,454 SQ. FT.

TOTAL LIVING AREA: *1,454 SQ. FT.*

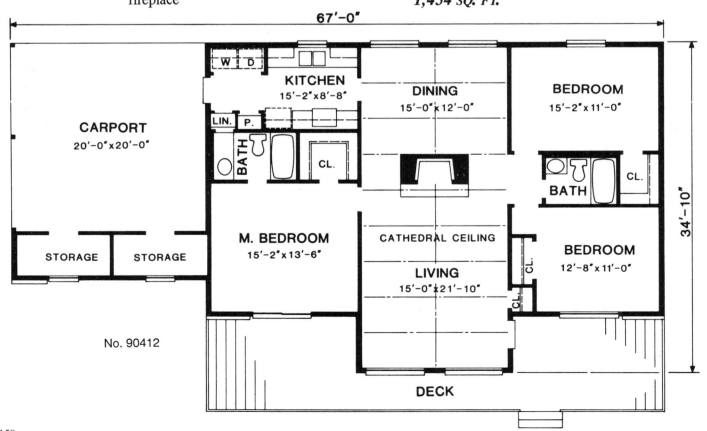

67'-0"

34'-10"

CARPORT
20'-0"x20'-0"

STORAGE   STORAGE

M. BEDROOM
15'-2"x13'-6"

W D

KITCHEN
15'-2"x8'-8"

LIN.   P.

BATH

CL.

DINING
15'-0"x12'-0"

CATHEDRAL CEILING

LIVING
15'-0"x21'-10"

CL.

CL.

BEDROOM
15'-2"x11'-0"

BATH

CL.

BEDROOM
12'-8"x11'-0"

No. 90412

DECK

No. 90433
Cabin in the Country

■ This plan features:

— Two bedrooms

— One full and one half baths

■ A screened porch for enjoyment of your outdoor surroundings

■ A combination Living and Dining area with cozy fireplace for added warmth

■ An efficiently laid out Kitchen with a built-in pantry

■ Two large bedrooms located at the rear of the home

■ An optional slab or crawl space foundation — please specify when ordering

FIRST FLOOR — 928 SQ. FT.
SCREENED PORCH — 230 SQ. FT.
STORAGE — 14 SQ. FT.

TOTAL LIVING AREA: 928 SQ. FT.

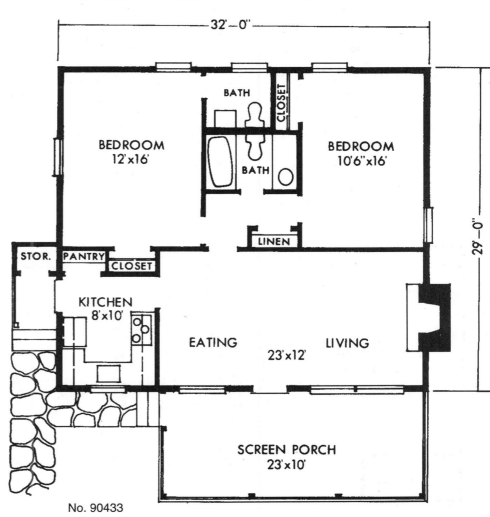

No. 90433

No. 91411
Master Suite with Private Sun Deck

■ This plan features:

— Four bedrooms

— Two and one half baths

■ A sunken Living Room, formal Dining Room, and island Kitchen enjoying an expansive view of the patio and backyard

■ A fireplaced Living Room keeping the house toasty after the sun goes down

■ Skylights brightening the balcony and Master Bath

■ An optional crawl space or basement foundation — please specify when ordering

FIRST FLOOR — 1,249 SQ. FT.
SECOND FLOOR — 890 SQ. FT.
GARAGE — 462 SQ. FT.

TOTAL LIVING AREA:
2,139 SQ. FT.

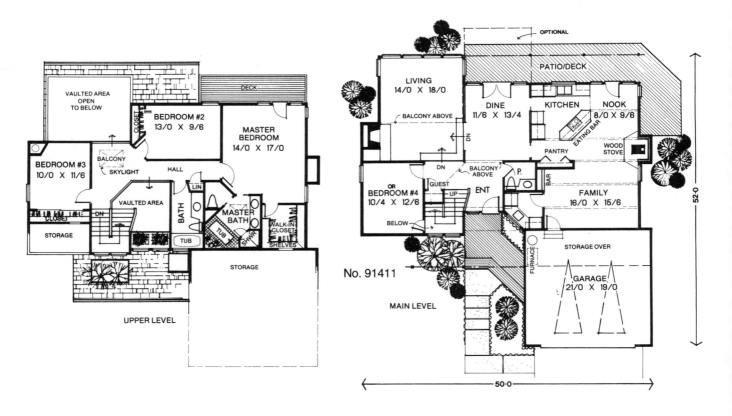

No. 99314

Contemporary Classic with a Custom Look

■ This plan features:

— Two bedrooms

— Two and a half baths

■ A well-appointed Kitchen with angular Nook

■ A two-story Great Room accentuated by a massive fireplace and glass sliders to the rear Deck

■ A bump-out window seat and private bath with double vanities in the Master Suite

FIRST FLOOR — 1,044 SQ. FT.
SECOND FLOOR — 454 SQ. FT.

TOTAL LIVING AREA: 1,498 SQ. FT.

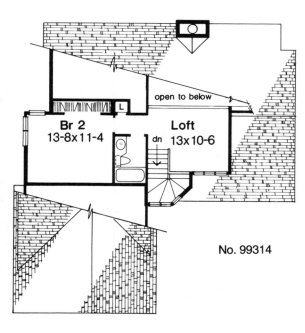

No. 99314

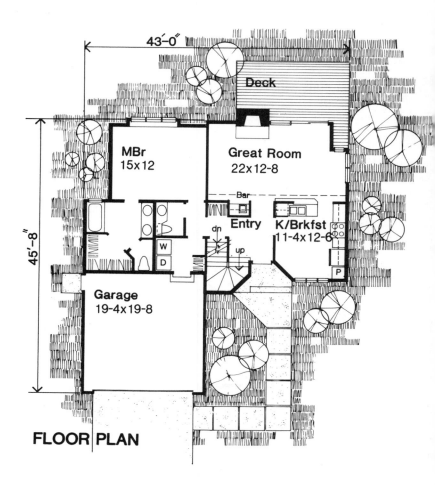

FLOOR PLAN

No. 90624

First Floor Master Suite is Special

■ This plan features:

— Three bedrooms

— Two and one half baths

■ A two-story foyer lit from above by a skylight

■ Access to the terrace or Garage through the Family Room

■ A heat-circulating fireplace

■ A Master Suite with vaulted ceilings and spectacular windows

FIRST FLOOR — 1,440 SQ. FT.
SECOND FLOOR — 613 SQ. FT.
BASEMENT — 1,340 SQ. FT.
GARAGE — 462 SQ. FT.

TOTAL LIVING AREA:
2,053 SQ. FT.

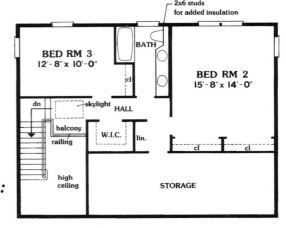

SECOND FLOOR

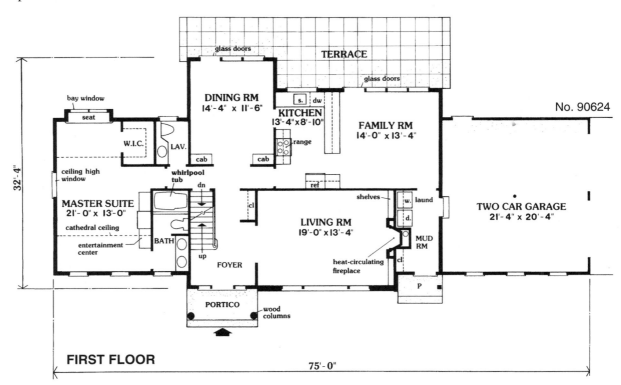

FIRST FLOOR

No. 90665
Visual Excitement

■ This plan features:

— Three bedrooms

— Two and one half baths

■ A sunken Living Room with a brick walled fireplace and a two-story ceiling height

■ A bow windowed, elegant formal Dining room with close access to the Kitchen

■ A Kitchen with a cooktop peninsula flowing into the Family Dining area

FIRST FLOOR — 1,458 SQ. FT.
SECOND FLOOR — 470 SQ. FT.

TOTAL LIVING AREA:
1,928 SQ. FT.

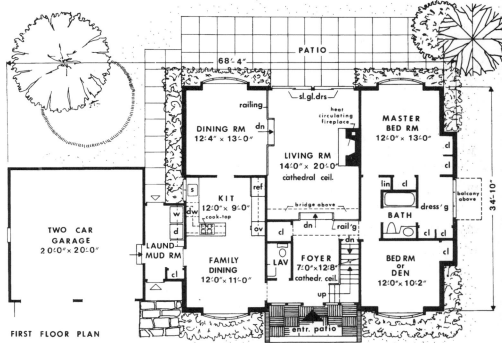

No. 90665

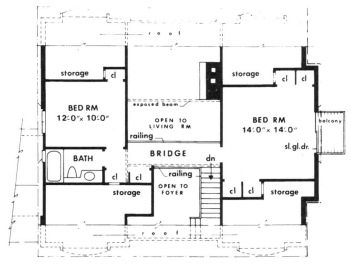

No. 90397

Country Classic Full Of Character

■ This plan features:

— Three bedrooms

— Two full and one half baths

■ A fireplace dividing the vaulted ceiling Living Room and Dining Room

■ An efficiently designed country Kitchen with a corner sink overlooking the deck and family sitting area

■ A vaulted ceiling Master Suite with a double-vanity, bath, and a walk-in closet

FIRST FLOOR — 834 SQ. FT.
SECOND FLOOR — 722 SQ. FT.

TOTAL LIVING AREA:
1,556 SQ. FT.

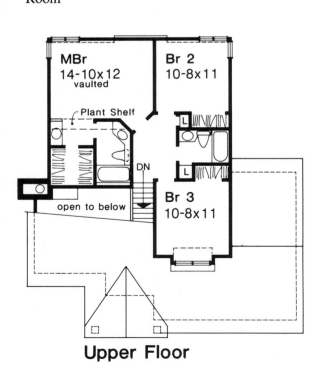

Upper Floor

MBr
14-10x12
vaulted

Br 2
10-8x11

Plant Shelf

DN

open to below

Br 3
10-8x11

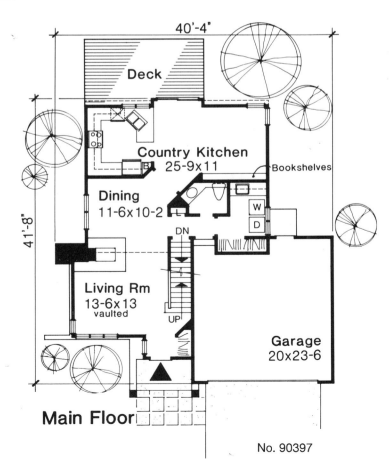

Main Floor

40'-4"

41'-8"

Deck

Country Kitchen
25-9x11

Bookshelves

Dining
11-6x10-2

W
D

DN

Living Rm
13-6x13
vaulted

UP

Garage
20x23-6

No. 90397

No. 90356

Balcony Overlooks Living Room Below

■ This plan features:

— Three bedrooms

— Two full and one half baths

■ A vaulted ceiling Living Room with a balcony above and a fireplace

■ An efficient, well-equipped Kitchen with stovetop island and easy flow of traffic into the Dining Room

■ A deck accessible from the Living Room

■ A luxurious Master Suite with a window seat bay, walk-in closet, dressing area, and a private shower

■ Two additional bedrooms that share a full hall bath

FIRST FLOOR — 674 SQ. FT.
SECOND FLOOR — 677 SQ. FT.

TOTAL LIVING AREA: 1,351 SQ. FT.

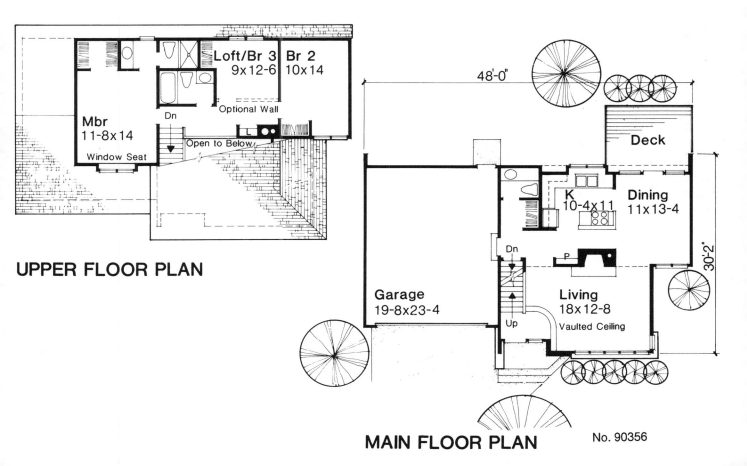

UPPER FLOOR PLAN

MAIN FLOOR PLAN   No. 90356

No. 91726

The Illusion of Spaciousness

■ This plan features:

— Three bedrooms

— Two full and one half baths

■ A vaulted ceiling in the combined Living and Dining Rooms with a fireplace to add warmth and visual interest

■ A step-in pantry, lazy Susan shelving in the corner cupboard, and an eating bar in the modern Kitchen

■ A Family Room with sliding glass doors that open to the patio

■ A Master Suite with a large walk-in closet, private bath and sliding glass doors that open to a private deck

■ Two additional bedrooms served by a full hall bath

FIRST FLOOR — 960 SQ. FT.
SECOND FLOOR — 768 SQ. FT.
GARAGE — 576 SQ. FT.
WIDTH — 50'-0"
DEPTH — 37'-0"

TOTAL LIVING AREA: 1,728 SQ. FT.

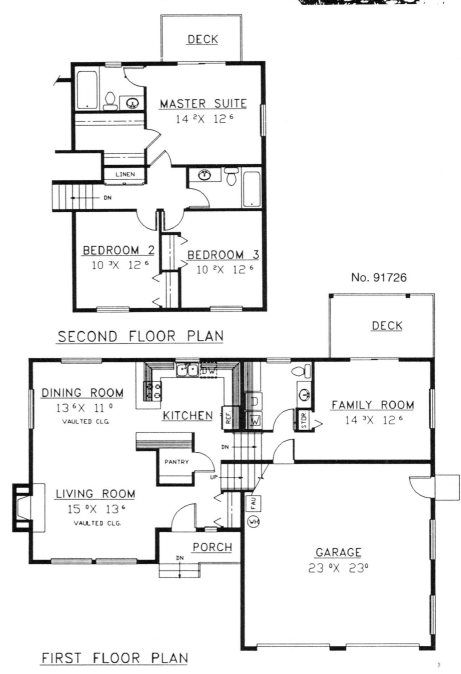

DECK

MASTER SUITE
14 ²X 12 ⁶

LINEN

DN

BEDROOM 2
10 ³X 12 ⁶

BEDROOM 3
10 ²X 12 ⁶

SECOND FLOOR PLAN

No. 91726

DECK

DINING ROOM
13 ⁶X 11 ⁰
VAULTED CLG.

KITCHEN

REF.

FAMILY ROOM
14 ³X 12 ⁶

STOR

DN

PANTRY

UP

W

LIVING ROOM
15 ⁰X 13 ⁶
VAULTED CLG.

FAU

VH

PORCH

DN

GARAGE
23 ⁰X 23 ⁰

FIRST FLOOR PLAN

No. 91212

Celebration of Light and Space

■ This plan features:

— Three bedrooms

— Two full baths

■ A massive fireplace dominating the Great Room

■ A country Kitchen with an efficient island that serves as the breakfast bar

■ A luxurious Master Bedroom with a walk-in closet and a complete Master Bath

■ Large vertical windows and generous closets in the two additional bedrooms

FIRST FLOOR — 1,873 SQ. FT.
GARAGE — 467 SQ. FT.

TOTAL LIVING AREA:
1,873 SQ. FT.

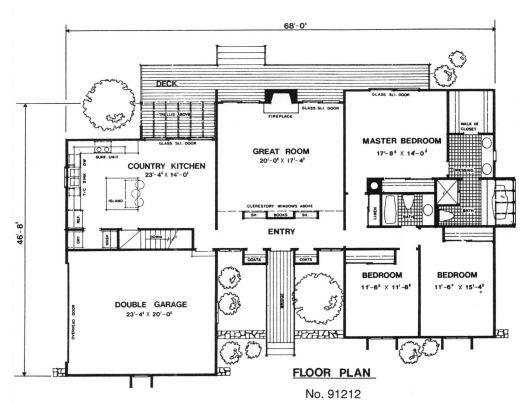

68'-0'

46'-8'

DECK

TRELLIS ABOVE

GLASS SLI. DOOR

SURF. UNIT

COUNTRY KITCHEN
23'-4' X 14'-0'

ISLAND

T/C SINK DW

REF.

DRY WASH

DOWN

FIREPLACE

GLASS SLI. DOOR

GREAT ROOM
20'-0' X 17'-4'

CLERESTORY WINDOWS ABOVE

SH. BOOKS SH.

ENTRY

GLASS SLI. DOOR

MASTER BEDROOM
17'-8' X 14'-0'

WALK IN CLOSET

DRESSING

LINEN BATH BATH

COATS COATS

BRIDGE

BEDROOM
11'-6' X 11'-8'

BEDROOM
11'-6' X 15'-4'

DOUBLE GARAGE
23'-4' X 20'-0'

OVERHEAD DOOR

FLOOR PLAN

No. 91212

No materials list available

No. 99229
Contemporary

- This plan features:
- — Three bedrooms
- — Two full and one half baths
- A huge skylight in the stairwell giving light to a typically dark area
- Two second-floor bedrooms with use of a full hall bath and a balcony lounge area
- A Master Suite with well-proportioned dressing suite and sliding doors to the patio
- A Kitchen area that combines with an open Breakfast Room, and has a handy pass-through counter and snack bar
- A large Gathering Room with cozy fireplace

FIRST FLOOR — 1,342 SQ. FT.
SECOND FLOOR — 619 SQ. FT.
GARAGE — 506 SQ. FT.

TOTAL LIVING AREA: 1,961 SQ. FT.

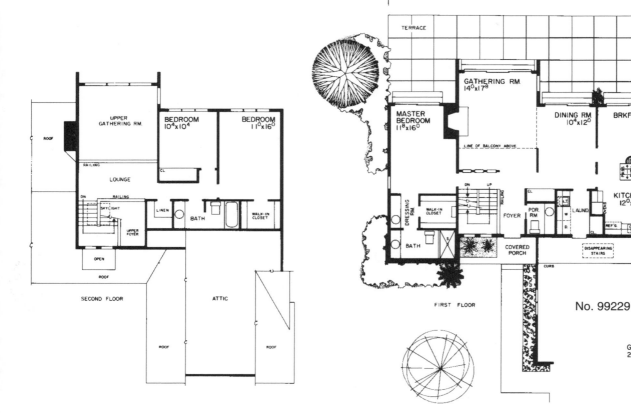

No. 99246

Unique Rooms Add Character

■ This plan features:

— Three bedrooms

— Two full and two half baths

■ A Master Suite with matching walk-in closets, a dressing area, and Master Bath with whirlpool tub

■ A country Kitchen with a fireplace, a four-seat breakfast bar, and ample storage and cabinet space

■ A Living Room with a cozy fireplace that easily flows into the formal Dining Room

■ A Clutter Room with laundry area, workbench, tool storage and a center work island

FIRST FLOOR — 2,758 SQ. FT.
GREENHOUSE — 149 SQ. FT.
BASEMENT — 2,758 SQ. FT.

TOTAL LIVING AREA: 2,758 SQ. FT.

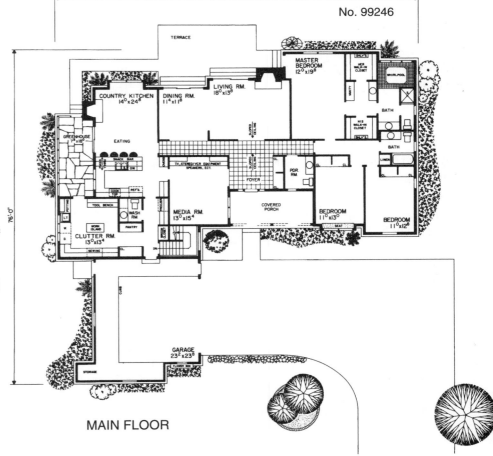

MAIN FLOOR

No. 91638

Many Windows Add Eye-Appeal

■ This plan features:

— Three bedrooms (with optional fourth)

— Three full baths

■ A fireplaced Family Room and Living Room

■ An efficient Kitchen with an adjoining eating Nook and easy access to the formal Dining Room

■ A coved ceiling Master Bedroom with a private bath and a walk-in closet

FIRST FLOOR — 1,181 SQ. FT.
SECOND FLOOR — 918 SQ. FT.
BONUS ROOM — 242 SQ. FT.

TOTAL LIVING AREA: 2,099 SQ. FT.

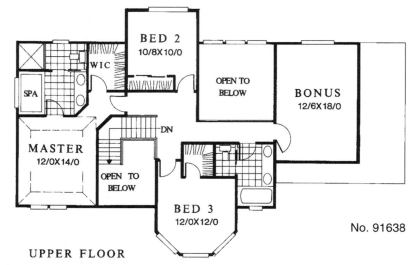

UPPER FLOOR

No. 91638

No materials list available

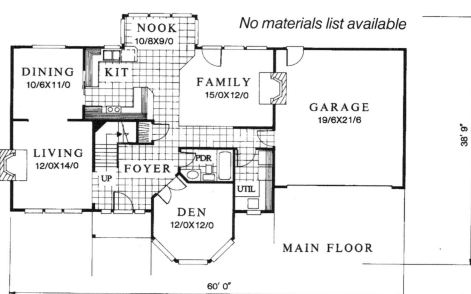

MAIN FLOOR

60' 0"

38' 9"

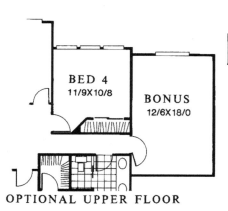

OPTIONAL UPPER FLOOR

No. 91776

Spread Out Living

■ This plan features:

— Three bedrooms

— Two full baths

■ A formal Dining Room overlooking a flower garden and a sun soaked Living Room

■ A Living Room with high ceilings and large windows at the front of the house

■ A Family Room with a strategically placed fireplace and access to a rear deck through sliding doors

■ A Master Suite with a walk-in closet, full bath and access to a rear deck

FIRST FLOOR — 1,798 SQ. FT.
GARAGE — 484 SQ. FT.

TOTAL LIVING AREA: 1,798 SQ. FT.

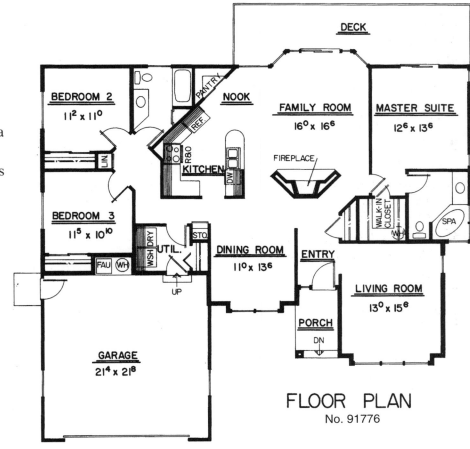

FLOOR PLAN
No. 91776

No. 91701

Spacious Country Home

■ This plan features:

— Three bedrooms

— Three full baths

■ A vaulted ceiling in the rambling Family Room/Nook/Kitchen combination

■ A vegetable sink in the work island of the large Kitchen which also has a walk-in pantry

■ A cozy, corner fireplace in the Family Room

■ A Master Suite with an L-shaped walk-in closet, private spa tub, separate shower, and double vanities

■ Two additional bedrooms that share a full, compartmentalized bath

FIRST FLOOR — 1,957 SQ. FT.
SECOND FLOOR — 531 SQ. FT.
GARAGE — 639 SQ. FT.

TOTAL LIVING AREA: 2,488 SQ. FT.

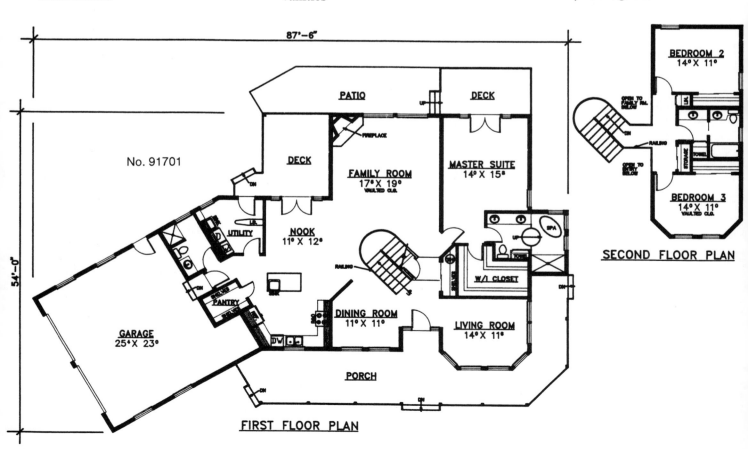

172

No. 91700

Country Style For Today

■ This plan features:

— Three bedrooms

— Two full and one half baths

■ A wide wrap-around porch for a farmhouse style

■ A spacious Living Room with double doors and a large front window

■ A garden window over the double sink in the huge, country Kitchen with two islands, one a butcher block, and the other an eating bar

■ A corner fireplace in the Family Room enjoyed throughout the Nook and Kitchen, thanks to an open layout

■ A Master Suite with a spa tub, and a huge walk-in closet as well as a shower and double vanities

FIRST FLOOR — 1,785 SQ. FT.
SECOND FLOOR — 621 SQ. FT.

TOTAL LIVING AREA: 2,406 SQ. FT.

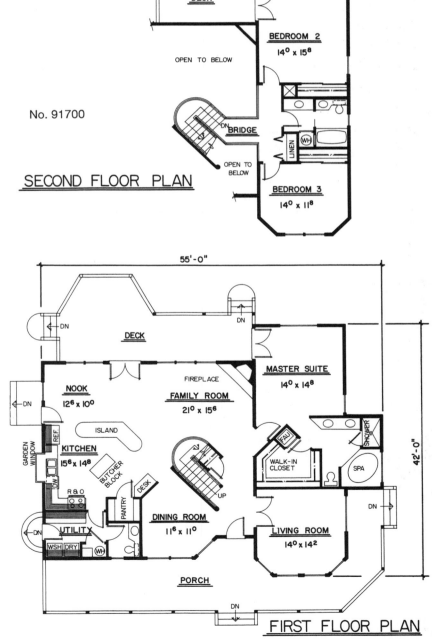

No. 91700

SECOND FLOOR PLAN

FIRST FLOOR PLAN

No. 90419

Country Kitchen and Great Room

■ This plan features:

— Three bedrooms

— Two full baths

■ Front porch, dormers, shutters and multi-paned windows

■ An eat-in country Kitchen with an island counter and bay window

■ A large utility room which can be entered from the Kitchen or Garage

■ A Great Room with an informal Dining Nook and double doors opening to the rear deck

■ A Master Suite featuring a walk-in closet and a compartmentalized bath with a linen closet

■ An optional basement, slab or crawl space foundation — please specify when ordering

FIRST FLOOR — 1,318 SQ. FT.
SECOND FLOOR — 718 SQ. FT.
BASEMENT — 1,221 SQ. FT.
GARAGE — 436 SQ. FT.

TOTAL LIVING AREA: 2,036 SQ. FT.

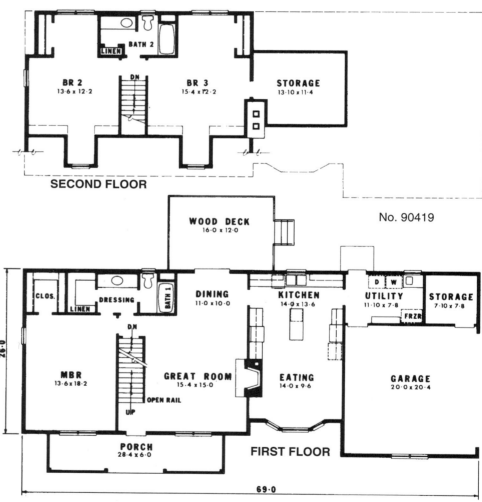

SECOND FLOOR PLAN

BED RM 4
10' x 10'

DRESS.
RM.

cl

BATH

vanity

cl

BED RM 3
12'-6"x11'-4"

HALL

LIN.

cl

MASTER
BED RM
16'-8"x11'-4"

dn

cl

cl

cl

cl

cl

BED RM 2
12'-6"x11'-4"

rail

open

BATH

No. 90615

Built In Entertainment Center for Family Fun

■ This plan features:

— Four bedrooms

— Two and one half baths

■ A heat circulating fireplace in the Living Room framed by decorative pilasters that support dropped beams

■ A convenient mudroom providing access to the two car Garage

■ A spacious Master Suite with a separate dressing area

■ An optional slab foundation

FIRST FLOOR — 1,094 SQ. FT.
SECOND FLOOR — 936 SQ. FT.
GARAGE — 441 SQ. FT.

TOTAL LIVING AREA:
2,030 SQ. FT.

FIRST FLOOR PLAN

No. 90615

60'-0"

35'-6"

TERRACE

sliding glass doors

s. dw

range

service entry

sliding glass doors

MUD RM

cl

DINING RM
12'-6" x 11'-6"

KITCHEN
10'-8" x 10'

ref.

DINETTE
8'-8" x 8'-8"

LAUNDRY

d. w.

TWO CAR GARAGE
21'-4" x 19'-8"

LAV.

heat-circulating fireplace

dn

railing

open

FAMILY RM
16' x 12'-2"(avg.)

entertainment center

LIVING RM
19'-8" x 12'-6"

FOYER

cl

up

high ceiling

PORCH

No. 99208

Cozy Traditional with Style

■ This plan features:

— Three bedrooms

— Two full baths

■ A convenient one-level design

■ A galley-style Kitchen that shares a snack bar with the spacious Gathering Room

■ A focal point fireplace making the Gathering Room warm and inviting

■ An ample Master Suite with a luxury bath which includes a whirlpool tub and separate dressing room

■ Two additional bedrooms, one that could double as a Study, located at the front of the house

FIRST FLOOR — 1,830 SQ. FT.
BASEMENT — 1,830 SQ. FT.

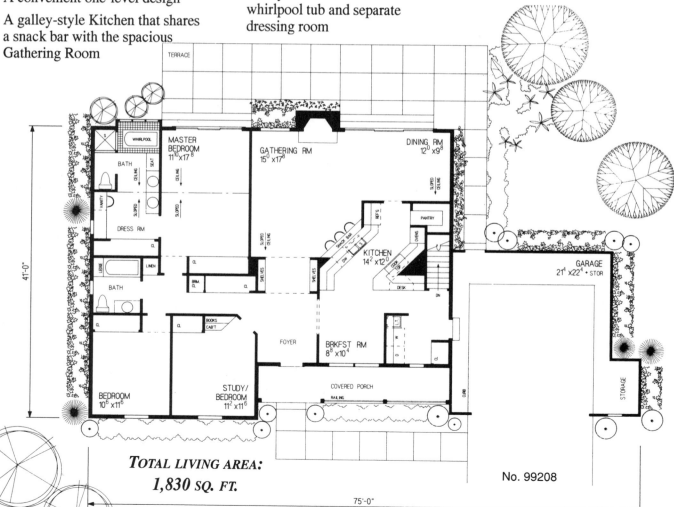

TOTAL LIVING AREA:
1,830 SQ. FT.

No. 99208

No. 90439
Romance Personified

■ This plan features:

— Three bedrooms

— Two full and one half baths

■ A spacious Family Room including a fireplace flanked by bookshelves

■ A sunny Breakfast Bay and adjoining country Kitchen with a peninsula counter

■ An expansive Master Suite spanning the width of the house including built-in shelves, walk-in closet, and a private bath with every amenity

■ A full bath that serves the two other bedrooms tucked into the gables at the front of the house

■ An optional basement or crawl space foundation — please specify when ordering

FIRST FLOOR — 1,366 SQ. FT.
SECOND FLOOR — 1,196 SQ. FT.
BASEMENT — 1,250 SQ. FT.
GARAGE — 484 SQ. FT.

TOTAL LIVING AREA: *2,562 SQ. FT.*

No. 90439

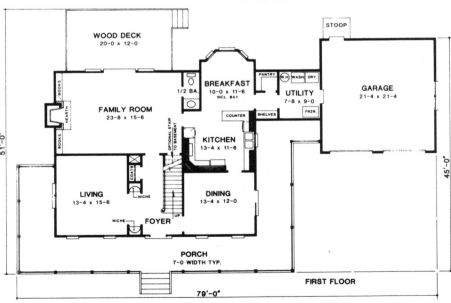

No. 90697

Carefree Contemporary

■ This plan features:

— Three bedrooms

— Two full baths

■ A corner fireplace adding intrigue to the sunny Living Room

■ Skylights in the high sloping ceiling of the Family Room which also has a greenhouse bay window and heat-circulating fireplace

■ An elegant formal Dining Room with a window alcove

■ A Master Bedroom with a private Master Bath and two closets

■ Two additional bedrooms which share a full hall bath

FIRST FLOOR — 1,597 SQ. FT.
BASEMENT — 1,512 SQ. FT.

TOTAL LIVING AREA:
1,597 SQ. FT.

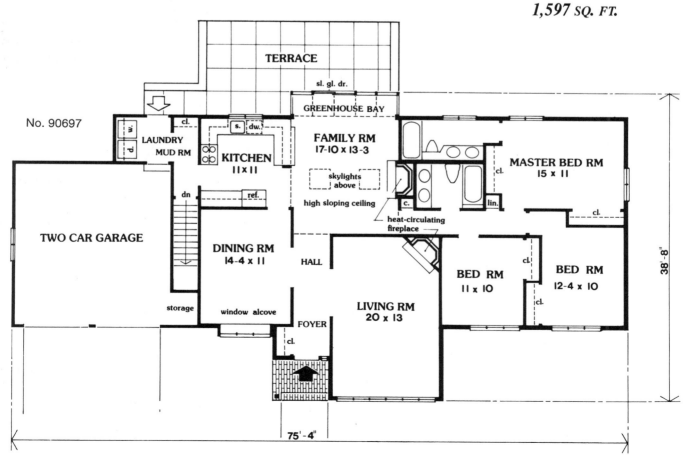

No. 90413

Rear of Home as Attractive as Front

■ This plan features:

— Three bedrooms

— Two full and one half baths

■ A sunken Family Room with a cathedral ceiling and a massive stone fireplace

■ Two front bedrooms having ample closet space and sharing a unique bath-and-a-half arrangement

■ A Master Bedroom with a walk-in closet and compartmentalized bath with double vanity and linen closet

■ A U-shaped Kitchen, well-equipped and efficient, serving the Breakfast Nook and the formal Dining Room with ease

■ A second floor with a large Studio

■ An optional basement, slab or crawl space foundation — please specify when ordering

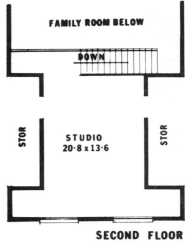

FAMILY ROOM BELOW

DOWN

STOR   STUDIO 20·8 x 13·6   STOR

SECOND FLOOR

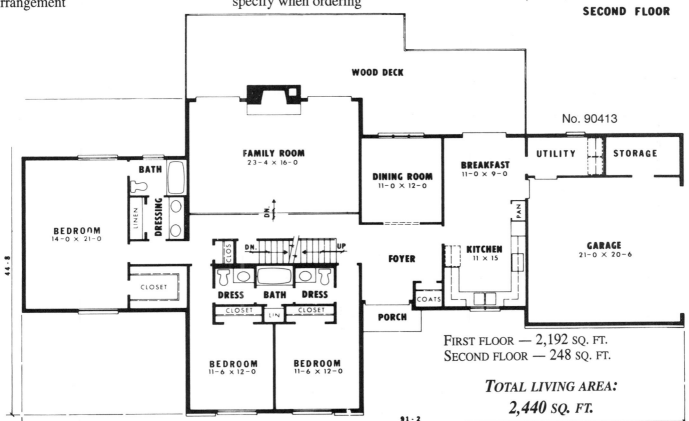

WOOD DECK

No. 90413

BATH

FAMILY ROOM
23-4 × 16-0

DINING ROOM
11-0 × 12-0

BREAKFAST
11-0 × 9-0

UTILITY   STORAGE

LINEN   DRESSING

DN.

BEDROOM
14-0 × 21-0

44·8

CLOSET

CLOS   DN.   UP

DRESS   BATH   DRESS

CLOSET   LIN   CLOSET

FOYER

COATS

PAN

KITCHEN
11 × 15

GARAGE
21-0 × 20-6

PORCH

BEDROOM
11-6 × 12-0

BEDROOM
11-6 × 12-0

91 - 2

FIRST FLOOR — 2,192 SQ. FT.
SECOND FLOOR — 248 SQ. FT.

TOTAL LIVING AREA:
2,440 SQ. FT.

No. 91660

Sunny and Open

■ This plan features:

— Four bedrooms

— Two full and one half baths

■ A vaulted ceiling in the foyer

■ A coved ceiling in the elegant Living Room enhanced by a fireplace

■ A sunken Family Room with a fireplace and French doors to the patio

■ A spacious Kitchen with a center island, snack bar, and a butler's pantry

■ A Master Suite with a coved ceiling, a private sitting area, and a lavish Master Bath

■ Three additional bedrooms served by a full hall bath

FIRST FLOOR — 1,843 SQ. FT.
SECOND FLOOR — 1,371 SQ. FT.
BONUS ROOM — 221 SQ. FT.

TOTAL LIVING AREA:
3,214 SQ. FT.

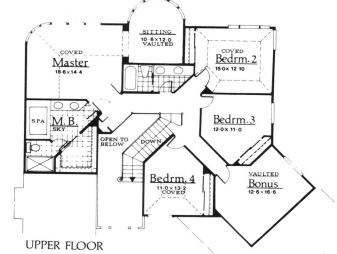

UPPER FLOOR

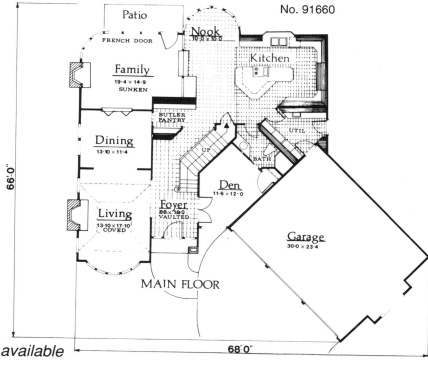

No. 91660

MAIN FLOOR

No materials list available

No. 91351

Students Love the Alcove

■ This plan features:

— Three bedrooms

— Two full baths

■ A Living Room enhanced by a stone hearth fireplace that flows into the Dining Room with built-in shelves

■ An efficiently designed Kitchen with a corner double sink, a built-in pantry and a breakfast bar

■ A Master Suite with a private Master Bath and a large walk-in closet

■ Two additional bedrooms, one with a study alcove, sharing a full hall bath

FIRST FLOOR — 1,477 SQ. FT.

TOTAL LIVING AREA:
1,477 SQ. FT.

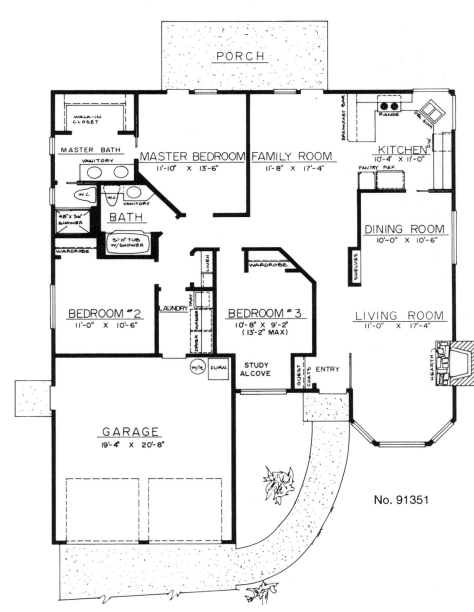

No. 91351

No. 90249
Tudor Sun Catcher

■ This plan features:

— Three bedrooms

— Two full baths

■ Sloped ceilings in the Living Room and Dining Room with rear-facing glass walls and a massive fireplace

■ A centrally-located Kitchen with a handy snack bar and a built-in pantry and planning desk

■ A Master Bedroom equipped with a walk-in closet and private Master Bath

■ Two additional bedrooms with ample closet space sharing a full hall bath

FIRST FLOOR — 1,584 SQ. FT.

TOTAL LIVING AREA: 1,584 SQ. FT.

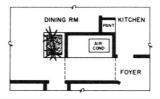

OPTIONAL NON-BASEMENT

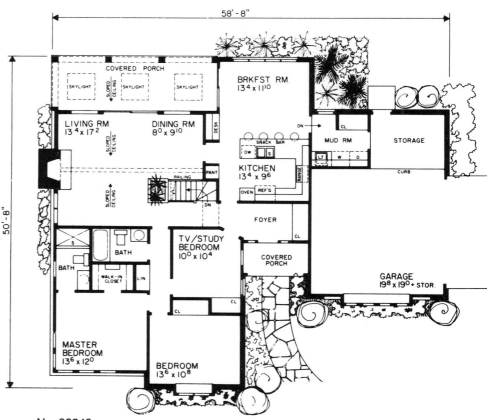

No. 90249

No. 90130
Energy Efficient

■ This plan features:

— Three bedrooms

— Two full baths

■ A galley-style Kitchen efficiently laid out to accommodate a busy life style

■ A Great Room with an open area for Dining space giving a feeling of spaciousness

■ A Master Bedroom with ample closet space and private full bath

■ Two additional bedrooms that share a full hall bath

■ An optional basement or crawl space foundation — please specify when ordering

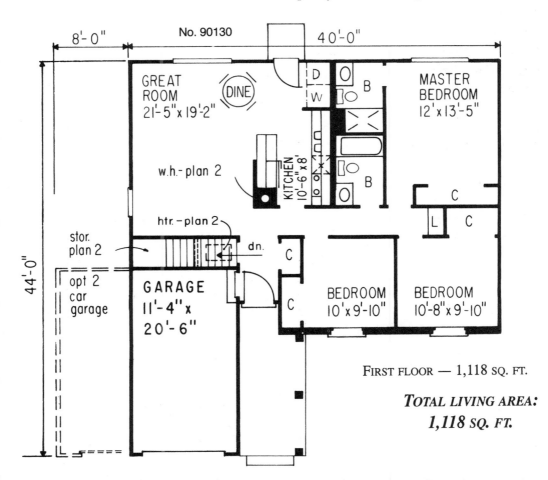

FIRST FLOOR — 1,118 SQ. FT.

TOTAL LIVING AREA: 1,118 SQ. FT.

No. 99214
Unusual Contemporary Flair

■ This plan features:

— Two bedrooms

— Two and one half baths

■ A large Media Room with custom built-ins for stereo and video equipment

■ A two-story Gathering Room with continuous window wall and cathedral ceiling

■ A fireplaced Master Bedroom with lavish, private bath including whirlpool tub, dressing area, and his and her walk-in closets

FIRST FLOOR — 1,128 SQ. FT.
SECOND FLOOR — 844 SQ. FT.
GARAGE — 441 SQ. FT.

**TOTAL LIVING AREA:
1,972 SQ. FT.**

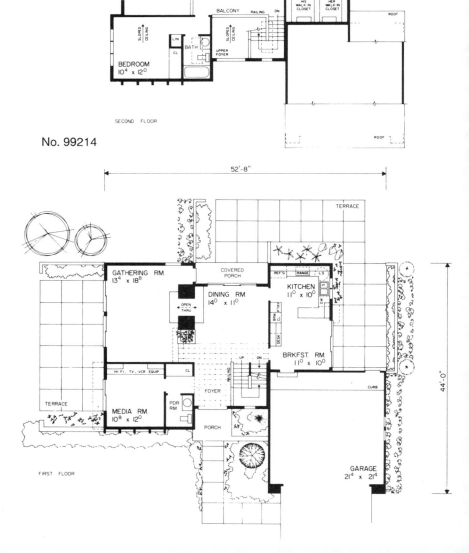

No. 99214

No. 90633
When There's a Hill

- This plan features:
— Three bedrooms
— Three full baths

- A design for a site that slopes down

- A sky-lit Dining Room with a high sloping ceiling and heat-circulating fireplace

- An efficient Kitchen with a peninsula counter and all the amenities

- A second floor Master Suite with a private balcony, deck and bath

- A basement foundation only

FIRST FLOOR — 790 SQ. FT.
SECOND FLOOR — 453 SQ. FT.
LOWER FLOOR — 340 SQ. FT.

TOTAL LIVING AREA:
1,583 SQ. FT.

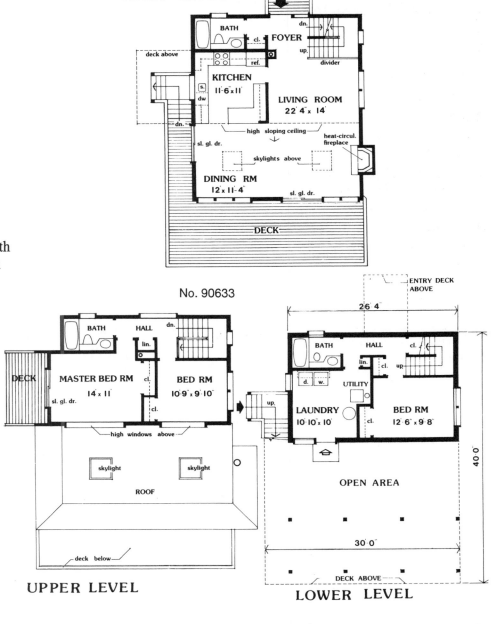

MAIN LEVEL

ENTRY DECK

BATH
FOYER
dn.
cl.
up.
deck above
ref.
divider
KITCHEN
11'·6" x 11'
s.
dw
LIVING ROOM
22'·4" x 14'
dn.
high sloping ceiling
sl. gl. dr.
heat-circul. fireplace
skylights above
DINING RM
12' x 11'·4"
sl. gl. dr.
DECK

No. 90633

BATH HALL dn.
lin.
DECK
MASTER BED RM
14' x 11'
cl.
BED RM
10'·9" x 9'·10"
sl. gl. dr.
cl.
high windows above
skylight
skylight
ROOF
deck below

UPPER LEVEL

ENTRY DECK ABOVE
26'·4"
BATH HALL cl.
lin. cl. up.
d. w.
UTILITY
LAUNDRY
10'·10" x 10'
BED RM
12'·6" x 9'·8"
up.
OPEN AREA
40'·0"
30'·0"
DECK ABOVE

LOWER LEVEL

No. 91903
Country Style Charmer

- This plan features:
- — Three bedrooms
- — Two and one half baths
- A classical symmetry and gracious front porch
- Formal areas zoned towards the front of the house
- A large Family Room with fireplace
- A winder staircase located off the Family Room
- A Master Bedroom with double vanities, separate glass shower and tub, and a built-in entertainment center

FIRST FLOOR — 910 SQ. FT.
SECOND FLOOR — 769 SQ. FT.
BASEMENT — 890 SQ. FT.

TOTAL LIVING AREA:
1,679 SQ. FT.

Mbr
14 x 12

Tv
L

Dn

Br 2
10 x 11·6

Open to below

Br 3
12 x 10

SECOND FLOOR

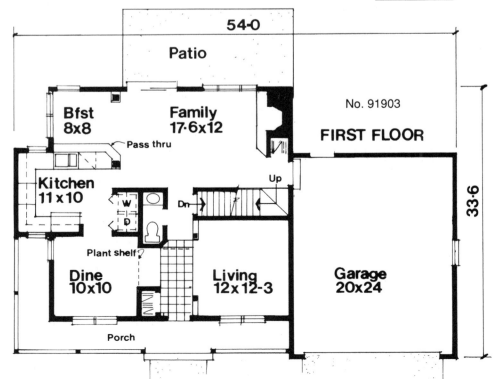

54-0

Patio

Bfst
8 x 8

Family
17·6 x 12

Pass thru

No. 91903

FIRST FLOOR

Kitchen
11 x 10

W
D

Up

Dn

33-6

Plant shelf

Dine
10 x 10

Living
12 x 12-3

Garage
20 x 24

Porch

No. 91757

Contemporary with Old-Country Porch

■ This plan features:

— Three bedrooms

— Two and one half baths

■ A fireplaced Parlor with built-in wood storage area

■ A Kitchen with a peninsula eating bar that runs into the Nook area

■ A vaulted ceiling in the fireplaced Family Room

■ A private, first floor Master Suite with Master Bath and walk-in closet

FIRST FLOOR — 1,971 SQ. FT.
SECOND FLOOR — 531 SQ. FT.
GARAGE — 600 SQ. FT.

TOTAL LIVING AREA: 2,084 SQ. FT.

No. 91757

SECOND FLOOR PLAN

No. 91618
Carefree and Cozy

■ This plan features:

— Three bedrooms

— Two full and one half baths

■ A convenient one floor layout

■ A coved ceiling, fireplace and massive front window in the Living Room

■ A built-in, corner china cabinet in the elegant, formal Dining Room

■ A Kitchen with a large cook top island and snack counter

■ A coved ceiling and fireplace in the Family Room

■ A secluded Master Suite with a bay window, coved ceiling, and a private bath with double vanities and garden spa tub

FIRST FLOOR — 2,087 SQ. FT.

TOTAL LIVING AREA:
2,087 SQ. FT.

No. 91618

No materials list available

MAIN FLOOR

No. 91648

Perfect Hilltop Design

■ This plan features:

— Four bedrooms

— Two full and one half baths

■ A large picture window in the formal Living Room flowing efficiently into the formal Dining Room

■ A modern, efficient Kitchen with a cook-top island, corner double sinks, and a built-in pantry

■ A fireplace in the spacious Family Room

■ A Master Suite with a walk-in closet, spa tub and a step-in shower

■ Three additional bedrooms served by a full hall bath

FIRST FLOOR — 1,179 SQ. FT.
SECOND FLOOR — 1,034 SQ. FT.

TOTAL LIVING AREA: 2,213 SQ. FT.

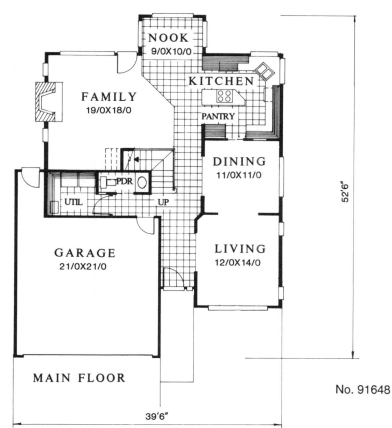

MAIN FLOOR

39'6"

No. 91648

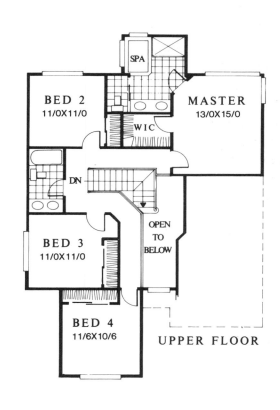

UPPER FLOOR

No. 91508

Entertain This Idea

■ This plan features:

— Three bedrooms

— Two full and one half baths

■ A spacious Living Room with a fireplace that flows into the elegant Dining Room

■ A vaulted ceiling in the Dining Room accentuated by expansive windows

■ A cook top island Kitchen with a built-in pantry and corner double sink

■ An informal Family Room warmed by a fireplace

■ A vaulted ceiling in the Master Suite with a lavish private bath and a walk-in closet

■ Two additional bedrooms served by a full bath

FIRST FLOOR — 1,519 SQ. FT.
SECOND FLOOR — 946 SQ. FT.

TOTAL LIVING AREA:
2,465 SQ. FT.

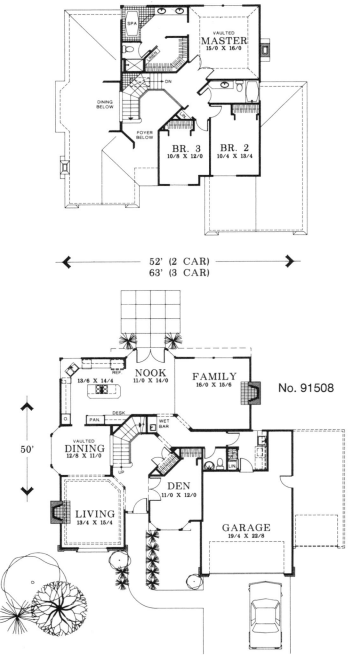

No. 91508

No. 91900
Traditional Elements

■ This plan features:

— Three bedrooms

— Two full and one half baths

■ A vaulted ceiling in the elegant Dining Room

■ A see-through fireplace in the Great Room and Kitchen

■ A roomy Kitchen with a step-in pantry, separate ovens, built-in desk, and sit-down snack bar

■ A gazebo Breakfast area

■ A Master Suite with a vaulted ceiling, large walk-in closet and a private bath

■ A dramatic, sky-lit staircase leading to two additional bedrooms and a full bath

FIRST FLOOR — 1,855 SQ. FT.
SECOND FLOOR — 530 SQ. FT.

TOTAL LIVING AREA: 2,385 SQ. FT.

No materials list available

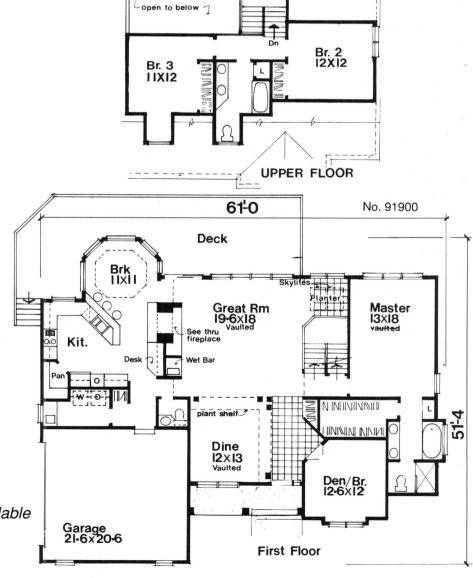

UPPER FLOOR

Br. 3 11X12
Br. 2 12X12
open to below
Dn
L

No. 91900

61'-0

Deck
Brk 11X11
Kit.
Great Rm 19-6X18 Vaulted
See thru fireplace
Desk
Wet Bar
Pan
Skylites
Planter
Master 13X18 vaulted
plant shelf
Dine 12X13 Vaulted
Den/Br. 12-6X12
51'-4
Garage 21-6X20-6

First Floor

No. 91346

Four Bedroom Charmer

■ This plan features:

— Four bedrooms

— Two full baths

■ A vaulted ceiling in the naturally lighted entry

■ A Living Room with a masonry fireplace, large windowed bay and vaulted ceiling

■ A coffered ceiling and built-in china cabinet in the Dining Room

■ A large Family Room with a wood stove alcove

■ An island cook top, built-in pantry and a telephone desk in the efficient Kitchen

■ A luxurious Master Bedroom with whirlpool garden tub, walk-in closet and double sink vanity

■ Two additional bedrooms sharing a full bath

■ A Study with a window seat and built-in bookshelves

FIRST FLOOR — 2,185 SQ. FT.

TOTAL LIVING AREA:
2,185 SQ. FT.

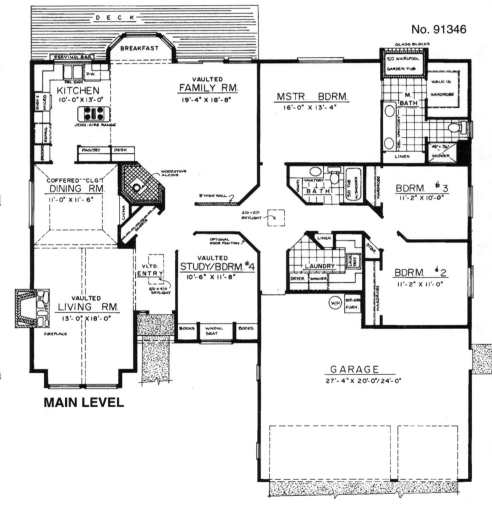

No. 91346

MAIN LEVEL

No. 91324

For a Fifty Foot Wide Lot

■ This plan features:

— Three bedrooms

— One full and one half baths

■ An entry with a two-story ceiling

■ A Living Room and Dining Room that flow easily into each other and share the warmth of a fireplace

■ Sliding glass doors to the patio from the Dining Room

■ An efficient, Kitchen with ample counter and cabinet space

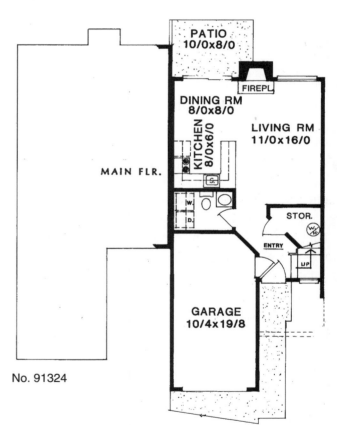

No. 91324

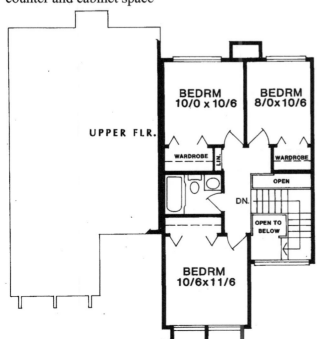

FIRST FLOOR(PER UNIT) — 432 SQ. FT.
SECOND FLOOR(PER UNIT) — 494 SQ. FT.

TOTAL LIVING AREA:
1,852 SQ. FT.
(926 PER UNIT)

No. 91511
Practical, Yet Pretty

■ This plan features:

— Four bedrooms

— Two full and one half baths

■ A Living Room with a dramatic vaulted ceiling and a fireplace

■ An elegant formal Dining Room with a decorative ceiling and direct access to the Kitchen

■ A cook top island Kitchen with a built-in pantry, desk, and corner double sink

■ A bright, bay-windowed Breakfast Nook

■ A spacious Family Room with a cozy fireplace

■ A vaulted ceiling in the Master Suite and a double vanity and skylight in the private full bath

FIRST FLOOR — 1,462 SQ. FT.
SECOND FLOOR — 1,013 SQ. FT.
BONUS ROOM — 180 SQ. FT.

TOTAL LIVING AREA:
2,475 SQ. FT.

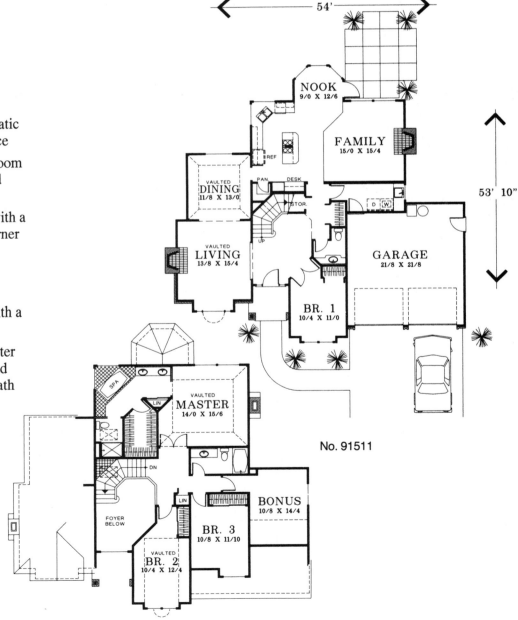

No. 91511

No. 91509
Angular Elegance

■ This plan features:

— Three bedrooms

— Two full and one half baths

■ A unique Living Room with a vaulted ceiling and columns separating it from the formal Dining Room

■ A wide-open arrangement between the Family Room, Nook and island Kitchen

■ A fireplace in both the Family Room and the Living Room

■ A skylight and double vanities in the full hall bath

■ A Master Suite with a walk-in closet, garden spa tub, and bay window

FIRST FLOOR — 1,675 SQ. FT.
SECOND FLOOR — 1,032 SQ. FT.
BONUS ROOM — 450 SQ. FT.

**TOTAL LIVING AREA:
2,707 SQ. FT.**

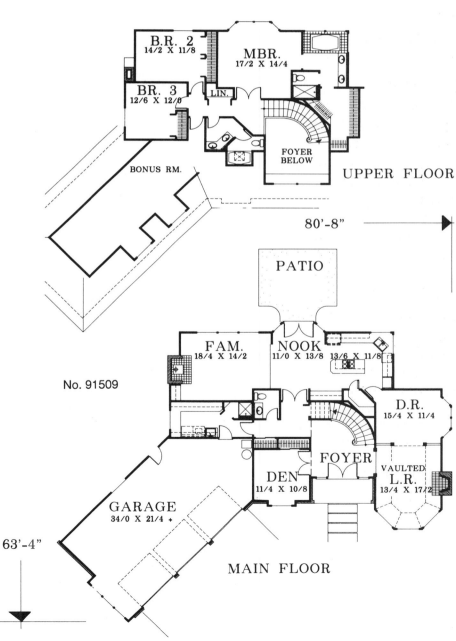

No. 91509

No. 99205
Farmhouse Feeling, Family-Style

■ This plan features:

— Four bedrooms

— Two full and two half baths

■ A sunny Breakfast bay with easy access to the efficient Kitchen

■ A large and spacious Family Room with a fireplace and a pass-through to the Kitchen

■ Sliders that link the Family and Dining Rooms with the rear terrace

■ A private Master Suite with his-and-her walk-in closets, dressing room with built-in vanity and convenient step-in shower

FIRST FLOOR — 1,590 SQ. FT.
SECOND FLOOR — 1,344 SQ. FT.

TOTAL LIVING AREA: 2,934 SQ. FT.

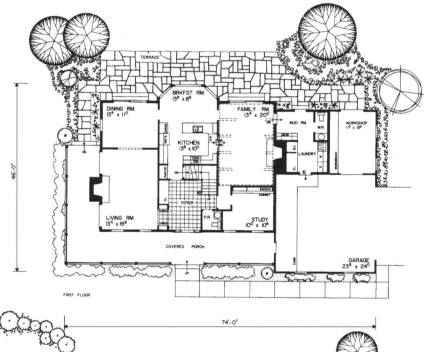

FIRST FLOOR

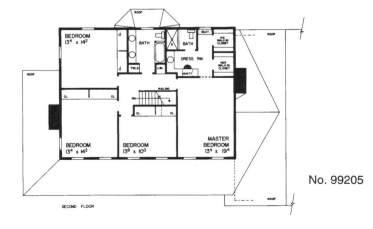

SECOND FLOOR

No. 99205

No. 90142
Master Bedroom on First Level

■ This plan features:

— Four bedrooms

— Two full and one half baths

■ A first floor Master Bedroom equipped with a walk-in closet and large bath area with a skylight over the tub

■ A large bay window allowing lots of natural light in the Living Room

■ Built-in bookshelves and a fireplace in the Family Room

■ An abundance of cabinet space and a pantry in the Kitchen

■ Three additional bedrooms that share a full hall bath

■ An optional basement or crawl space foundation — please specify when ordering

FIRST FLOOR — 1,633 SQ. FT.
SECOND FLOOR — 727 SQ. FT.

TOTAL LIVING AREA: 2,360 SQ. FT.

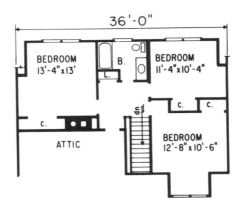

SECOND FLOOR

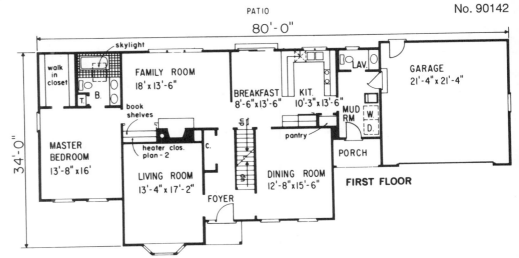

No. 91607
Daytime Delight

■ This plan features:

— Three bedrooms

— Two full baths

■ A large, vaulted ceiling in the Living Room and Dining Room that flows together and is accentuated by huge windows

■ A centrally-located Kitchen with a double sink, and ample cabinet and counter space

■ A glass-walled eating Nook with access to a covered porch

■ A vaulted ceiling in the Family Room with a focal point fireplace

■ An exciting Master Suite with a vaulted ceiling, a walk-in closet and a private double-vanity bath

■ Two additional bedrooms, one with French doors, served by a full hall bath

FIRST FLOOR — 1,653 SQ. FT.

TOTAL LIVING AREA: 1,653 SQ. FT.

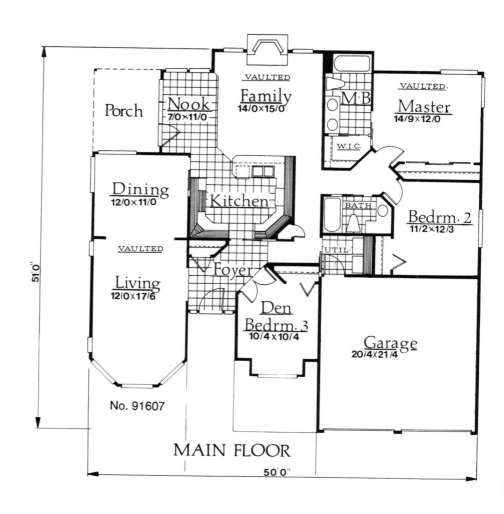

MAIN FLOOR

No. 91811
Spectacular Rambler

■ This plan features:

— Three bedrooms

— Two full baths

■ A twelve foot high ceiling over the foyer, Living Room, Kitchen and Dining Rooms

■ A sunken Living Room with custom cut windows

■ A spacious Master Suite with a dressing area, walk-in closet, and a private bath

■ A Family Room with a fireplace, separated from the Kitchen by an eating bar

■ An efficient Kitchen with a double sink, built-in pantry, and a peninsula counter

■ A formal Dining Room with sliding glass doors to the patio

FIRST FLOOR — 1,546 SQ. FT.
OPTIONAL BASEMENT — 1,588 SQ. FT.
GARAGE — 549 SQ. FT.

TOTAL LIVING AREA:
1,546 SQ. FT.

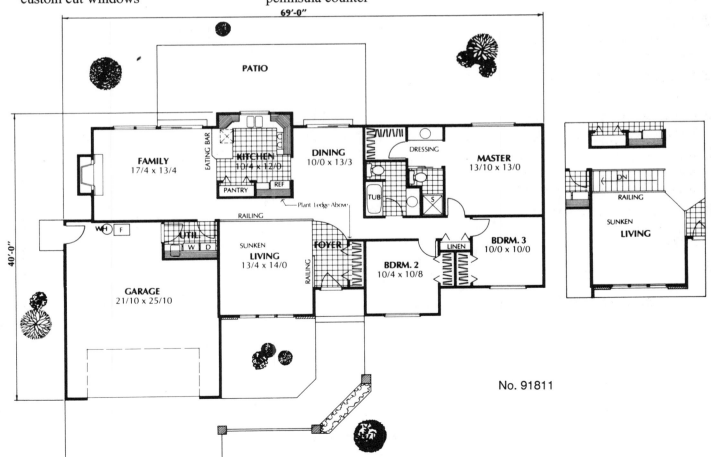

No. 91811

No. 90048
Three Porches Offer Outdoor Charm

■ This plan features:

— Three bedrooms

— Two full baths

■ An oversized log burning fireplace in the spacious Living/Dining area which is two stories high with sliding glass doors

■ Three porches offering the maximum in outdoor living space

■ A private bedroom located on the second floor

■ An efficient Kitchen including an eating bar and access to the covered Dining Porch

FIRST FLOOR — 972 SQ. FT.
SECOND FLOOR — 321 SQ. FT.

TOTAL LIVING AREA:
1,293 SQ. FT.

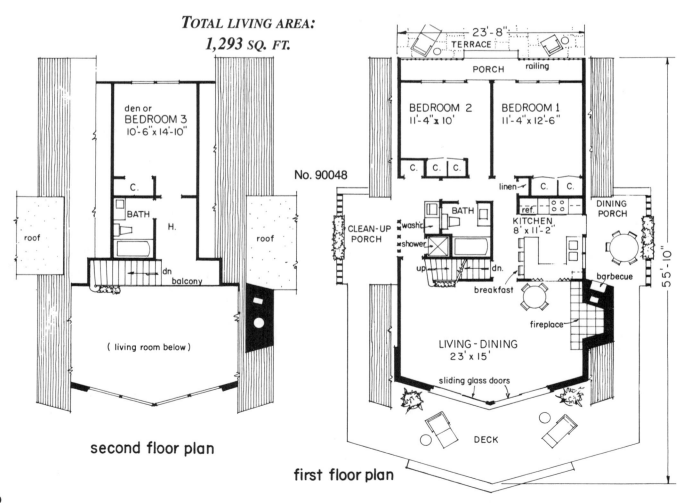

second floor plan

first floor plan

No. 90066

Get Out the Telescope

■ This plan features:

— Three bedrooms

— One full bath

■ Two upper level decks which take advantage of the view

■ A lounge area with a fireplace flowing into the Dining are

■ A well-equipped Kitchen, with a pass through to the Dining area

■ A first floor Master Bedroom with ample closet space

■ A second floor bedroom with a private covered porch

FIRST FLOOR — 1,155 SQ. FT.
SECOND FLOOR — 306 SQ. FT.

TOTAL LIVING AREA: 1,461 SQ. FT.

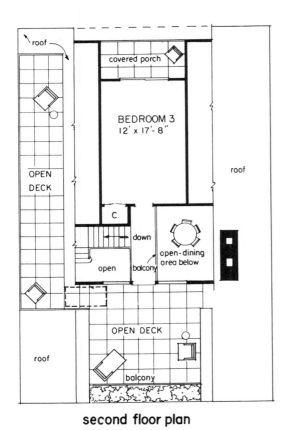

second floor plan

No. 90066

first floor plan

No. 91343

Customized for Sloping View Site

■ This plan features:

— Three bedrooms

— Two full and one half baths

■ A stone-faced fireplace and vaulted ceiling in the Living Room

■ An island food preparation center with a sink and a Breakfast bar in the Kitchen

■ Sliding glass doors leading from the Dining Room to the adjacent deck

■ A Master Suite with a vaulted ceiling, a sitting room, and a lavish Master Bath with a whirlpool tub, skylights, double vanity, and a walk-in closet

FIRST FLOOR — 1,338 SQ. FT.
SECOND FLOOR — 763 SQ. FT.
LOWER FLOOR — 61 SQ. FT.

TOTAL LIVING AREA: 2,162 SQ. FT.

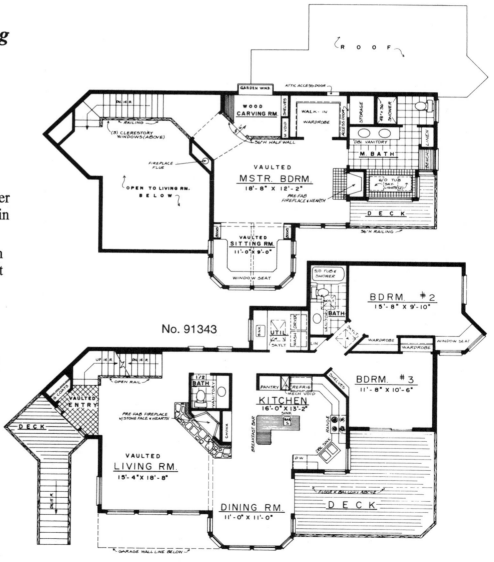

No. 91343

No. 90611

Solar Room More Than Just a Greenhouse

■ This plan features:

— Three bedrooms

— Two full baths

■ A passive design that will save on heating costs

■ A heat-circulating fireplace in the Living Room adding atmosphere as well as warmth

■ A Master Suite, with lofty views of the living area

■ Two additional bedrooms with ample closet space and a shared full hall bath

■ A slab foundation only

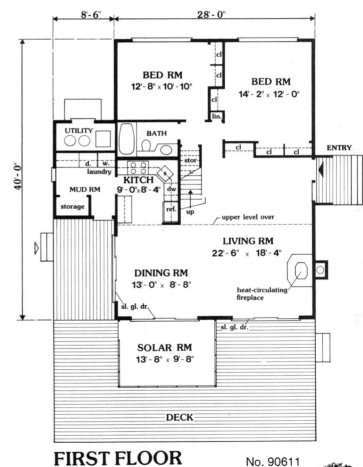

FIRST FLOOR No. 90611

BED RM 12'-8" x 10'-10"
BED RM 14'-2" x 12'-0"
UTILITY
BATH
ENTRY
d. w.
laundry
KITCH 9'-0" x 8'-4"
stor.
MUD RM
storage
ref.
up
upper level over
LIVING RM 22'-6" x 18'-4"
DINING RM 13'-0" x 8'-8"
heat-circulating fireplace
sl. gl. dr.
sl. gl. dr.
SOLAR RM 13'-8" x 9'-8"
DECK

8'-6" 28'-0" 40'-0"

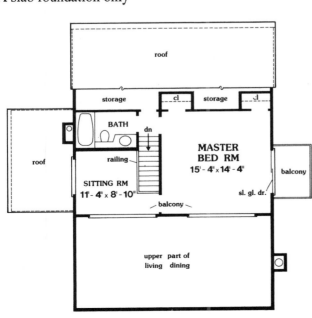

roof
storage cl storage cl
BATH
dn
railing
roof
SITTING RM 11'-4" x 8'-10"
MASTER BED RM 15'-4" x 14'-4"
balcony
sl. gl. dr.
balcony
upper part of living dining

FIRST FLOOR — 1,120 SQ. FT.
SECOND FLOOR — 490 SQ. FT.
UTILITY ROOM — 122 SQ. FT.

TOTAL LIVING AREA: 1,732 SQ. FT.

No. 90435

Classic and Comfortable

■ This plan features:

— Three bedrooms

— Two full and one half baths

■ A central staircase dominating the spacious foyer

■ A convenient L-shaped arrangement of Kitchen, formal and informal Dining Rooms making meal service a breeze

■ An elegant, massive fireplace, French doors, and an adjoining rear deck add to the Great Room

■ A lavish Master Suite including a private Study, walk-in closet and a sky-lit, private bath

■ Two additional bedrooms share a full hall bath

■ An optional basement, slab or crawl space foundation — please specify when ordering

FIRST FLOOR — 1,032 SQ. FT.
SECOND FLOOR — 1,050 SQ. FT.

TOTAL LIVING AREA:
2,082 SQ. FT.

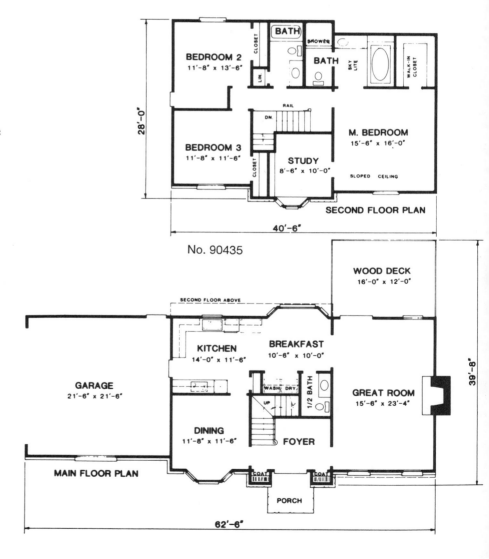

No. 90435

No. 98315

Packed with Efficiency

■ This plan features:

— Three bedrooms

— Two and one half baths

■ An open plan with minimum circulation

■ A Kitchen large enough for informal eating

■ A Master Suite with a large walk-in closet and private bath

■ An upper level laundry area

Please note there is no Material List available for this plan

MAIN FLOOR — 684 SQ. FT.
UPPER FLOOR — 727 SQ. FT.
BASEMENT — 684 SQ. FT.
GARAGE — 400 SQ. FT.

TOTAL LIVING AREA:
1,411 SQ. FT.

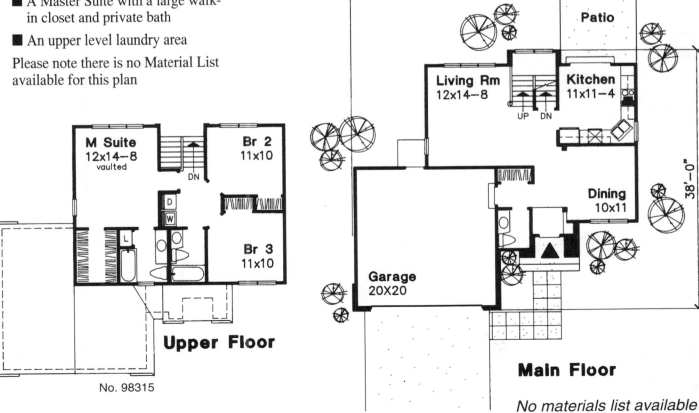

M Suite
12x14−8
vaulted

Br 2
11x10

DN

D
W

L

Br 3
11x10

Upper Floor

No. 98315

41'−4"

Patio

Living Rm
12x14−8

UP   DN

Kitchen
11x11−4

Dining
10x11

38'−0"

Garage
20X20

Main Floor

No materials list available

No. 90669

Dinner on the Deck

■ This plan features:

— Three bedrooms

— Two full baths

■ A Living Room with a sloped ceiling and a built-in window seat

■ Four outdoor decks insure you'll never run out of room

■ An eat-in Kitchen with an efficient and convenient layout

■ A mudroom with a shower area

■ A Master Bedroom with his and her closets and a private bath

■ Two additional bedrooms located on the second floor that share a full hall bath

■ A crawl space foundation only

FIRST FLOOR — 877 SQ. FT.
SECOND FLOOR — 455 SQ. FT.

TOTAL LIVING AREA: 1,332 SQ. FT.

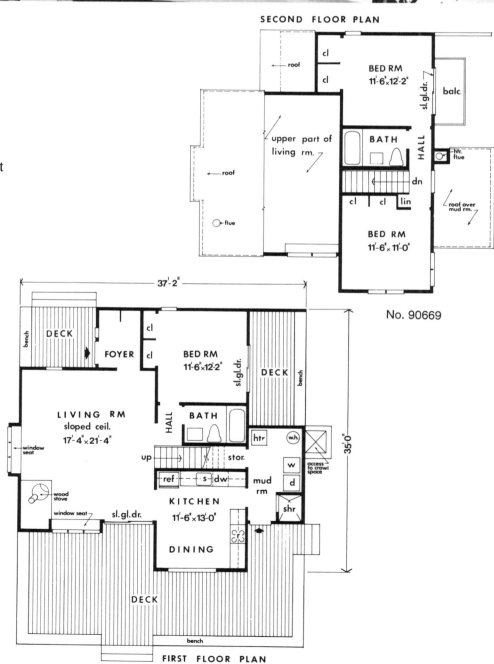

SECOND FLOOR PLAN

No. 90669

FIRST FLOOR PLAN

No. 90072

Perfect Vacation Retreat

■ This plan features:

— Three bedrooms

— Two full baths

■ An eating bar in the self-contained, efficient Kitchen

■ A Living Room and Dinette with cathedral ceilings and a fireplace in the Living Room

■ A second floor bedroom with a private full bath

■ A lower level Recreation Room with optional fireplace

FIRST FLOOR — 975 SQ. FT.
SECOND FLOOR — 316 SQ. FT.
BASEMENT — 255 SQ. FT.
GARAGE — 280 SQ. FT.

**TOTAL LIVING AREA:
1,291 SQ. FT.**

No. 90072

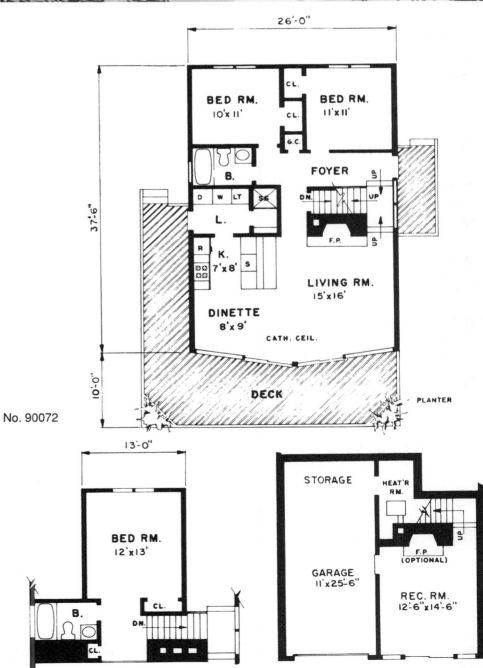

No. 91657

Elegant First Floor Master Suite

■ This plan features:

— Three bedrooms

— Two full and one half baths

■ A sunny, formal Living Room with a fireplace

■ A formal Dining Room directly accessing the Kitchen

■ An efficient, well-equipped Kitchen with an informal eating Nook

■ A corner fireplace in the Family Room

■ A bay window and private bath in the Master Suite

■ Two additional, second floor bedrooms sharing a full bath

FIRST FLOOR — 1,558 SQ. FT.
SECOND FLOOR — 560 SQ. FT.
BONUS ROOM — 280 SQ. FT.

TOTAL LIVING AREA: 2,118 SQ. FT.

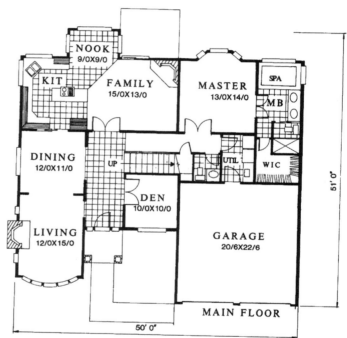

No. 91730
Country Exterior with Many Amenities

■ This plan features:

— Four bedrooms

— Two full and one half baths

■ Curved arches flanked by formal columns marking the passages between the Living Room and the family living area

■ A semi-formal Parlor with see-through fireplace linked to the Family Room

■ A Master Suite with his-and-her walk-in closets and a private Master Bath

■ A Family Room that is accessible from the bright, window-lined eating Nook

■ Three additional bedrooms upstairs that share a compartmentalized bath

FIRST FLOOR — 1,979 SQ. FT.
SECOND FLOOR — 905 SQ. FT.
BASEMENT — 1,961 SQ. FT.
GARAGE — 588 SQ. FT.
WIDTH — 62'-0"
DEPTH — 62'-0"

TOTAL LIVING AREA: 2,884 SQ. FT.

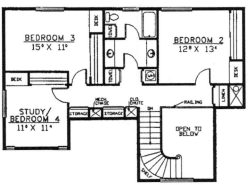

SECOND FLOOR

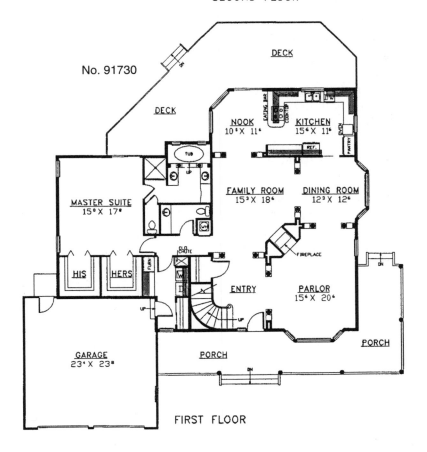

No. 91730

FIRST FLOOR

No. 91613

Stucco Splendor

■ This plan features:

— Three bedrooms

— Three full baths

■ A cozy Den with an adjoining full bath and French doors

■ A coved ceiling in both the Living and Dining Rooms

■ An efficient, cook-top island Kitchen with more than ample counter and storage space

■ A glass-walled eating Nook

■ A built-in wetbar and a fireplace in the Family Room

■ An enchanting Master Suite with a private sitting room, fabulous spa bath and a walk-in closet

FIRST FLOOR — 2,268 SQ. FT.
SECOND FLOOR — 1,484 SQ. FT.
BONUS ROOM — 300 SQ. FT.

TOTAL LIVING AREA: 3,752 SQ. FT.

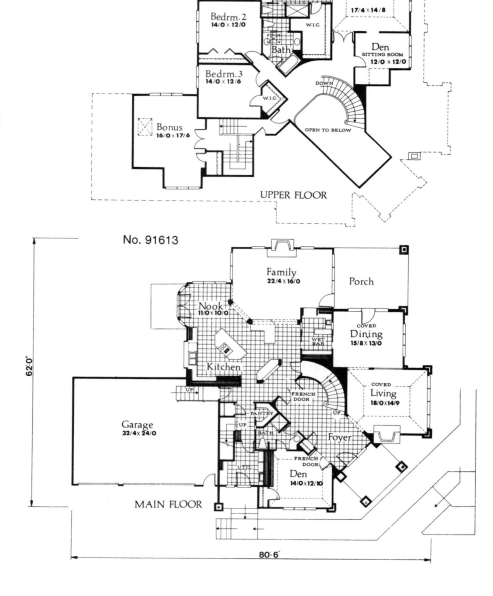

No. 91655

Attractive Modern Design

■ This plan features:

— Three bedrooms

— Two full and one half baths

■ A coved ceiling and a five-sectioned window in the formal Living Room

■ A well-appointed Kitchen with convenient access to both the formal Dining Room and the informal eating Nook

■ A Family Room with direct access to the patio and a lovely fireplace

■ A coved ceiling in the Master Suite including a full private bath with all the amenities

■ Two additional bedrooms served by a full, double-vanity hall bath

FIRST FLOOR — 1,173 SQ. FT.
SECOND FLOOR — 823 SQ. FT.
BONUS ROOM — 204 SQ. FT.

TOTAL LIVING AREA: 1,996 SQ. FT.

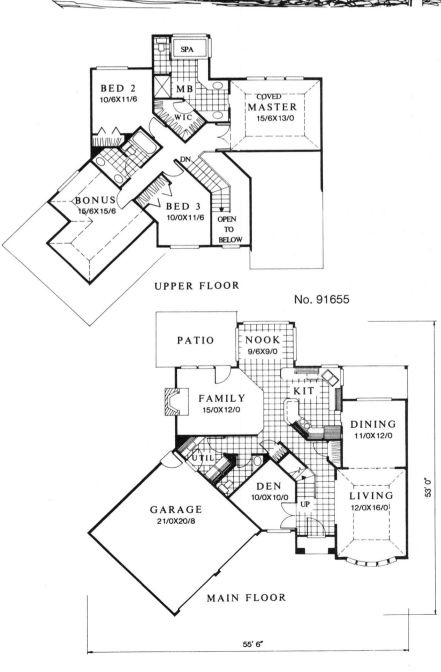

No. 91409

Built-Ins Add Convenience to Light and Airy One-Level

■ This plan features:

— Three bedrooms

— Two full baths

■ Two front bedrooms, each with a bump-out window and easy access to a full bath

■ A luxurious Master Suite with sliding glass doors to a private, covered patio, double vanities, and a huge, sunken tub

■ An elegant vaulted ceiling in the Dining Room crowned by a skylight

■ A two-way fireplace separating the Living Room and the Family Room

■ A well-equipped Kitchen with a range top island and a sunny eating bay

FIRST FLOOR — 2,215 SQ. FT.
GARAGE — 539 SQ. FT.

TOTAL LIVING AREA:
2,215 SQ. FT.

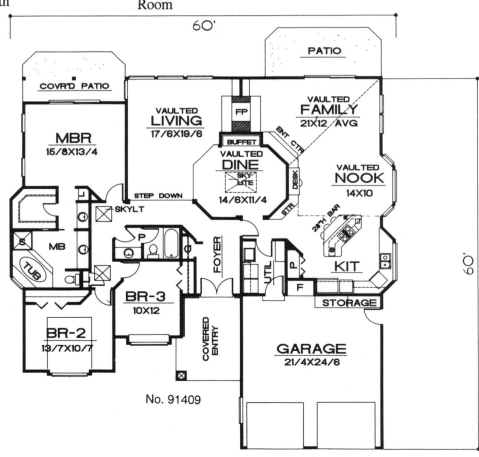

No. 91409

No. 90686
Dutch Colonial Accent

■ This plan features:

— Three bedrooms

— Two full baths

■ A greenhouse bay window in the Dining Room accentuating the sunny atmosphere

■ A spacious Living Room with a skylight and a heat-circulating fireplace

■ A central Kitchen location with a peninsula counter separating it from the Family Room

■ A Master Bedroom with a walk-in closet, and a private bath with a whirlpool tub and double vanity

■ Two additional bedrooms that share a full hall bath

FIRST FLOOR — 1,544 SQ. FT.
LAUNDRY/MUDROOM — 74 SQ. FT.
GARAGE/STORAGE — 516 SQ. FT.

TOTAL LIVING AREA:
1,618 SQ. FT.

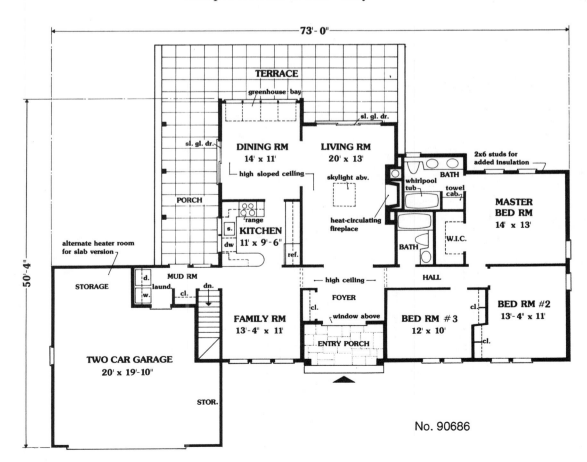

No. 90686

No. 90267

Split-Level Spanish Design

■ This plan features:

— Four bedrooms

— Three full and one half baths

■ An activity room with a raised-hearth fireplace, soda bar and sliding glass doors to a covered terrace

■ A Master Bedroom with a large walk-in closet, dressing room and private Master Bath

■ An efficient Kitchen equipped with an island located next to both the Breakfast Room and the formal Dining Room

■ A Living Room which flows into the Dining Room for ease in entertaining

■ A spacious Family Room enhanced by a fireplace with a raised hearth

FIRST FLOOR — 1,530 SQ. FT.
SECOND FLOOR — 984 SQ. FT.
LOWER FLOOR — 951 SQ. FT.
GARAGE — 3-CAR

TOTAL LIVING AREA: 3,465 SQ. FT.

No. 90267

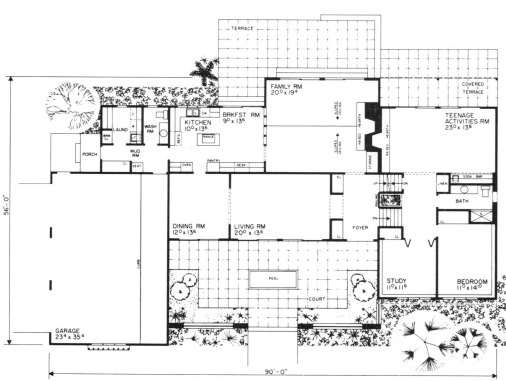

No. 90232

Imposing Staircase Graces Elegantly Designed Home

■ This plan features:

— Four bedrooms

— Three full baths

■ A two-story entrance

■ The Living and Dining Rooms complimented by large windows and window seats

■ A central cooking island and walk-in pantry, a desk, a lazy Susan and an extra large storage closet in the efficient Kitchen

■ A very large Master Bedroom including a fireplace and two double closets, a dressing room with a walk-in closet and vanity, plus a private full bath

■ Two of the three additional bedrooms having double closets and sharing a bath; the other bedroom with a private bath and two closets

FIRST FLOOR — 2,345 SQ. FT.
SECOND FLOOR — 1,687 SQ. FT.

TOTAL LIVING AREA: 4,032 SQ. FT.

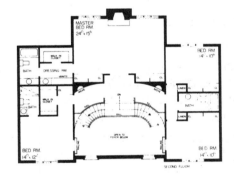

No. 90232

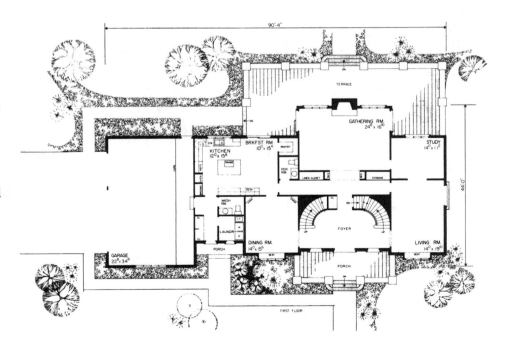

No. 91771
Hexagon at its Core

■ This plan features:

— Two bedrooms

— Two full baths

■ A lofty, vaulted ceiling in the Living/Dining/Kitchen area

■ A huge, walk-in pantry providing visual separation between the Living Room/Dining Room and the Kitchen

■ A secluded Master Suite with a generous walk-in closet, a private bath equipped with an oversized spa tub, and a second vanity in the dressing area

■ Wide decks expanding the usable living space and wrapping around most of the back of the home

FIRST FLOOR — 2,095 SQ. FT.
GARAGE — 515 SQ. FT.
WIDTH — 95'-6"
DEPTH — 59'-0"

TOTAL LIVING AREA: 2,095 SQ. FT.

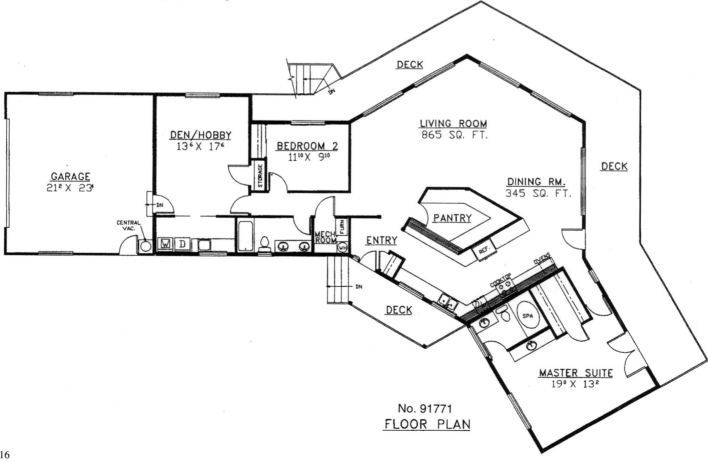

No. 91771
FLOOR PLAN

No. 92110
Skylights Brighten Rooms

■ This plan features:

— Four bedrooms

— Three full baths

■ A Kitchen with a skylight, plenty of cabinet space, an eat-in Nook and exits to an extra-long deck

■ A sunken Living Room with a fireplace and natural light from two large windows

■ A convenient first-floor Laundry Room with built-in shelving and ample space for appliances

■ A Master Suite with a sky-lit bath equipped with a double vanity, an elegant window seat, his and her showers, and an enormous walk-in closet

■ A Recreation Room with a fireplace

FIRST FLOOR — 2,314 SQ. FT.
FINISHED BASEMENT — 1,302 SQ. FT.
GARAGE — 1,017 SQ. FT.

TOTAL LIVING AREA:
3,616 SQ. FT.

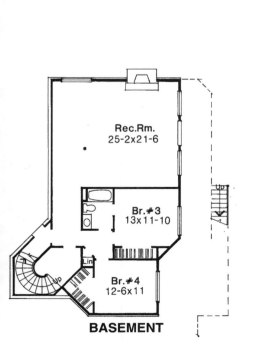

Rec.Rm.
25-2x21-6

Br.#3
13x11-10

Br.#4
12-6x11

BASEMENT

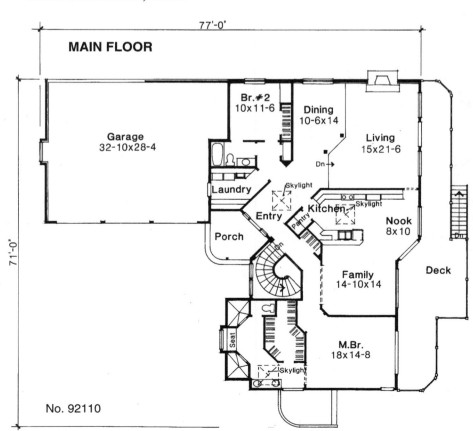

MAIN FLOOR

77'-0"

71'-0"

Garage
32-10x28-4

Br.#2
10x11-6

Dining
10-6x14

Living
15x21-6

Dn →

Laundry

Skylight

Entry

Kitchen

Skylight

Nook
8x10

Porch

Pantry

Family
14-10x14

Deck

Seat

Skylight

M.Br.
18x14-8

No. 92110

No. 91507
Built-In Beauty

■ This plan features:

— Three bedrooms

— Two full baths

■ A sky-lit foyer

■ A bump-out window enhancing the wide-open arrangement in the Living/Dining Room

■ An efficient island Kitchen with a built-in pantry, and a corner double sink

■ An informal Family Room with a lovely fireplace

■ A Master Suite with elegant double doors, and a luxurious private Master Bath

■ Two additional bedrooms flanking the laundry area

FIRST FLOOR — 1,687 SQ. FT.

TOTAL LIVING AREA:
1,687 SQ. FT.

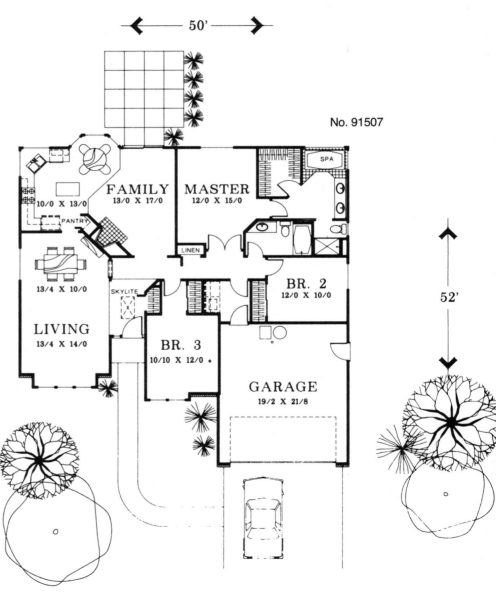

No. 91507

50'

52'

FAMILY
13/0 X 17/0

MASTER
12/0 X 15/0

SPA

PANTRY

LINEN

13/4 X 10/0

SKYLITE

BR. 2
12/0 X 10/0

LIVING
13/4 X 14/0

BR. 3
10/10 X 12/0

GARAGE
19/2 X 21/8

10/0 X 13/0

No. 99614

Triangular Entrance Extends Into Foyer

■ This plan features:

— Three bedrooms

— Two full and one half baths

■ A triangular ceiling in the entrance porch that extends into the foyer

■ A large glazed bay window that extends the full width of the Living Room

■ A heat-circulating fireplace flanked by shelves and cabinets in the Living Room

■ A Dinette with a six-sided shape, four sides being windows

■ A Family Room with a sloped ceiling, sliding glass doors to the terrace and easy access to an angled Kitchen counter acting as a snack bar

■ A Master Suite with walk-in closet, private terrace, private Master Bath with whirlpool tub, a separate shower and a double vanity

■ Two additional bedrooms that share a full hall bath

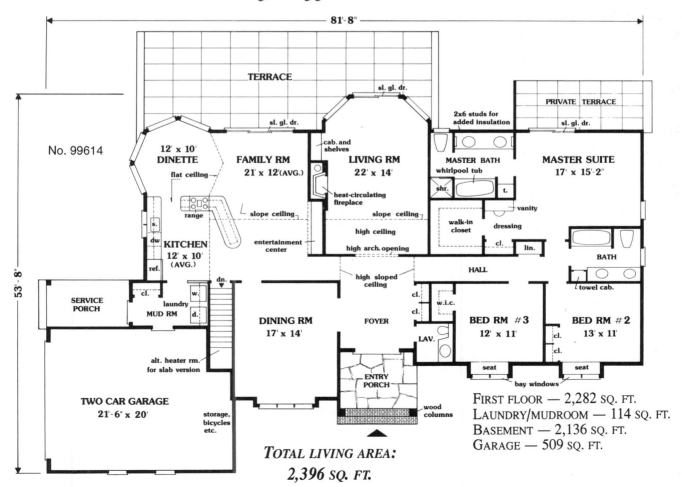

FIRST FLOOR — 2,282 SQ. FT.
LAUNDRY/MUDROOM — 114 SQ. FT.
BASEMENT — 2,136 SQ. FT.
GARAGE — 509 SQ. FT.

TOTAL LIVING AREA:
2,396 SQ. FT.

No. 90407

L-Shaped Bungalow With Two Porches

■ This plan features:

— Three bedrooms

— Two full baths

■ A Master Suite with a lavish Master Bath including a garden tub, shower, his and her vanities and separate walk-in closets

■ Two additional bedrooms having ample closet space and share full hall bath

■ A large Family Room accentuated by a fireplace

■ A U-shaped Kitchen with a built-in pantry, double sink and ample storage and counter space

■ A sunny, bay Breakfast Nook for informal eating

■ An optional basement, slab or crawl space foundation — please specify when ordering

FIRST FLOOR — 1,950 SQ. FT.

TOTAL LIVING AREA: 1,950 SQ. FT.

No. 90407

MAIN AREA

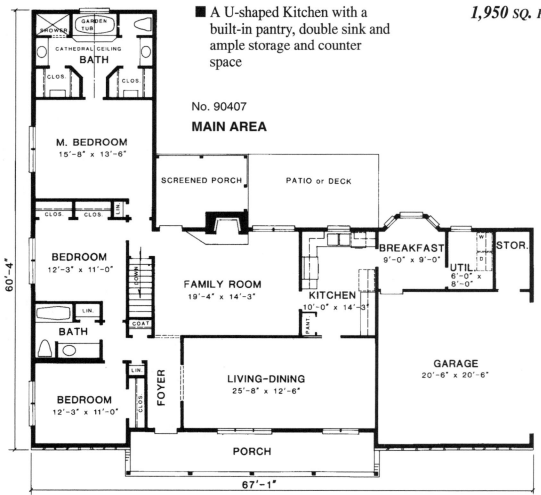

No. 90441

Moderate Ranch Has Features of Much Larger Plan

■ This plan features:

— Three bedrooms

— Two full baths

■ A large Great Room with a vaulted ceiling and a stone

fireplace with book shelves on either side

■ A spacious Kitchen with ample cabinet space conveniently located next to the large Dining Room

■ A Master Suite having a large bath with a garden tub, double vanity and a walk-in closet

■ Two other large bedrooms, each with a walk-in closet and access to the full bath

■ An optional basement or crawl space foundation — please specify when ordering

FIRST FLOOR — 1,811 SQ. FT.

TOTAL LIVING AREA: 1,811 SQ. FT.

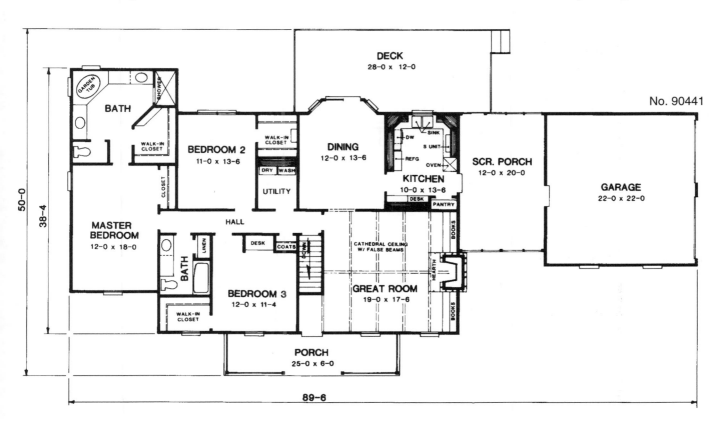

No. 91501

Sprawling Sun-Catcher

■ This plan features:

— Three bedrooms

— Two full and one half baths

■ A central foyer opening to every area of the house

■ A fabulous Master Suite with a garden spa, double vanity and a room-size walk-in closet

■ A cozy Den with French doors to the rear patio

■ Columns separating the Living Room with fireplace from the octagonal, vaulted-ceiling Dining Room

■ An island Kitchen with twin ovens and a peninsula counter

■ An eating Nook area open to the Kitchen

■ An informal Family Room with a cozy fireplace

FIRST FLOOR — 3,160 SQ. FT.

TOTAL LIVING AREA: 3,160 SQ. FT.

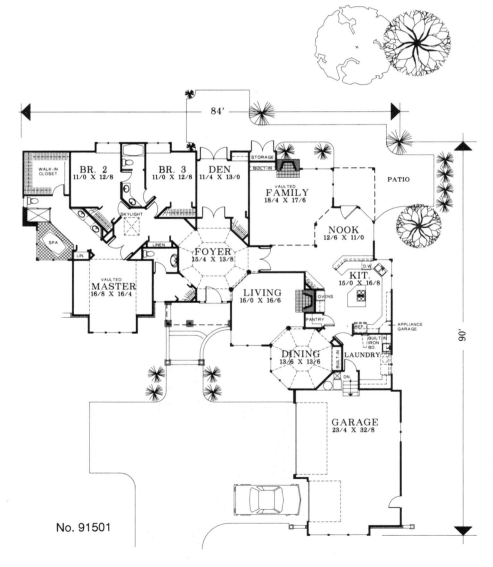

No. 91501

No. 91654

Spacious Kitchen Completes Special Design

- ■ This plan features:
- — Three or four bedrooms
- — Two or three full baths and one half bath
- ■ A picture window and fireplace accentuating the Living Room

- ■ An island Kitchen with a built-in pantry, corner double sink, built-in desk and a sunny eating Nook
- ■ A spacious Family Room with a cozy fireplace and direct access to the deck
- ■ A Master Suite with a decorative ceiling, walk-in closet, and a private Master Bath
- ■ Three (optional four) additional bedrooms with easy access to a full hall bath

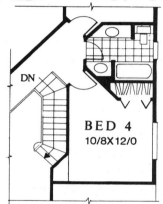

DN

BED 4
10/8X12/0

OPTIONAL UPPER FLOOR

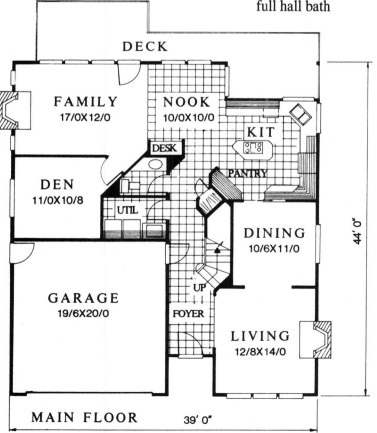

DECK

FAMILY
17/0X12/0

NOOK
10/0X10/0

KIT

DESK

PANTRY

DEN
11/0X10/8

UTIL

DINING
10/6X11/0

GARAGE
19/6X20/0

UP

FOYER

LIVING
12/8X14/0

44' 0"

MAIN FLOOR   39' 0"

No. 91654   *No materials list available*

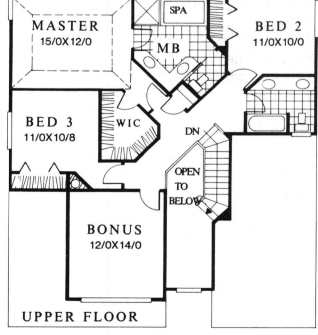

MASTER
15/0X12/0

SPA

MB

BED 2
11/0X10/0

BED 3
11/0X10/8

WIC

DN

OPEN TO BELOW

BONUS
12/0X14/0

UPPER FLOOR

FIRST FLOOR — 1,233 SQ. FT.
SECOND FLOOR — 902 SQ. FT.
BONUS ROOM — 168 SQ. FT.

TOTAL LIVING AREA:
2,135 SQ. FT.

No. 91426

Contemporary with Class

■ This plan features:

— Three bedrooms

— Two full and one half baths

■ A vaulted foyer

■ A Great Room with decorative beams, a built-in bar and a wood stove

■ A Kitchen that is open to the Breakfast Room, and equipped with a peninsula counter

■ A Master Bedroom with a large walk-in closet, double-vanity bath and private access to the deck

■ Two additional bedrooms sharing a full hall bath

FIRST FLOOR — 1,686 SQ. FT.
SECOND FLOOR — 674 SQ. FT.

TOTAL LIVING AREA:
2,360 SQ. FT.

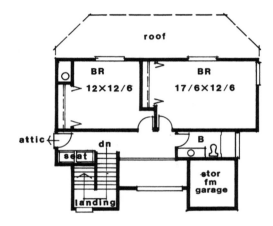

UPPER LEVEL

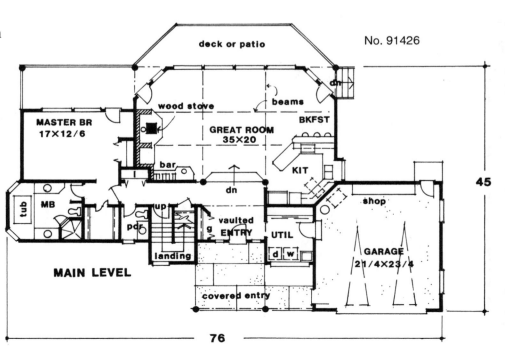

MAIN LEVEL

No. 99313

One-Level Living with a Wide-Open Feeling

■ This plan features:

— Two bedrooms

— Two full baths

■ A dramatic arched transom window over the entry

■ A vaulted ceiling and fireplace in the spacious Great Room

■ Sliding glass doors to the deck from the Great Room

■ A U-shaped Kitchen with double sink and ample cabinet and counter space

■ A greenhouse window in the informal Breakfast Nook

■ A Master Bedroom with a vaulted ceiling, walk-in closet, and private Master Bath

■ A second bedroom that adjoins a full compartmentalized bath

FIRST FLOOR — 1,955 SQ. FT.

TOTAL LIVING AREA: 1,955 SQ. FT.

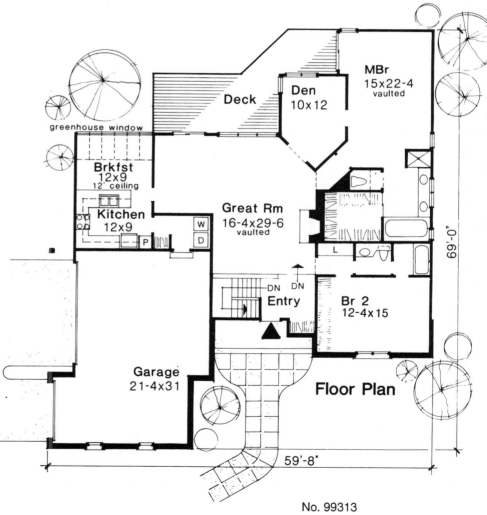

No. 99313

No. 91424

Infinite Possibilities

■ This plan features:

— Three bedrooms

— Two full and one half baths

■ A dramatic vaulted entry

■ An arched floor-to-ceiling window, a vaulted ceiling, and a fireplace in the Living Room

■ A formal Dining Room adjoining the Living Room

■ An open layout between the Kitchen, eating Nook and the Family Room making for a spacious atmosphere

■ A peninsula counter in the efficient Kitchen

■ Direct access to the patio from the Family Room which also has a fireplace

■ A Master Suite with a vaulted ceiling, walk-in closet and private Master Bath

FIRST FLOOR — 1,290 SQ. FT.
SECOND FLOOR — 932 SQ. FT.
BONUS ROOM — 228 SQ. FT.

TOTAL LIVING AREA: 2,222 SQ. FT.

UPPER FLOOR PLAN

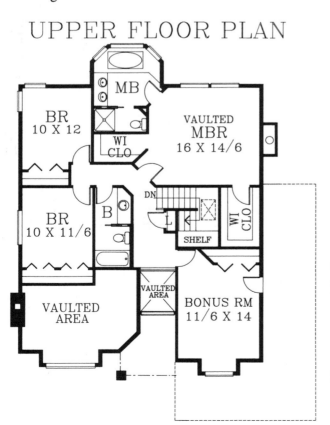

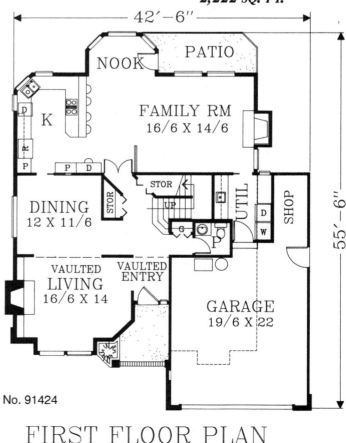

No. 91424

FIRST FLOOR PLAN

No. 91429

Kitchen has Gourmet in Mind

■ This plan features:

— Three bedrooms

— Three full baths

■ A spacious, sunken Great Room with a fireplace and large arched window

■ A gourmet Kitchen with an island rangetop and a snack bar also equipped with a built-in pantry

■ A formal Dining Room elegantly placed just steps up from the Great Room

■ A second-floor Master Suite with a walk-in closet, compartmentalized bath and a private deck

■ An additional bedroom on the second floor that is also equipped with a private bath

FIRST FLOOR — 1,392 SQ. FT.
SECOND FLOOR — 832 SQ. FT.

TOTAL LIVING AREA:
2,224 SQ. FT.

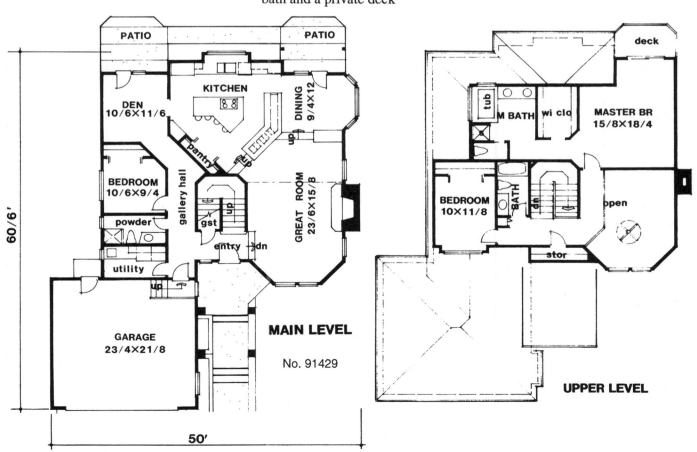

MAIN LEVEL

No. 91429

UPPER LEVEL

No. 90147

Abundance of Cabinets in Ranch Design

■ This plan features:

— Three bedrooms

— Two full baths

■ A Kitchen connected with the Dining/Family Room providing a very relaxed atmosphere

■ Laundry facilities located next to the bedroom area, both convenient and practical

■ A Master Bedroom with a private full bath

■ A Study that can double as a guest bedroom with ample closet space

■ An optional basement or crawl space foundation — please specify when ordering

FIRST FLOOR — 1,288 SQ. FT.

TOTAL LIVING AREA: 1,288 SQ. FT.

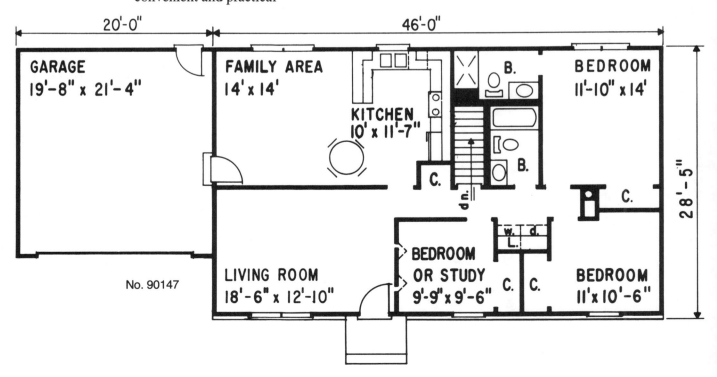

No. 90147

GARAGE 19'-8" x 21'-4"

FAMILY AREA 14' x 14'

KITCHEN 10' x 11'-7"

B.

B.

BEDROOM 11'-10" x 14'

C.

C.

LIVING ROOM 18'-6" x 12'-10"

BEDROOM OR STUDY 9'-9" x 9'-6"

w. d.

C. C.

BEDROOM 11' x 10'-6"

20'-0"

46'-0"

28'-5"

No. 90124

Focus on Family Activities

■ This plan features:

— Three bedrooms

— Two full and one half baths

■ A Master Bedroom with a walk-in closet and private full bath

■ A Family Room with an exposed beam ceiling and fireplace

■ An efficient Kitchen with an eating bar open to the Family Room

■ A mudroom entrance combined with laundry facilities

■ An optional basement or crawl space foundation — please specify when ordering

FIRST FLOOR — 1,080 SQ. FT.
SECOND FLOOR — 868 SQ. FT.

TOTAL LIVING AREA: 1,948 SQ. FT.

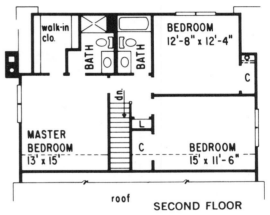

SECOND FLOOR

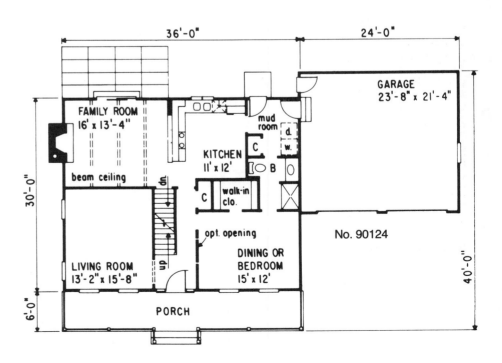

No. 90124

No. 91349

Two Separate Dining Areas

■ This plan features:

— Two bedrooms

— Two full baths

■ A vaulted ceiling entry

■ A Living Room with a vaulted ceiling and accented by a bay window and an optional fireplace

■ A garden window, eating bar, and an abundance of storage space in the efficient Kitchen

■ A Master Bedroom with its own bath having a double sink vanity and a walk-in closet

■ A Library with a vaulted ceiling option and a window seat

FIRST FLOOR — 1,694 SQ. FT.

TOTAL LIVING AREA: 1,694 SQ. FT.

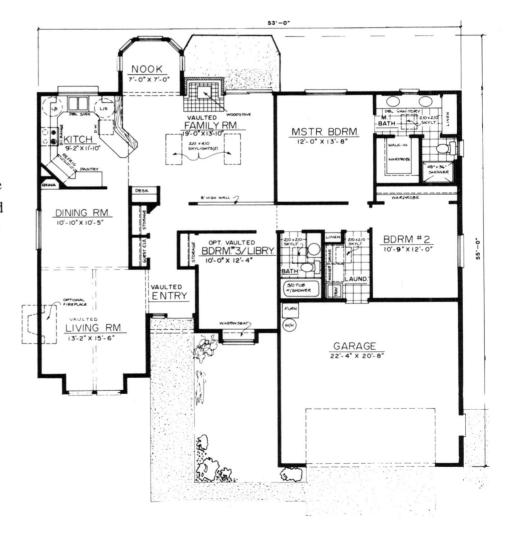

No. 91349

No. 99241
You've Got the Choice

■ This plan features:
— Three bedrooms
— Two full baths

■ A galley-style Kitchen with easy access to both the formal Dining Room with built-in china closet and the eating Nook with a sunny bay

■ A spacious Gathering Room with a raised hearth fireplace

■ A Master Bedroom with a walk-in closet, and a private bath

■ Two additional bedrooms served by a full hall bath

FIRST FLOOR — 1,366 SQ. FT.
BASEMENT — 1,281 SQ. FT.
GARAGE — 484 SQ. FT.

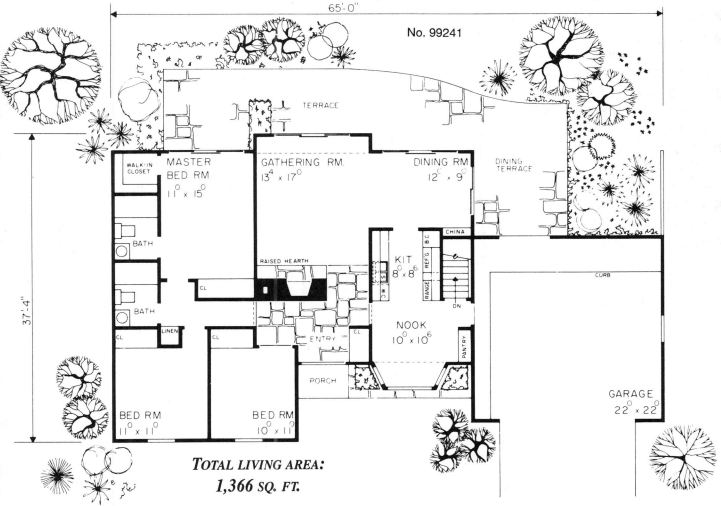

No. 99241

65'-0"

37'-4"

TERRACE

WALK-IN CLOSET

MASTER BED RM
11⁰ x 15⁰

GATHERING RM.
13⁴ x 17⁰

DINING RM
12⁰ x 9⁰

DINING TERRACE

BATH

RAISED HEARTH

CHINA

KIT
8⁰ x 8⁶

REFG. B.C.

RANGE

CURB

BATH

CL

CL

LINEN

CL

CL

ENTRY

DW

DN

NOOK
10⁰ x 10⁶

PANTRY

BED RM
11⁰ x 11⁰

BED RM
10⁰ x 11⁰

PORCH

GARAGE
22⁰ x 22⁰

TOTAL LIVING AREA:
1,366 SQ. FT.

No. 91227

English Elegance with a Twist

■ This plan features:

— Three bedrooms

— Two full and one half baths

■ A two-story foyer

■ A first-floor Master Suite with two walk-in closets, a private Master Bath and access to an outdoor deck

■ A magnificent Great Room with a sloping ceiling, a massive fireplace and a built-in wetbar

■ An island Kitchen with a double-sized pantry and a Breakfast area

■ Two additional bedrooms on the second floor that share a full bath

FIRST FLOOR — 1,772 SQ. FT.
SECOND FLOOR — 674 SQ. FT.
GARAGE AND STORAGE — 667 SQ. FT.

TOTAL LIVING AREA: 2,446 SQ. FT.

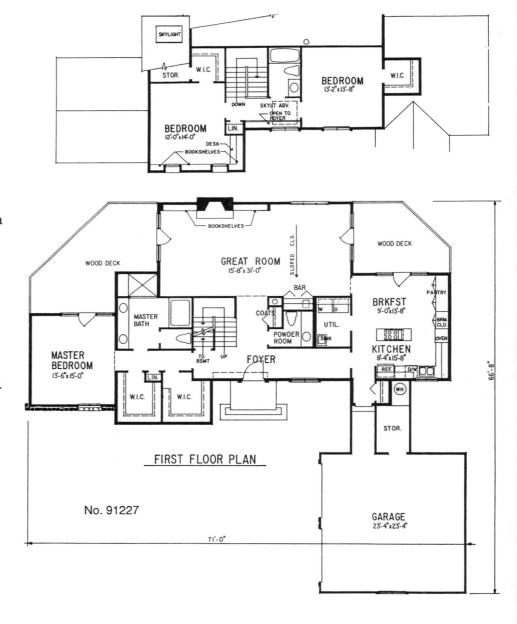

FIRST FLOOR PLAN

No. 91227

No. 91204

Country Comfort

- This plan features:
- — Three bedrooms
- — Two full baths
- A convenient, eat-in, country Kitchen with sliding panels, built-in pantry, and a broom closet

- A sloped ceiling and a fireplace in the sunken Great Room which has sliding glass doors to the deck
- A private Master Bath and two walk-in closets in the spacious Master Suite

- Two additional bedrooms, one with a walk-in closet, that share a full hall bath

FIRST FLOOR — 1,974 SQ. FT.
GARAGE AND STORAGE — 612 SQ. FT.

TOTAL LIVING AREA:
1,974 SQ. FT.

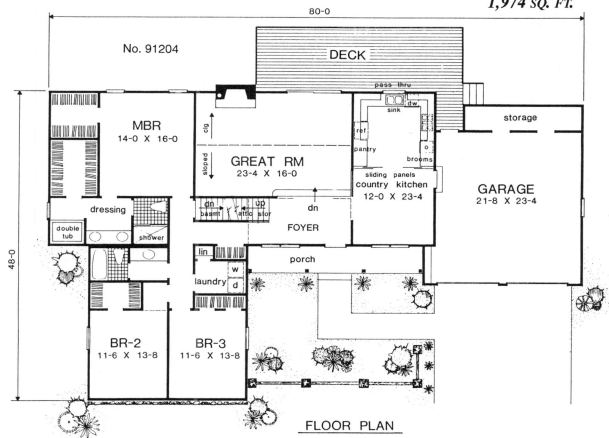

FLOOR PLAN

No. 91420
Build for the Future

■ This plan features:

— Three bedrooms

— Two full baths

■ A sky-lit Master Suite with a walk-in closet, and private, well-appointed bath

■ A Library balcony area off the Master Suite

■ A vaulted ceiling in the Great Room with a fireplace and a view of the Library balcony

■ A built-in bar in the formal Dining Room

■ An island Kitchen with an eating bar and pantry

FIRST FLOOR — 1,632 SQ. FT.
SECOND FLOOR — 910 SQ. FT.
BONUS ROOM — 456 SQ. FT.
GARAGE — 2-CAR

TOTAL LIVING AREA: 2,542 SQ. FT.

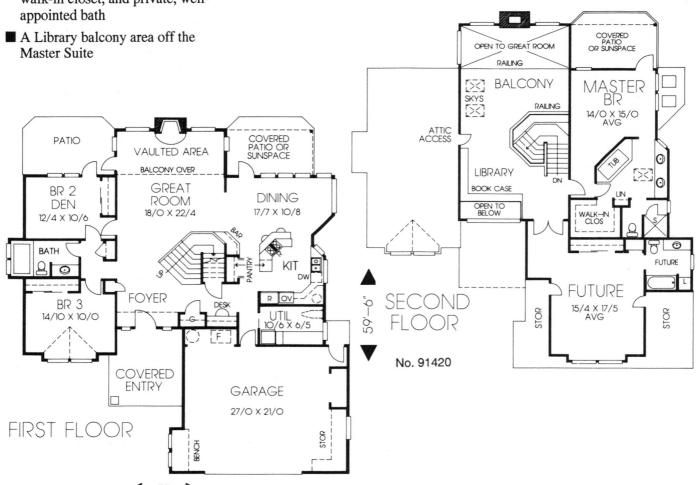

57′

No. 91413
Compact Classic

■ This plan features:

— Three bedrooms

— Two full and one half baths

■ A spacious Family Room with a cozy fireplace and direct access to the patio

■ A well-appointed Kitchen with an eating bar peninsula, double sink and sunny eating Nook

■ A formal Living Room and Dining Room located at the front of the house

■ A Master Suite equipped with a walk-in closet, a double vanity and a full Master Bath

FIRST FLOOR — 963 SQ. FT.
SECOND FLOOR — 774 SQ. FT.

TOTAL LIVING AREA:
1,737 SQ. FT.

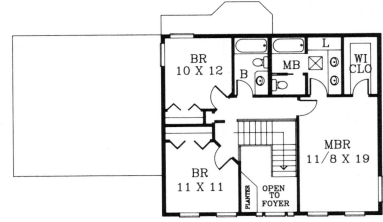

SECOND FLOOR PLAN

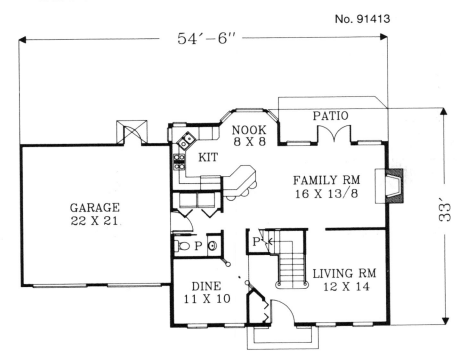

No. 91413

No. 91414
Luxury Living

■ This plan features:

— Four bedrooms

— Three full baths

■ A vaulted ceiling foyer

■ A Living Room with a vaulted ceiling and elegant fireplace

■ A formal Dining Room that adjoins the Living Room, with a built-in buffet

■ An island cook top in the well-appointed Kitchen with a walk-in pantry and an open layout to the Family Room

■ A vaulted ceiling in the Family Room with a cozy, corner fireplace

■ A huge walk-in closet, built-in entertainment center, and a full bath with every amenity in the Master Suite

FIRST FLOOR — 2,125 SQ. FT.
SECOND FLOOR — 1,095 SQ. FT.
GARAGE — 3-CAR

**TOTAL LIVING AREA:
3,220 SQ. FT.**

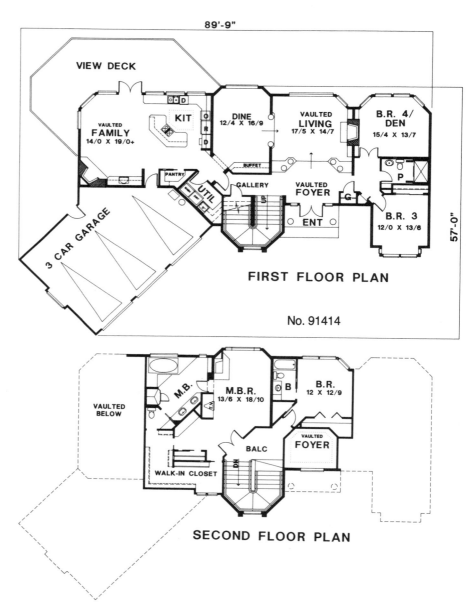

89'-9"

VIEW DECK

VAULTED FAMILY 14/0 X 19/0+

KIT

DINE 12/4 X 16/9

VAULTED LIVING 17/5 X 14/7

B.R. 4/ DEN 15/4 X 13/7

PANTRY

BUFFET

UTIL

GALLERY

VAULTED FOYER

P

ENT

B.R. 3 12/0 X 13/6

3 CAR GARAGE

57'-0"

FIRST FLOOR PLAN

No. 91414

VAULTED BELOW

M.B.

M.B.R. 13/6 X 18/10

B

B.R. 12 X 12/9

WALK-IN CLOSET

BALC

VAULTED FOYER

SECOND FLOOR PLAN

No. 91412

Two-Story Arched Window Makes Dramatic Statement

■ This plan features:

— Three bedrooms

— Two full and one half baths

■ A spacious Family Room/Kitchen combination

■ A sunken Living Room with a warm and cozy fireplace

■ An impressive Dining Room with a vaulted ceiling in close proximity to the Kitchen

■ A Master Suite with a walk-in closet, a double-vanity bath, and a private deck

First floor — 1,416 sq. ft.
Second floor — 1,056 sq. ft.
Garage — 504 sq. ft. or 729 with option

Total living area:
2,472 sq. ft.

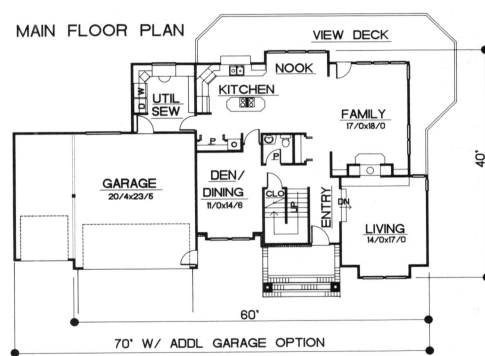

MAIN FLOOR PLAN

VIEW DECK

NOOK

KITCHEN

UTIL SEW

FAMILY
17/0x18/0

GARAGE
20/4x23/5

DEN/ DINING
11/0x14/6

CLO

ENTRY

UP

DN

LIVING
14/0x17/0

40'

60'

70' W/ ADDL GARAGE OPTION

No. 91412

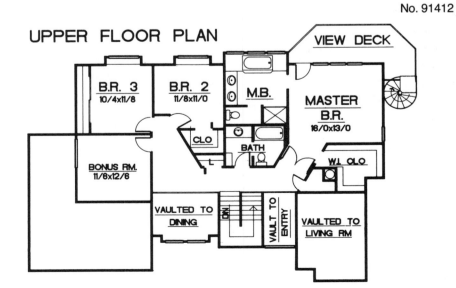

UPPER FLOOR PLAN

VIEW DECK

B.R. 3
10/4x11/8

B.R. 2
11/8x11/0

M.B.

MASTER B.R.
18/0x13/0

CLO

BATH

W.I. CLO

BONUS RM.
11/8x12/8

VAULTED TO DINING

DN

VAULT TO ENTRY

VAULTED TO LIVING RM

No. 90040

Design Portrays Expensive Look

■ This plan features:

— Three bedrooms

— Two full and one half baths

■ A sunny and spacious Living Room with a log burning fireplace and French doors opening to the porch

■ A well-equipped and efficient Kitchen located between the formal Dining Room and the informal Family Room

■ A Master Suite with a walk-in closet and a lavish Master Bath located in the turret

■ Two additional bedrooms sharing the full hall bath

FIRST FLOOR — 1,069 SQ. FT.
SECOND FLOOR — 948 SQ. FT.

TOTAL LIVING AREA: 2,017 SQ. FT.

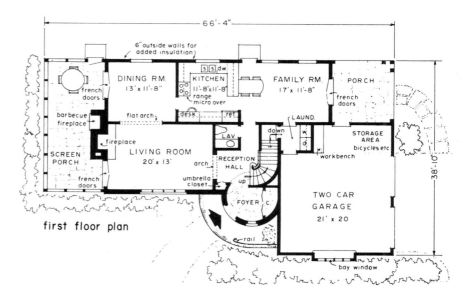

first floor plan

No. 90040

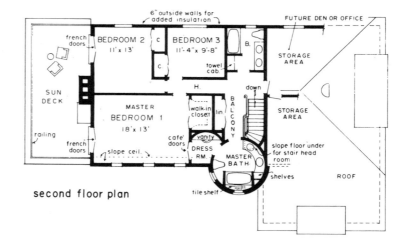

second floor plan

No. 90014
Stately Home Features Formal Courtyard

■ This plan features:

— Three bedrooms

— Two full and one half baths

■ A conveniently organized Kitchen located between the Dining Room and the Family Room

■ A grand foyer leading to the large Living Room which features a fireplace and window seats

■ A Master Bedroom with private Master Bath and his and her closets

■ Two additional bedrooms sharing a full hall bath

FIRST FLOOR — 943 SQ. FT.
SECOND FLOOR — 772 SQ. FT.

TOTAL LIVING AREA: 1,715 SQ. FT.

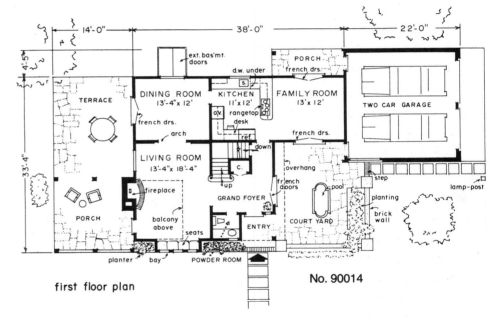

first floor plan

No. 90014

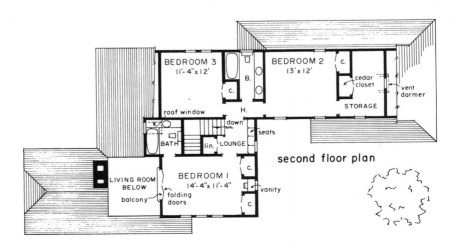

second floor plan

No. 91347
Functional Angles

■ This plan features:

— Four bedrooms

— Three full baths

■ A vaulted ceiling entry

■ A sunken, vaulted ceiling Living Room accented by a large bay window

■ An angular-shaped Kitchen with a boxed bay window, island cooktop and vaulted ceiling Breakfast area

■ A Family Room with a wood stove alcove

■ A spacious Master Suite with a private deck, deluxe bath and a walk-in closet

■ Two additional bedrooms, one with a walk-in closet, that are served by a full hall bath

FIRST FLOOR — 1,392 SQ. FT.
SECOND FLOOR — 940 SQ. FT.

TOTAL LIVING AREA:
2,332 SQ. FT.

No. 91643

Prestigious Executive Design

■ This plan features:

— Four bedrooms

— Three full and one half baths

■ A spacious Living Room with a lovely fireplace

■ A formal Dining Room with direct access to the Kitchen

■ A large, modern Kitchen with an island cook top, corner double sink, built-in desk, and a walk-in pantry

■ A fireplace in the Family Room made more spacious by the open layout into the Kitchen and Nook

■ A coved ceiling in the Master Suite with a private and lavish Master Bath

■ Two full baths serving the three additional bedrooms, each with walk-in closets

FIRST FLOOR — 1,703 SQ. FT.
SECOND FLOOR — 1,739 SQ. FT.
BONUS ROOM — 291 SQ. FT.

TOTAL LIVING AREA:
3,442 SQ. FT.

UPPER FLOOR

No. 91643

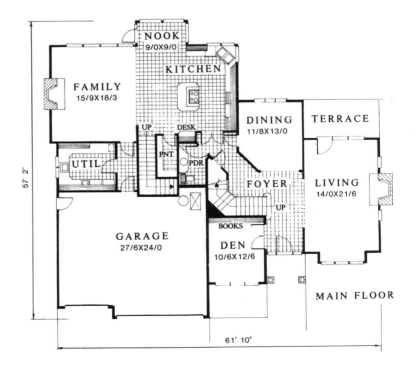

MAIN FLOOR

No. 90696
Energy-Saving Cape

■ This plan features:

— Four bedrooms

— Two full baths

■ A large Living Room with an exposed wood beam ceiling, heat-circulating fireplace and a bay window

■ A sunny Dining and Family Room enlarged by a bay window with sliding glass doors to rear deck

■ A country Kitchen with generous cabinet and counter space

■ A first floor Master Bedroom with his and her closets

■ Two additional upstairs bedrooms with sitting areas and skylights

FIRST FLOOR — 1,298 SQ. FT.
SECOND FLOOR — 542 SQ. FT.

TOTAL LIVING AREA: 1,840 SQ. FT.

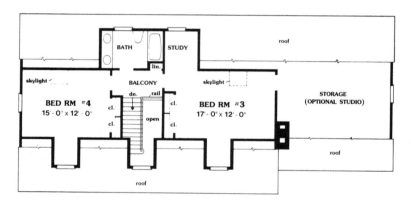

SECOND FLOOR PLAN

No. 90696

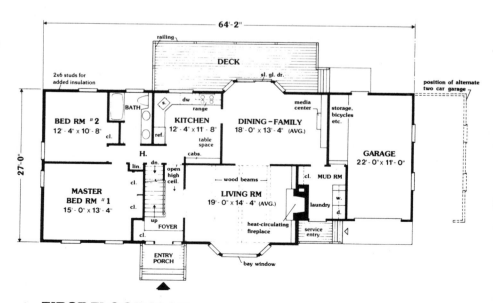

FIRST FLOOR PLAN

242

No. 99608
Classic Farmhouse with Elegant Amenities

■ This plan features:

— Four bedrooms

— Two full and one half baths

■ A decorative curved stairway in the roomy foyer

■ A Living Room with an ornamental heat-circulating fireplace

■ A Dining Room enhanced by a large bay window

■ A sky-lit Family Room with a heat-circulating fireplace and sliding glass doors to the terrace

■ An efficient well-equipped Kitchen with a window over the sink and a peninsula counter

■ A Master Suite with a Master Bath equipped with a whirlpool tub and double vanities

FIRST FLOOR — 1,269 SQ. FT.
SECOND FLOOR — 1,006 SQ. FT.
MUDROOM — 58 SQ. FT.
BASEMENT — 854 SQ. FT.
GARAGE — 403 SQ. FT.

TOTAL LIVING AREA:
2,333 SQ. FT.

SECOND FLOOR PLAN

2x6 studs for added insulation

master BATH

whirlpool tub

MASTER BED RM 15' x 14'

BED RM # 2 13'-4" x 11'

walk-in closet

dn.

open   BALC.

HALL

cl.

closet

lin.

closet

BED RM #4 11'-8" x 10'

BED RM # 3 11'-8" x 11'

BATH

whirlpool tub

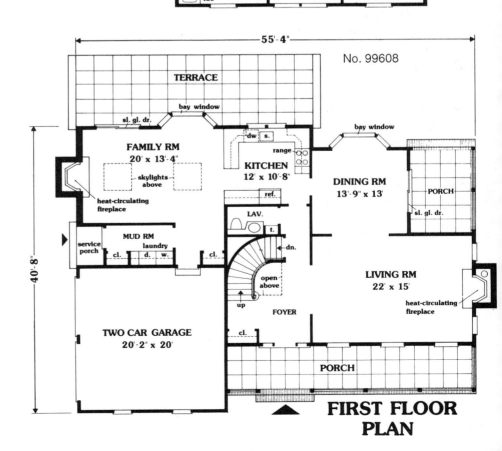

No. 99608

— 55'-4" —

TERRACE

bay window

sl. gl. dr.

dw   s.

FAMILY RM 20' x 13'-4"

bay window

range

skylights above

KITCHEN 12' x 10'-8"

DINING RM 13'-9" x 13'

PORCH

heat-circulating fireplace

ref.

sl. gl. dr.

40'-8"

service porch

MUD RM laundry

LAV.

t.

d. w.

cl.

cl.

dn.

open above

up

LIVING RM 22' x 15'

heat-circulating fireplace

TWO CAR GARAGE 20'-2" x 20'

cl.

FOYER

PORCH

FIRST FLOOR PLAN

No. 90833

Enjoy the View

■ This plan features:

— Three bedrooms

— Three full baths

■ A Family Room complete with a fireplace and bay window

■ A second fireplace in the Living Room that flows easily into the Dining Room with sliding glass doors to the deck

■ A Family Kitchen with an eat-in Nook and built-in pantry

■ A Master Bedroom with a walk-in closet and a private bath

■ Two additional bedrooms sharing a full hall bath

FIRST FLOOR — 1,318 SQ. FT.
BASEMENT — 994 SQ. FT.
GARAGE — 378 SQ. FT.
WIDTH — 40'-0"
DEPTH — 40'-0"

TOTAL LIVING AREA:
2,312 SQ. FT.

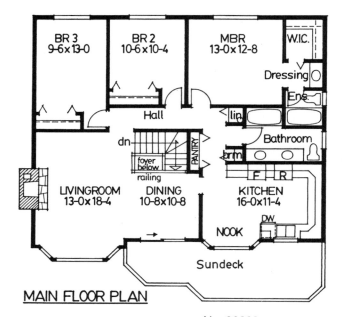

MAIN FLOOR PLAN

No. 90833

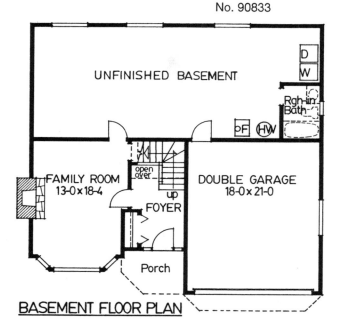

BASEMENT FLOOR PLAN

No. 91224

Breathtaking Views Inside and Out

■ This plan features:

— Three bedrooms

— Two full and one half baths

■ A Master Suite with sky-lit tub, private balcony and a fireplace

■ An island Kitchen efficiently located between the formal and informal eating areas

■ A spacious Living Room with a lovely fireplace

■ A built-in wetbar, which is just steps away from the Living Room

FIRST FLOOR — 997 SQ. FT.
SECOND FLOOR — 1,059 SQ. FT.
GARAGE — 506 SQ. FT.

TOTAL LIVING AREA: 2,056 SQ. FT.

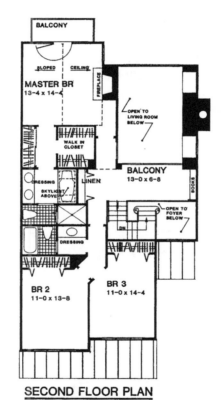

No materials list available

SECOND FLOOR PLAN

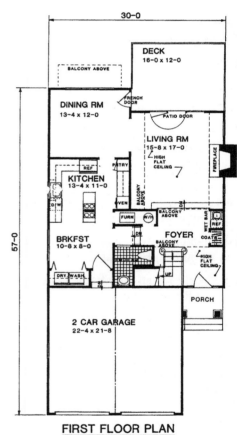

FIRST FLOOR PLAN

No. 91224

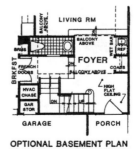

OPTIONAL BASEMENT PLAN

No. 90012

Modest Tudor with a Massive Look

■ This plan features:

— Three bedrooms

— Two full and one half baths

■ A large log-burning fireplace centrally located on the far wall of the Living Room

■ A formal Dining Room with access to either the screen porch, terrace, or Kitchen

■ A Kitchen with a cook top island and a built-in Breakfast Nook

■ A Family Room with French door access to another porch

■ A Master Suite with lounge area, private Master Bath, and a walk-in closet

■ Two additional bedrooms with access to the full hall bath

FIRST FLOOR — 1,078 SQ. FT.
SECOND FLOOR — 1,131 SQ. FT.

TOTAL LIVING AREA: 2,209 SQ. FT.

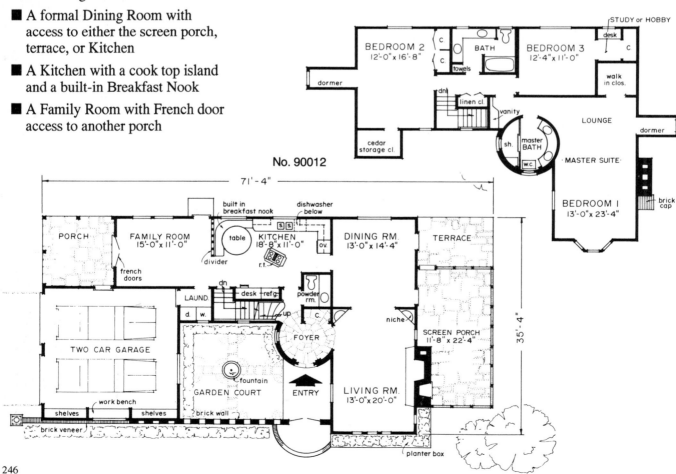

No. 99204

Five Fireplaces Add Uncommon Distinction

■ This plan features:

— Four bedrooms

— Four full and one half baths

■ A sprawling portico that opens to a two-story foyer

■ A fireplace in the Living Room, Library, Dining Room, Master Suite, and Family Rooms

■ An island Kitchen that is efficiently laid out with a snack bar peninsula

■ A Master Suite with an adjoining Exercise Room and a lavish Master Bath

■ Atrium doors that link every rear-facing room with the backyard

■ Two upstairs bedrooms with twin walk-in closets and private baths

FIRST FLOOR — 4,104 SQ. FT.
SECOND FLOOR — 979 SQ. FT.

TOTAL LIVING AREA: 5,083 SQ. FT.

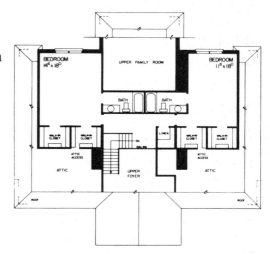

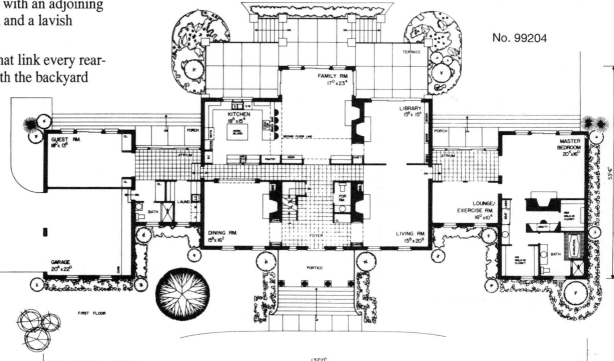

No. 99204

No. 91206

Friendly Porch Welcomes Guests

■ This plan features:

— Four bedrooms

— Two full and one half baths

■ A Master Suite with a huge, walk-in closet, a cozy window seat, double sinks and a garden tub

■ Three additional bedrooms that share a full hall bath

■ A sunken Family Room with French doors and a fireplace

■ A country Kitchen with a cook top island, a convenient Breakfast Bay and a large pantry

FIRST FLOOR — 1,346 SQ. FT.
SECOND FLOOR — 1,230 SQ. FT.
GARAGE AND STORAGE — 788 SQ. FT.

TOTAL LIVING AREA: 2,576 SQ. FT.

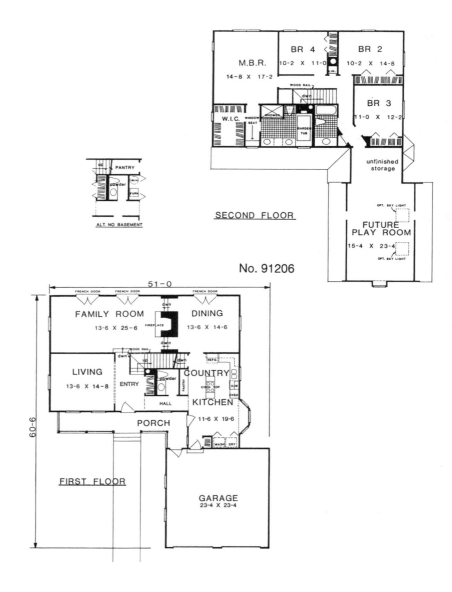

No. 90424
Call This Home

■ This plan features:

— Three bedrooms

— Two full and two half baths

■ A covered porch in the front and a screened porch in the back to take advantage of seasonal weather

■ A Great Room with a stone fireplace that occupies the center of the home

■ An island Kitchen that flows directly into the Dining Room and the Breakfast Bay

■ A secluded Master Bedroom with a five piece bath and his and her walk-in closets

■ Two upstairs bedrooms, each with plenty of closet space and private access to a shared bath

■ A basement, slab or crawl space foundation — please specify when ordering

FIRST FLOOR — 1,535 SQ. FT.
SECOND FLOOR — 765 SQ. FT.
BASEMENT — 1,091 SQ. FT.

TOTAL LIVING AREA:
2,300 SQ. FT.

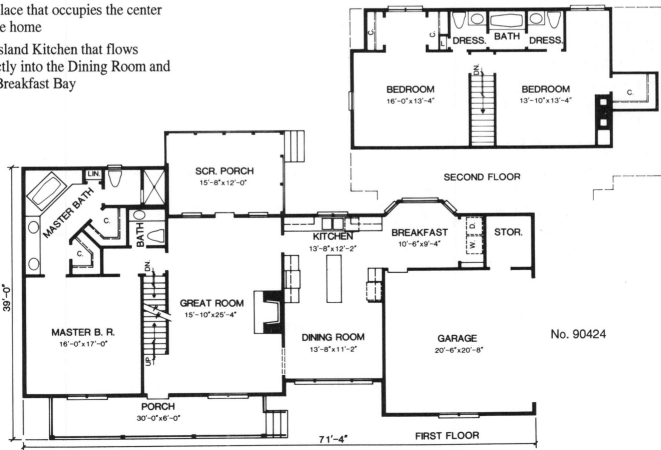

No. 91400

Create a Dramatic Impression

■ This plan features:

— Three bedrooms

— Two full baths

■ A two-story entry

■ A cook-top island and breakfast bar in the efficient Kitchen

■ A vaulted ceiling and wood stove in the Great Room

■ A built-in desk in each of the first-floor bedrooms

■ A luxurious Master Suite with an adjoining sky-lit bath and a dressing room

FIRST FLOOR — 1,450 SQ. FT.
SECOND FLOOR — 650 SQ. FT.
GARAGE — 558 SQ. FT.

TOTAL LIVING AREA:
2,100 SQ. FT.

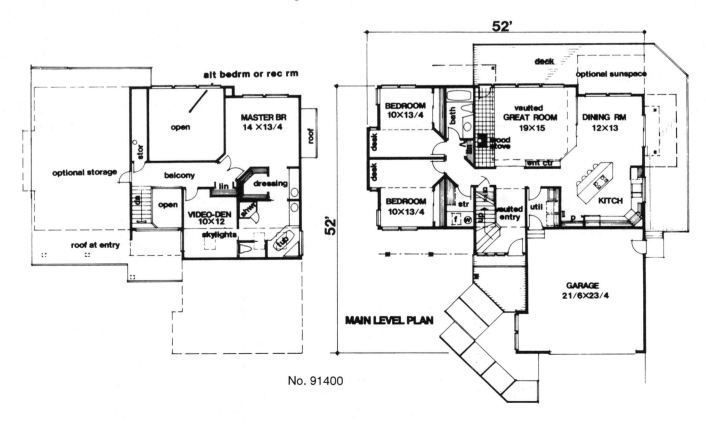

No. 91400

No. 90836

Tower Suite

■ This plan features:

— Three bedrooms

— Two full and one half baths

■ A Living Room and Dining Room that flow together and are separated by a single step

■ A Family Room that has a cozy fireplace and sliding doors to the patio

■ A handy breakfast bar, built-in planning desk and walk-in pantry in the efficient Kitchen

■ A Master Suite with a walk-in closet, cozy sitting nook and a private Master Bath

■ Two additional bedrooms, one with a walk-in closet, sharing a double-vanity, full hall bath

FIRST FLOOR — 1,306 SQ. FT.
SECOND FLOOR — 1,266 SQ. FT.
GARAGE — 572 SQ. FT.

TOTAL LIVING AREA: 2,572 SQ. FT.

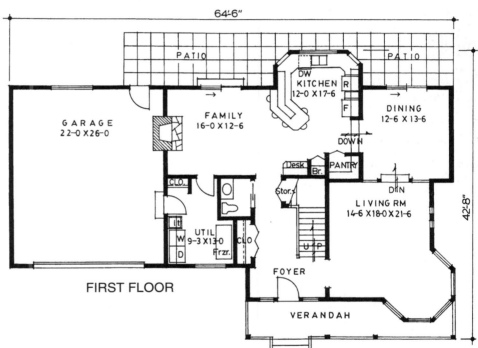

64'-6"

PATIO

PATIO

DW
KITCHEN
12-0 X 17-6
R
F

FAMILY
16-0 X 12-6

DINING
12-6 X 13-6

GARAGE
22-0 X 26-0

DOWN

Desk
Br.
PANTRY

CLO.

DN

Stor.

LIVING RM
14-6 X 18-0 X 21-6

UTIL
9-3 X 13-0

CLO

UP

W
D

Frzr.

FOYER

42'-8"

FIRST FLOOR

VERANDAH

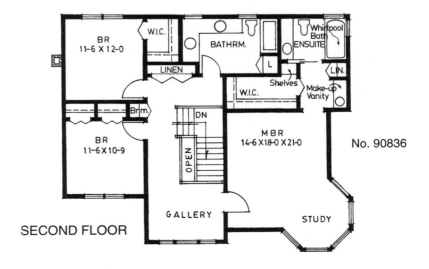

BR
11-6 X 12-0

W.I.C.

BATHRM.

Whirlpool
Bath
ENSUITE

LINEN

L

LIN.

Shelves

W.I.C.

Make-up
Vanity

Brm.

DN

No. 90836

BR
11-6 X 10-9

OPEN

MBR
14-6 X 18-0 X 21-0

SECOND FLOOR

GALLERY

STUDY

No. 90307

Open Floor Plan Enhances Home

■ This plan features:

— One bedroom

— Two full baths

■ A Fireside Room with a vaulted ceiling and a unique built-in sofa enclosed in glass with a focal point fireplace

■ A centrally-located island Kitchen efficiently laid out and flowing into the Dining Room

■ A second floor bedroom incorporating a bump-out window and a sitting room

FIRST FLOOR — 768 SQ. FT.
SECOND FLOOR — 419 SQ. FT.

TOTAL LIVING AREA:
1,187 SQ. FT.

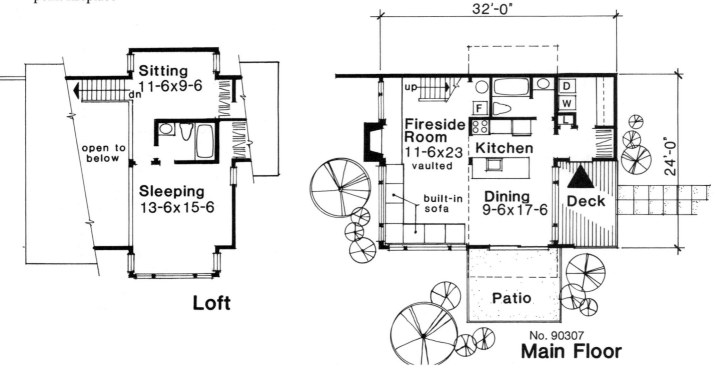

Sitting
11-6x9-6

dn

open to below

Sleeping
13-6x15-6

Loft

32'-0"

up

Fireside Room
11-6x23
vaulted

Kitchen

F

D

W

built-in sofa

Dining
9-6x17-6

Deck

24'-0"

Patio

No. 90307
Main Floor

No. 90934

A Nest for Empty-Nesters

■ This plan features:

— Two bedrooms

— One full bath

■ An economical design

■ A covered sun deck adding
outdoor living space

■ A mudroom/laundry area inside
the side door, trapping dirt before
it can enter the house

■ An open layout between the
Living Room with fireplace,
Dining Room and Kitchen

FIRST FLOOR — 884 SQ. FT.
WIDTH — 34'-0"
DEPTH — 28'-0"

TOTAL LIVING AREA:
884 SQ. FT.

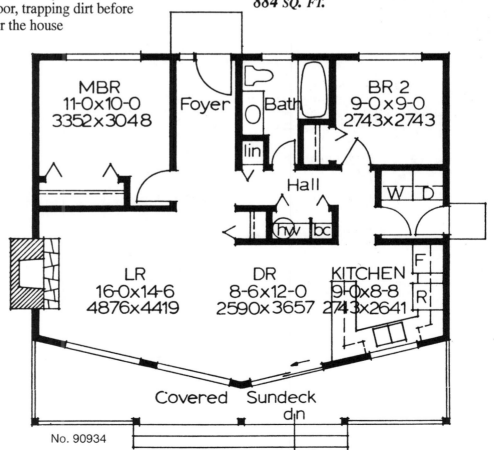

MBR
11-0x10-0
3352x3048

Foyer

Bath

lin

BR 2
9-0 x 9-0
2743x2743

Hall

W D

hw   bc

LR
16-0x14-6
4876x4419

DR
8-6x12-0
2590x3657

KITCHEN
9-0x8-8
2743x2641

F

R

Covered   Sundeck
dn

No. 90934

No. 91022
Double Decks Adorn Luxurious Master Suite

■ This plan features:

— Three bedrooms

— Two full and one half baths

■ Abundant windows, indoor planters and three decks uniting every room with the outdoors

■ An efficient Kitchen with direct access to the Nook and the formal Dining Room

■ A wood stove warming the spacious Family Room

■ A secluded Master Suite with private deck, Den and Master Bath

■ An optional basement, slab or crawl space foundation — please specify when ordering

FIRST FLOOR — 1,985 SQ. FT.
SECOND FLOOR — 715 SQ. FT.

TOTAL LIVING AREA:
2,700 SQ. FT.

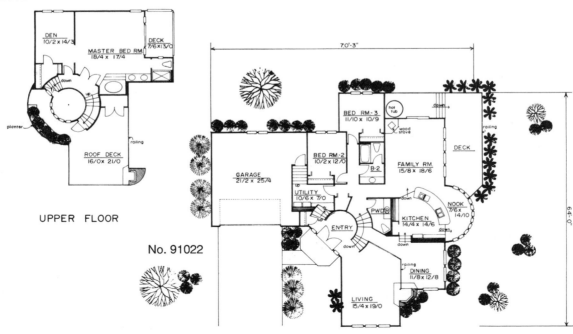

UPPER FLOOR

No. 91022

MAIN FLOOR

254

No. 91026

Home on a Hill

■ This plan features:

— Two bedrooms

— Two full baths

■ Sweeping panels of glass and a wood stove, creating atmosphere for the Great Room

■ An open plan that draws the Kitchen into the warmth of the Great Room's wood stove

■ A sleeping loft that has a full bath all to itself

■ A basement foundation only

FIRST FLOOR — 988 SQ. FT.
SECOND FLOOR — 366 SQ. FT.
BASEMENT — 988 SQ. FT.

TOTAL LIVING AREA:
1,354 SQ. FT.

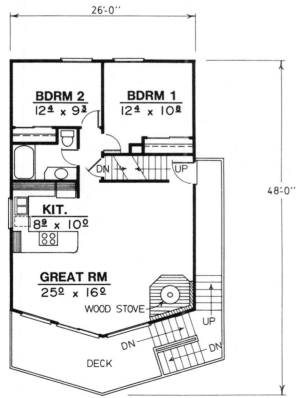

26'-0"

48'-0"

BDRM 2
12⁴ x 9³

BDRM 1
12⁴ x 10⁸

DN   UP

KIT.
8⁹ x 10⁰

GREAT RM
25⁰ x 16⁰

WOOD STOVE

UP

DN   DN

DECK

MAIN LEVEL

No. 91026

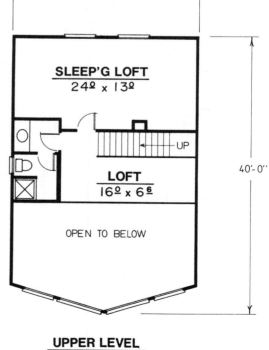

26'-0"

40'-0"

SLEEP'G LOFT
24⁰ x 13⁰

UP

LOFT
16⁰ x 6⁶

OPEN TO BELOW

UPPER LEVEL

No. 90011
Breezeway Connects to Angled Garage

■ This plan features:

— Three bedrooms

— Three full baths

■ A sunken Living Room with a fireplace and sliding glass doors to a covered porch

■ A step up from the Living Room to the Dining Room with a built-in china cabinet and sliding glass doors to the covered porch

■ A well-equipped Kitchen with a breakfast/snack bar adjoining the Family Room

■ A Master Bedroom with a private Master Bath and more than ample closet space

■ A glazed hot house for the plant enthusiast

■ A private Den right off breezeway

FIRST FLOOR — 1,867 SQ. FT.
BASEMENT — 1,020 SQ. FT.
GARAGE — 485 SQ. FT.

TOTAL LIVING AREA:
1,867 SQ. FT.

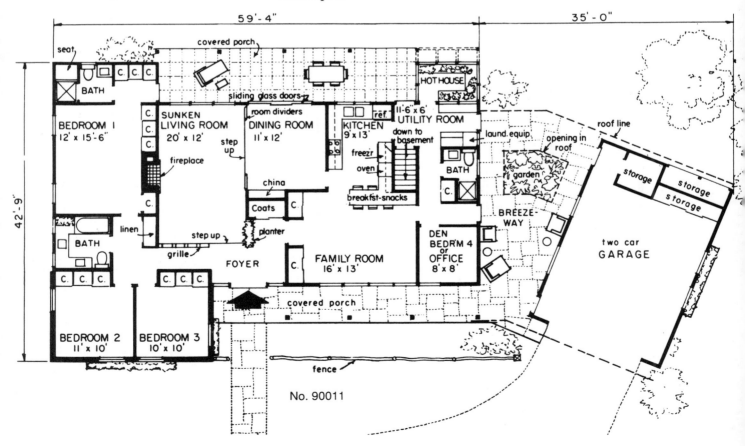

No. 90011

No. 90028

Modern Design Highlighted by Split Roofline

■ This plan features:

— Three bedrooms

— Two baths

■ An energy efficient solar hot water system with solar flat-plate collector panels and double glazed windows

■ A Living/Dining area accentuated by massive stonefaced, heat-circulating fireplace

■ An upstairs bedrooms sharing a sky lit full bath

FIRST FLOOR — 960 SQ. FT.
SECOND FLOOR — 580 SQ. FT.
WOOD DECK — 460 SQ. FT.

TOTAL LIVING AREA: 1,540 SQ. FT.

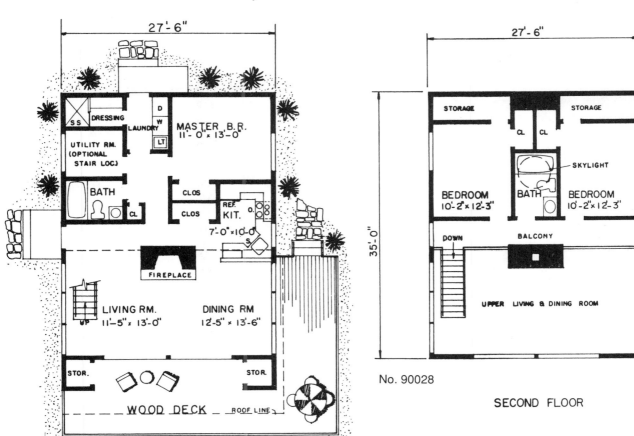

FIRST FLOOR

No. 90028

SECOND FLOOR

No. 90401

Basement with Drive-Under Garage

■ This plan features:

— Three bedrooms

— Two full baths

■ A first floor Master Suite with a large walk-in closet and a double vanity Master Bath

■ An L-shaped Kitchen, well-equipped and efficiently laid out, flowing easily into a bayed Dining Room

■ A Living Room with a raised-hearth fireplace to add warmth and a cozy atmosphere

■ A second floor with two bedrooms, both with large walk-in closets

■ An optional basement or crawl space foundation — please specify when ordering

FIRST FLOOR — 1,100 SQ. FT.
SECOND FLOOR — 660 SQ. FT.

TOTAL LIVING AREA:
1,760 SQ. FT

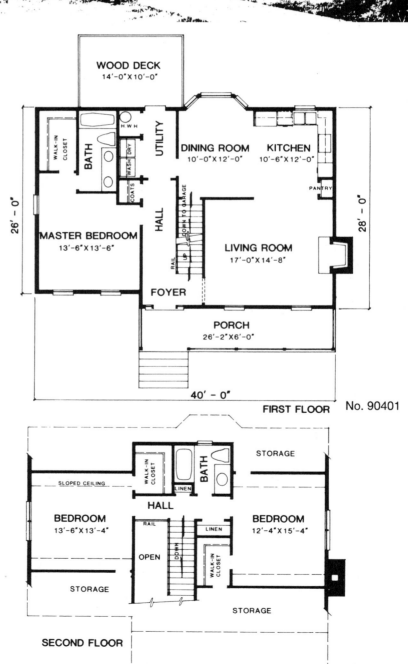

WOOD DECK
14'-0" X 10'-0"

WALK-IN CLOSET

BATH

H W H

UTILITY

WASH DRY

COATS

DINING ROOM
10'-0" X 12'-0"

KITCHEN
10'-6" X 12'-0"

PANTRY

MASTER BEDROOM
13'-6" X 13'-6"

HALL

DOWN TO GARAGE

RAIL

LIVING ROOM
17'-0" X 14'-8"

FOYER

26' - 0"

28' - 0"

PORCH
26'-2" X 6'-0"

40' - 0"

FIRST FLOOR   No. 90401

WALK-IN CLOSET

BATH

LINEN

STORAGE

SLOPED CEILING

HALL

BEDROOM
13'-6" X 13'-4"

RAIL

LINEN

BEDROOM
12'-4" X 15'-4"

OPEN

DOWN

WALK-IN CLOSET

STORAGE

STORAGE

SECOND FLOOR

No. 90822

Suited for a Hill

■ This plan features:

— Three bedrooms

— One and a half baths

■ Vaulted ceilings and a fieldstone fireplace in the Living/Dining Room

■ Two first floor bedrooms that have ample closet space and share a full hall bath

■ A Master Bedroom on the loft level including a private bath

■ A wrap-around sun deck offering an abundance of outdoor living space

FIRST FLOOR — 925 SQ. FT.
LOFT — 338 SQ. FT.
BASEMENT — 864 SQ. FT.
WIDTH — 33'-0"
DEPTH — 47'-0"

TOTAL LIVING AREA:
1,263 SQ. FT.

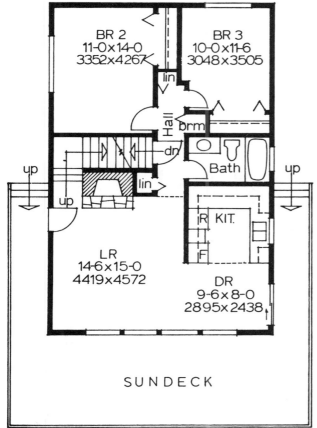

MAIN FLOOR

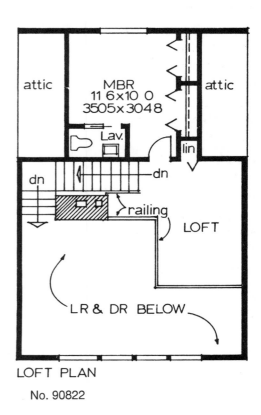

LOFT PLAN

No. 90822

No. 90691
Classic Features

■ This plan features:

— Three bedrooms

— Two full baths

■ A cathedral ceiling in the Living Room with a heat-circulating fireplace

No. 90691

■ A spectacular bow window and skylight in the Dining Room

■ A sliding glass door and skylight in the Kitchen

■ A Master Bedroom including a private Master Bath with whirlpool tub

■ Two additional bedrooms that share a full, double-vanity hall bath

FIRST FLOOR — 1,397 SQ. FT.
BASEMENT — 1,397 SQ. FT.

TOTAL LIVING AREA:
1,397 SQ. FT.

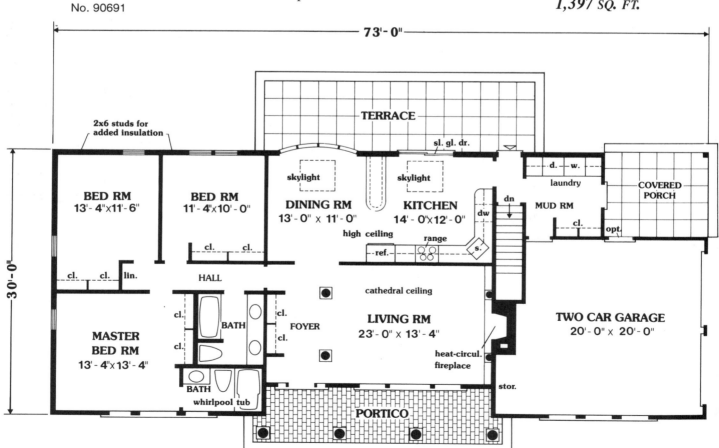

No. 92404
Traditional Ranch

■ This plan features:

— Three bedrooms

— Two full baths

■ A tray ceiling in the Master Suite that is equipped with his-and-her walk-in closets and a private Master Bath with a cathedral ceiling

■ A formal Living Room with a cathedral ceiling

■ A decorative tray ceiling in the elegant formal Dining Room

■ A spacious Family Room with a vaulted ceiling and a fireplace

■ A modern, well-appointed Kitchen with snack bar and bayed Breakfast area

■ Two additional bedrooms that share a full hall bath each having a walk-in closet

FIRST FLOOR — 2,275 SQ. FT.
BASEMENT — 2,207 SQ. FT.
GARAGE — 512 SQ. FT.

TOTAL LIVING AREA:
2,275 SQ. FT.

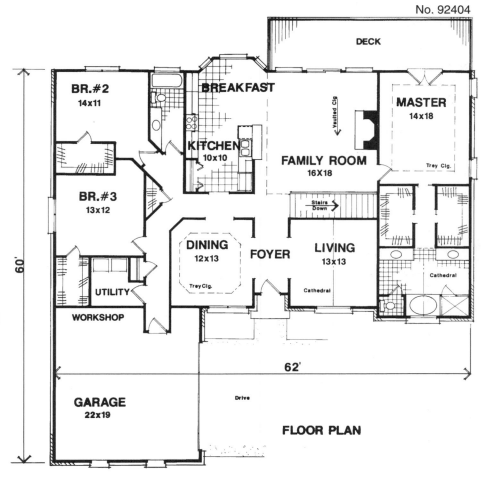

No. 92404

DECK

BR.#2
14x11

BREAKFAST

MASTER
14x18

KITCHEN
10x10

FAMILY ROOM
16X18

Trey Clg.

BR.#3
13x12

Stairs Down

DINING
12x13

FOYER

LIVING
13x13

Trey Clg.

Cathedral

UTILITY

WORKSHOP

Cathedral

62'

60'

GARAGE
22x19

Drive

FLOOR PLAN

No. 90684

Window Boxes Add Romantic Charm

- ■ This plan features:
- — Three bedrooms
- — Two full and one half baths
- ■ A spacious Living Room and formal Dining Room combination that's perfect for entertaining
- ■ A Family Room with a large fireplace and an expansive glass wall that overlooks the patio

- ■ An informal Dining bay convenient to both the Kitchen and the Family Room
- ■ An efficient and well-equipped Kitchen with a peninsula counter dividing it from the Family Room
- ■ A Master Bedroom with his and her closets and a private Master Bath

FIRST FLOOR — 1,486 SQ. FT.

TOTAL LIVING AREA: 1,486 SQ. FT.

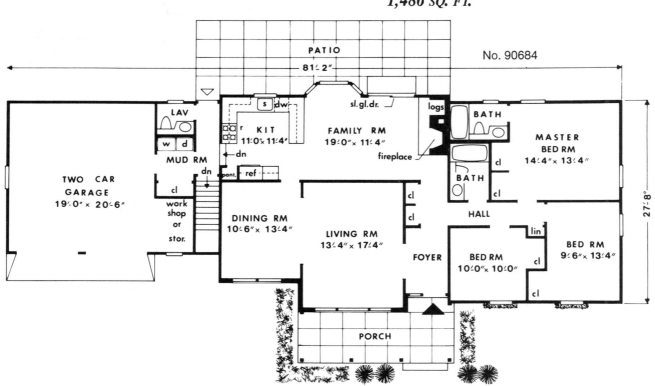

No. 91763

Designed for a Lot that Slopes Toward the Front

■ This plan features:

— Three bedrooms

— Two full and one half baths

■ A large study complete with a fireplace, overlooking the Living Room

■ A Master Suite illuminated by a skylight and equipped with a whirlpool tub, double-vanity sink and a walk-in closet

■ A vaulted ceiling in the Solarium/Family Room

■ A corner fireplace that enhances the Living Room

■ An efficient Kitchen with a cook top island and a built-in pantry

■ Two additional bedrooms that share a full hall bath

FIRST FLOOR — 1,856 SQ. FT.
SECOND FLOOR — 618 SQ. FT.
GARAGE — 704 SQ. FT.

TOTAL LIVING AREA: 2,474 SQ. FT.

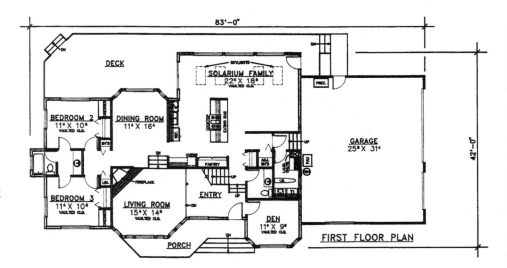

FIRST FLOOR PLAN

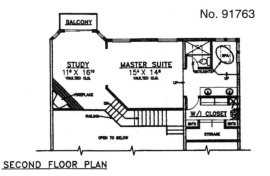

No. 91763

SECOND FLOOR PLAN

No. 90007

Truly Western Approach to the Ranch House

■ This plan features:

— Four bedrooms

— Three full baths

■ Authentic ranch styling with long loggia, posts and braces, hand-split shake roof and cross-buck doors

■ A Texas-sized hexagonal, sunken Living Room with two solid walls, one with a fireplace, and two 10' walls of sliding glass doors

■ A porch bounding the Living Room on three sides

■ A Master Suite with a private Master Bath

■ An efficient well-equipped Kitchen flowing into the Family Room

FIRST FLOOR — 1,830 SQ. FT.

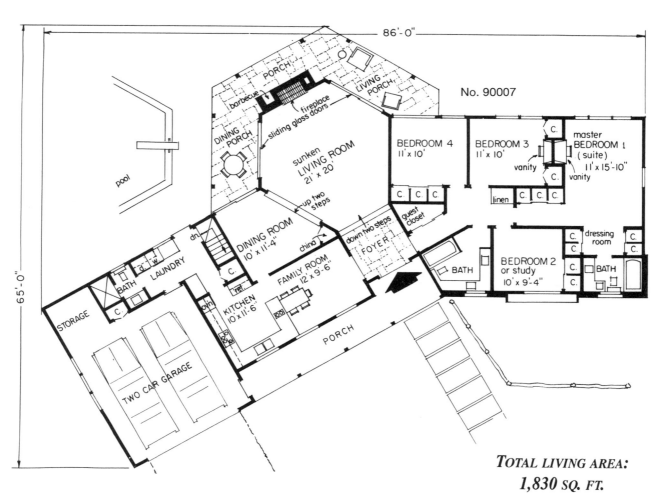

No. 90007

TOTAL LIVING AREA: 1,830 SQ. FT.

No. 90623

Expansive, Not Expensive

■ This plan features:

— Three bedrooms

— Two full baths

■ A Master Suite with his and her closets and a private Master Bath

■ Two additional bedrooms that share a full hall closet

■ A pleasant Dining Room that overlooks a rear garden

■ A well-equipped Kitchen with a built-in planning corner and eat-in space

■ A basement foundation only
FIRST FLOOR — 1,474 SQ. FT.

TOTAL LIVING AREA:
1,474 SQ. FT.

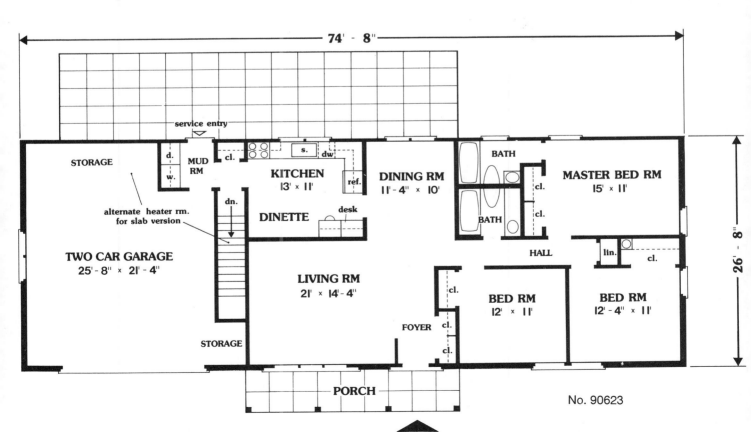

74' - 8"

26' - 8"

service entry

STORAGE

d. w.

MUD RM

cl.

s.

dw

KITCHEN
13' × 11'

ref.

DINING RM
11' - 4" × 10'

BATH

BATH

cl.

cl.

MASTER BED RM
15' × 11'

alternate heater rm. for slab version

dn.

DINETTE

desk

HALL

lin.

cl.

TWO CAR GARAGE
25' - 8" × 21' - 4"

LIVING RM
21' × 14' - 4"

cl.

BED RM
12' × 11'

BED RM
12' - 4" × 11'

STORAGE

FOYER

cl.

cl.

PORCH

No. 90623

No. 91304

Deck Surrounds House on Three Sides

■ This plan features:

— Three bedrooms

— Two full and one half baths

■ A sunken, circular Living Room with windows on four sides and a vaulted clerestory for a wide-open feeling

■ Back-to-back fireplaces in the Living Room and the adjoining Great Room

■ A convenient, efficient Kitchen with a sunny eating Nook

■ A Master Suite with a walk-in closet and a private Master Bath

■ Two additional bedrooms that share a full hall bath

FIRST FLOOR — 1,439 SQ. FT.
SECOND FLOOR — 873 SQ. FT.

TOTAL LIVING AREA:
2,312 SQ. FT.

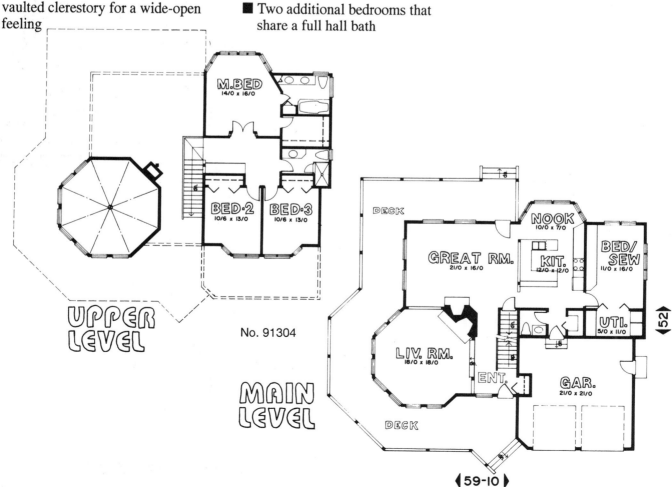

UPPER LEVEL

No. 91304

MAIN LEVEL

M. BED 14/0 x 16/0

BED-2 10/6 x 13/0

BED-3 10/6 x 13/0

DECK

GREAT RM. 21/0 x 16/0

NOOK 10/0 x 7/0

KIT. 12/0 x 12/0

BED/SEW 11/0 x 16/0

UTI. 5/0 x 11/0

LIV. RM. 18/0 x 18/0

ENT.

GAR. 21/0 x 21/0

52

59-10

No. 99620
Country Style for Today

■ This plan features:

— Four bedrooms

— Two full and one half baths

■ Two bay windows in the formal Living Room with a heat-circulating fireplace to enhance the mood and warmth

■ A spacious formal Dining Room with a bay window and easy access to the Kitchen

■ An octagon-shaped Dinette defined by columns, dropped beams and a bay window

■ An efficient island Kitchen with ample storage and counter space

■ A Master Suite equipped with a large whirlpool tub plus a double vanity

■ Three additional bedrooms that share a full hall bath

First floor — 1,132 sq. ft.
Second floor — 1,020 sq. ft.
Basement — 1,026 sq. ft.
Garage & storage — 469 sq. ft.
Laundry/mudroom — 60 sq. ft.

Total living area: 2,212 sq. ft.

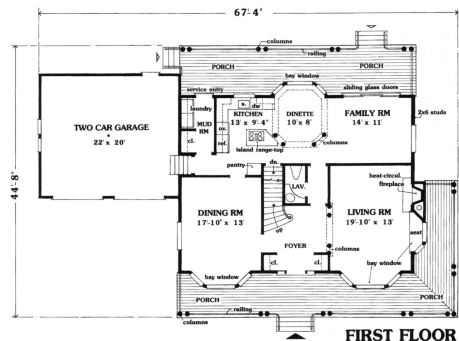

FIRST FLOOR

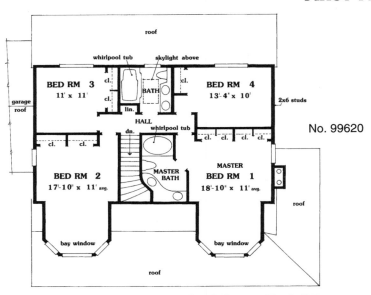

No. 99620

SECOND FLOOR

No. 90673
Zoned for Privacy

■ This plan features:

— Three bedrooms

— Two full baths

■ A cathedral ceiling in the huge Living Room which also has a heat-circulating fireplace

■ Skylights in the Dining Room and Kitchen

■ Sliding glass doors in the Living Room, Dining Room and Master Suite that open on to the wrap-around deck that runs the full length of the house

■ A Master Suite with three closets and a private bath

■ Two additional bedrooms that share a full hall bath

First floor — 1,324 SQ. FT.
Garage — 266 SQ. FT.

Total living area:
1,324 SQ. FT.

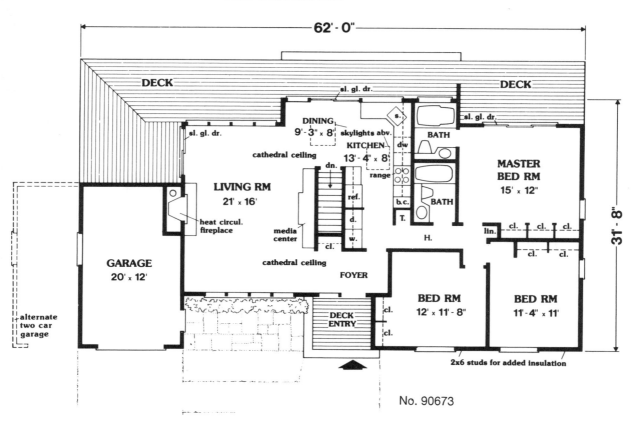

No. 90673

No. 91017

Inviting Porch Welcomes Guest

■ This plan features:

— Three bedrooms

— Two full baths

■ An open plan of the Family Room, Nook and island Kitchen giving a feeling of spaciousness

■ A fireplace in the Family Room adding warmth

■ An intimate formal Dining Room and an angular, glass-walled Living Room for formal entertaining

■ A Master Suite with a walk-in closet and a private Master Bath

■ A crawl space foundation only

FIRST FLOOR — 1,850 SQ. FT.

TOTAL LIVING AREA: 1,850 SQ. FT.

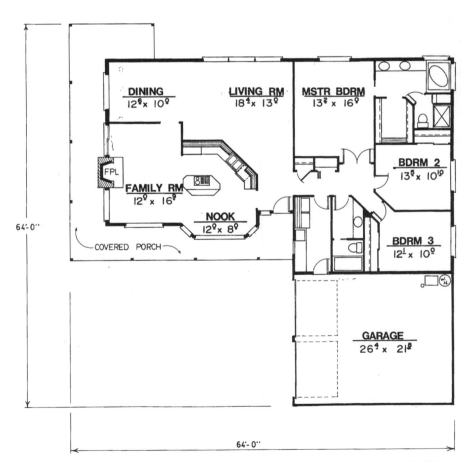

No. 91017

No. 90676

Easy Living, with a Hint of Drama

■ This plan features:

— Three bedrooms

— Two full baths

■ A cathedral ceiling in the Living Room with exposed beams and a heat-circulating fireplace

■ A formal Dining Room conveniently located next to the Kitchen and having sliding glass doors to the covered Porch

■ Bedrooms located in a separate wing for added privacy and quiet

■ A Master Bedroom with two walk-in closets and a private Master Bath

■ Two additional Bedrooms that have ample closet space and share a full hall bath

FIRST FLOOR — 1,575 SQ. FT.

TOTAL LIVING AREA: *1,575 SQ. FT.*

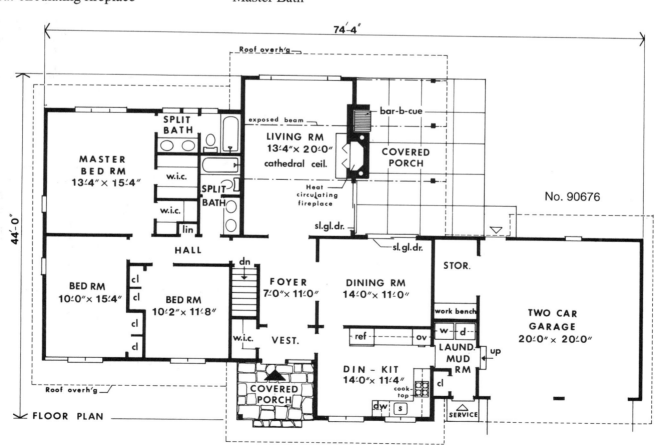

FLOOR PLAN

No. 90690
Family Favorite

■ This plan features:

— Five bedrooms

— Two full baths

■ An efficient Kitchen with a peninsula counter opening into the Family Room

■ A cozy bay window seat in the formal Dining Room

■ A first floor Master Bedroom with an adjoining private bath including double vanities

■ A heat-circulating fireplace in the Living Room which has sliding glass doors to the Terrace

■ Three bedrooms located on the second floor that share a full bath

FIRST FLOOR — 1,407 SQ. FT.
SECOND FLOOR — 675 SQ. FT.

TOTAL LIVING AREA:
2,082 SQ. FT.

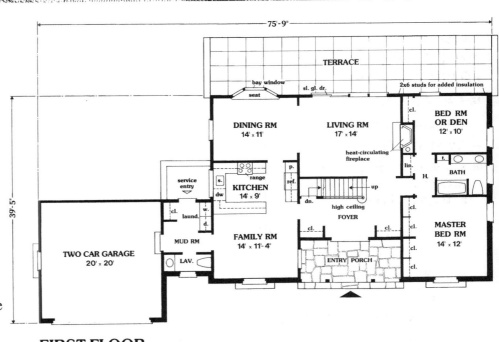

FIRST FLOOR
No. 90690

SECOND FLOOR

No. 91029

Sunny and Warm

■ This plan features:

— Four bedrooms

— Two full and one half baths

■ A pass-through between the island Kitchen and the Dining Room

■ Fireplaces that keep the Living Room and the Family Room warm

■ A luxurious Master Suite with a raised spa, double vanities, and a walk-in closet

■ Three additional bedrooms that share a full hall bath

■ An optional basement or crawl space foundation — please specify when ordering

FIRST FLOOR — 1,593 SQ. FT.
SECOND FLOOR — 1,224 SQ. FT.

TOTAL LIVING AREA: 2,817 SQ. FT.

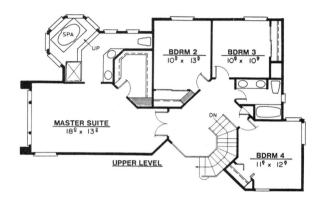

No. 91029

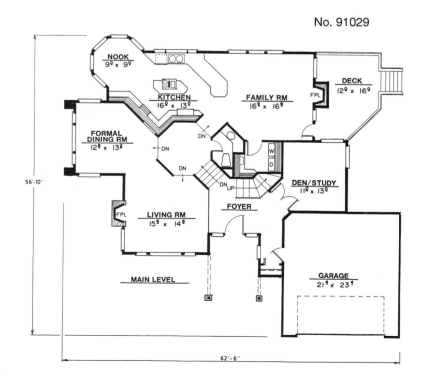

No. 90555

Dream House for a Growing Family

■ This plan features:

— Three bedrooms

— Three full baths

■ A Master Suite with private sitting area and lavish Master Bath

■ Two additional bedrooms, one with a window seat, sharing a hall bath

■ A vaulted ceiling in the Living and Dining Rooms with a brick-faced fireplace in the Living Room

■ An efficient Kitchen with an island cook top that serves the sunny Nook as well as the formal Dining Room

■ A large Family Room with a cozy fireplace sure to be the hub of family life

FIRST FLOOR — 1,360 SQ. FT.
SECOND FLOOR — 980 SQ. FT.

TOTAL LIVING AREA:
2,340 SQ. FT.

SECOND FLOOR

Sitting
9/4x9/4

Master
14/8x15/4

wardrobe

open to below

dn.

lin

Bedrm. 2
10/6x11/6

Bedrm. 3
10/0x11/0

wdw. seat

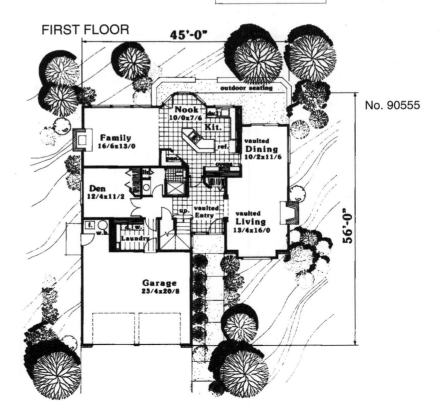

FIRST FLOOR

45'-0"

56'-0"

No. 90555

outdoor seating

Nook
10/0x7/6

Kit.

Family
16/6x13/0

ref.

vaulted
Dining
10/2x11/6

Den
12/4x11/2

up.

vaulted
Entry

vaulted
Living
13/4x16/0

Laundry

Garage
23/4x20/8

No. 91401

Spacious Living in a Small Package

- This plan features:
- — Three bedrooms
- — Two full and one half baths

- A Living Room with a vaulted ceiling made even larger by a two-story arched window

- An open layout between the Family Room, sunny Dining Bay, and well-appointed Kitchen

- A wood stove in the Family Room that, because of the open plan, circulates heat throughout the house

- A magnificent Master Suite with a private deck and a luxurious bath with double vanities, a shower and an oversized tub

FIRST FLOOR — 924 SQ. FT.
SECOND FLOOR — 860 SQ. FT.
GARAGE — 430 SQ. FT.

TOTAL LIVING AREA:
1,784 SQ. FT.

UPPER LEVEL FLOORPLAN

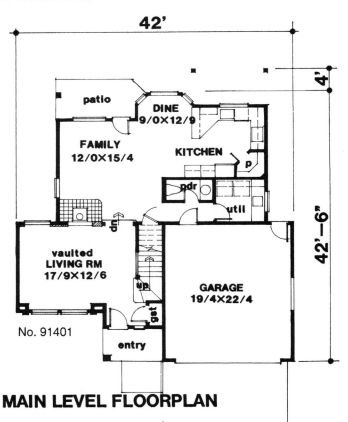

MAIN LEVEL FLOORPLAN

No. 90372
Country Contemporary

■ This plan features:

— Three bedrooms

— Two full baths

■ An inviting porch as a welcoming introduction for guests

■ A first floor Master Suite with a private Master Bath and walk-in closet

■ An efficient U-shaped Kitchen with sliding glass doors to the deck

■ A vaulted, sunken Living Room accentuated by a massive fireplace

FIRST FLOOR — 1,006 SQ. FT.
SECOND FLOOR — 437 SQ. FT.

TOTAL LIVING AREA:
1,443 SQ. FT.

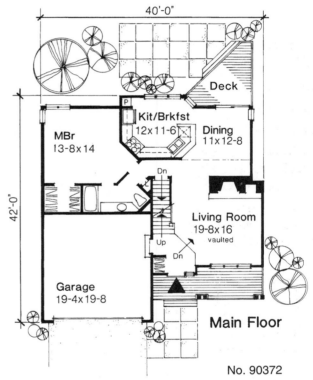

40'-0"

42'-0"

Deck

Kit/Brkfst
12x11-6

P

MBr
13-8x14

Dining
11x12-8

Dn

Living Room
19-8x16
vaulted

Up

Dn

Garage
19-4x19-8

Main Floor

No. 90372

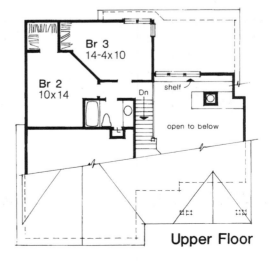

Br 3
14-4x10

Br 2
10x14

Dn

shelf

open to below

Upper Floor

No. 90358

Four Bedroom 1-1/2 Story Design

■ This plan features:

— Three bedrooms

— Two full baths

■ A vaulted ceiling in the Great Room with a fireplace

■ An efficient Kitchen with a peninsula counter and double sink

■ A Family Room with easy access to the wood Deck

■ A Master Bedroom with private bath entrance

■ Convenient laundry facilities outside the Master Bedroom

■ Two additional bedrooms upstairs with walk-in closets and the use of the full hall bath

FIRST FLOOR — 1,062 SQ. FT.
SECOND FLOOR — 469 SQ. FT.

TOTAL LIVING AREA: 1,531 SQ. FT.

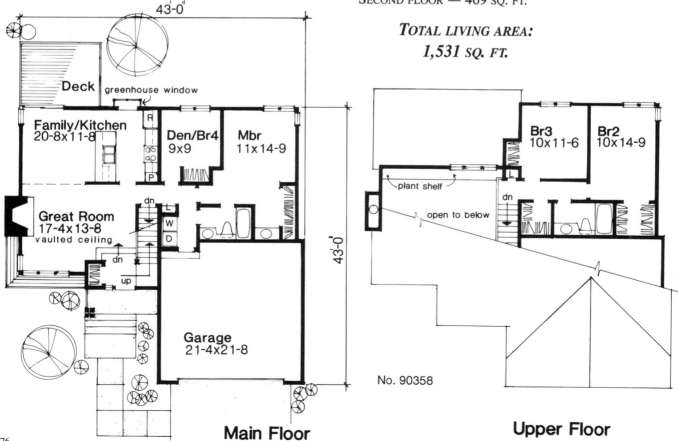

Main Floor

Upper Floor

No. 90358

No. 90355
Roomy 1-1/2 Story Design

■ This plan features:

— Three bedrooms

— Two full and one half baths

■ A luxurious Master Bedroom Suite with full bath and walk-in closet

■ An impact window wall, vaulted ceiling and fireplace enhancing the Living Room

■ An island Kitchen well-equipped and open to the Family Room and formal Dining Room

■ A built-in wetbar in the Dining Room

FIRST FLOOR — 1,022 SQ. FT.
SECOND FLOOR — 741 SQ. FT.

TOTAL LIVING AREA: 1,763 SQ. FT.

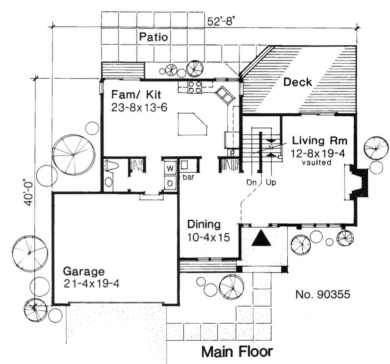

Patio

52'-8"

Deck

Fam/ Kit
23-8 x 13-6

Living Rm
12-8 x 19-4
vaulted

40'-0"

Dn   Up

W
D   bar

Dining
10-4 x 15

Garage
21-4 x 19-4

No. 90355

Main Floor

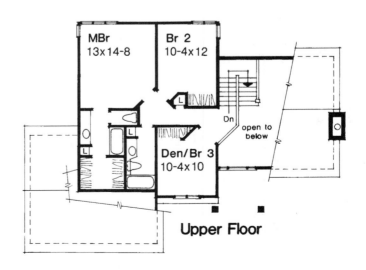

MBr
13 x 14-8

Br 2
10-4 x 12

Dn

open to below

Den/Br 3
10-4 x 10

Upper Floor

No. 90008
Spanish Two-Story Includes Distinctive Features

■ This plan features:

— Four bedrooms

— Two full and one half baths

■ A two-story Family Room with a semi-circular staircase and center fountain

■ A Living Room, including a fireplace, flowing easily into the Dining Room

■ A Master Suite with a private Master Bath and ample closet space

■ A balcony overlooking the Family Room

■ Terrace, porches and a roof garden making for enjoyable outdoor living

FIRST FLOOR — 1,249 SQ. FT.
SECOND FLOOR — 1,134 SQ. FT.

TOTAL LIVING AREA: 2,383 SQ. FT.

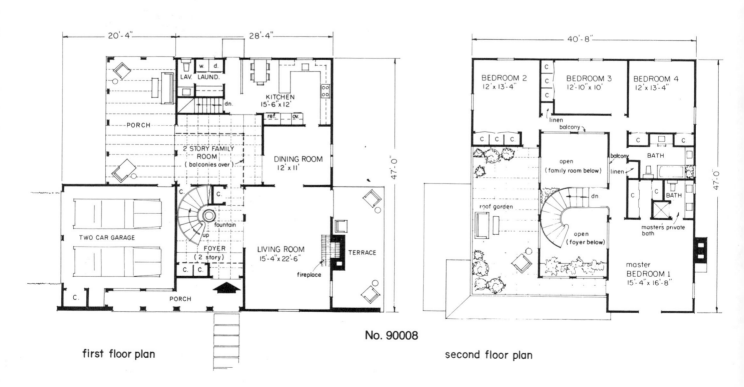

No. 90008

first floor plan

second floor plan

No. 90004
Rustic Vacation House

■ This plan features:

— Three bedrooms

— One full and one half baths

■ Two porches and an outdoor balcony for entertaining, relaxing or just enjoying a sunset

■ A spiral stairway leading to the balcony and upstairs bedroom

■ A Living Room with a massive stone fireplace, floor-to-ceiling windows at the gable end, and sliding glass doors to a rear porch

■ A pantry adjoining the Kitchen which has a small bay window over the sink

FIRST FLOOR — 1,020 SQ. FT.
SECOND FLOOR — 265 SQ. FT.

TOTAL LIVING AREA:
1,285 SQ. FT.

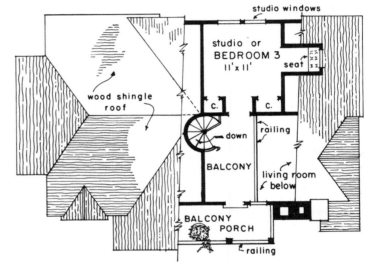

studio windows

studio or BEDROOM 3 11'x11'

seat

wood shingle roof

c.

c.

down

railing

BALCONY

living room below

BALCONY PORCH

railing

balcony level

No. 90004

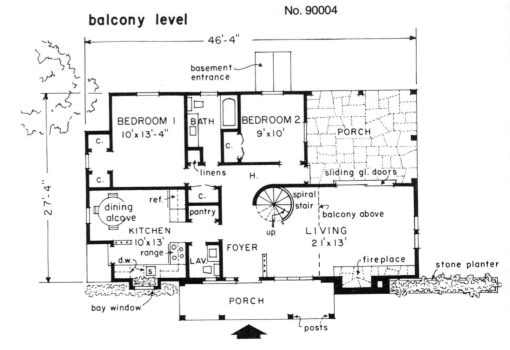

46'-4"

basement entrance

BEDROOM 1 10'x13'-4"

BATH

BEDROOM 2 9'x10'

PORCH

c.

c.

27'-4"

linens

H.

sliding gl. doors

c.

ref.

dining alcove

c.

pantry

spiral stair

balcony above

KITCHEN 10'x13'

range

LIVING 21'x13'

d.w.

S

LAV.

FOYER

fireplace

stone planter

bay window

PORCH

posts

first floor

REAR VIEW

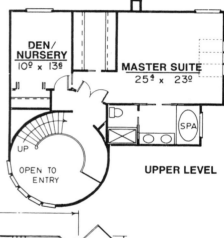

FRONT VIEW

No. 91023
Gracious Living

■ This plan features:

— Three bedrooms

— Two full and one half baths

■ A circular, two-story entry with clerestory windows

■ An efficient Kitchen with a large counter island that includes a double sink and a cook top

■ A bayed, sunny eating Nook opening from the Kitchen

■ A spacious Family Room with a cozy, corner fireplace

■ Two first-floor bedrooms that share a full hall bath

■ A sky-lit Master Suite with double sinks and a private spa

■ An optional slab or crawl space foundation — please specify when ordering

FIRST FLOOR — 1,901 SQ. FT.
SECOND FLOOR — 785 SQ. FT.

TOTAL LIVING AREA:
2,686 SQ. FT.

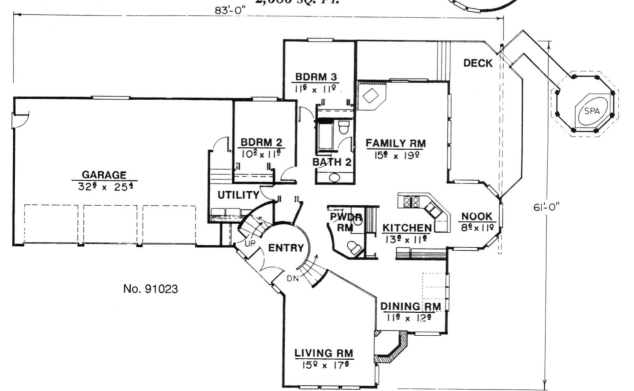

No. 91023

No. 90309

Modified A-Frame at Home Anywhere

■ This plan features:

— One or two bedrooms

— One full and one half bath

■ A combined Living Room/Dining Room with a ceiling that reaches to the second floor loft

■ A galley-styled Kitchen conveniently arranged and open to the Dining Room

■ A fireplace in the Living Room area with sliding glass doors to the Deck

■ A loft with a half bath and an optional bedroom

FIRST FLOOR — 735 SQ. FT.
SECOND FLOOR — 304 SQ. FT.

TOTAL LIVING AREA:
1,039 SQ. FT.

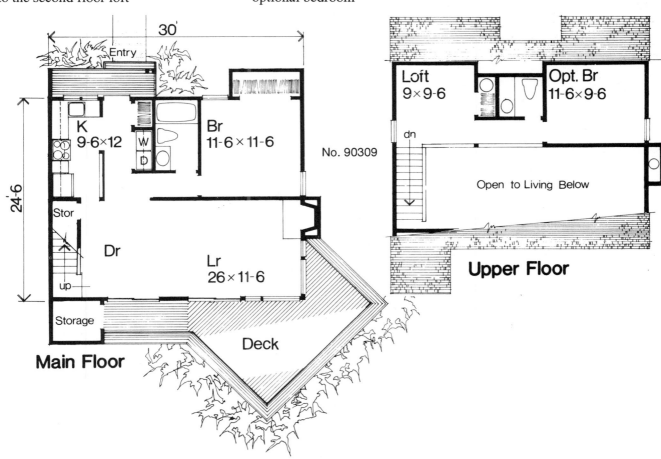

Main Floor

Entry
30'
24-6
K 9-6×12
W D
Br 11-6 × 11-6
Stor
Dr
Lr 26×11-6
up
Storage
Deck

No. 90309

Upper Floor

Loft 9×9-6
Opt. Br 11-6×9-6
dn
Open to Living Below

No. 90444

Traditional Ranch has Many Modern Features

■ This plan features:

— Three bedrooms

— Three full baths

■ A vaulted-ceiling Great Room with skylights and a fireplace

■ A double L-shaped Kitchen with an eating bar opening to a bayed Breakfast Room

■ A Master Suite with a walk-in closet, corner garden tub, separate vanities and a linen closet

■ Two additional bedrooms each with a walk-in closet and built-in desk, sharing a full hall bath

■ A loft that overlooks the Great Room which includes a vaulted ceiling and open rail balcony

■ A basement or crawl space foundation — please specify when ordering

FIRST FLOOR — 1,996 SQ. FT.
LOFT — 305 SQ. FT.

TOTAL LIVING AREA: 2,301 SQ. FT.

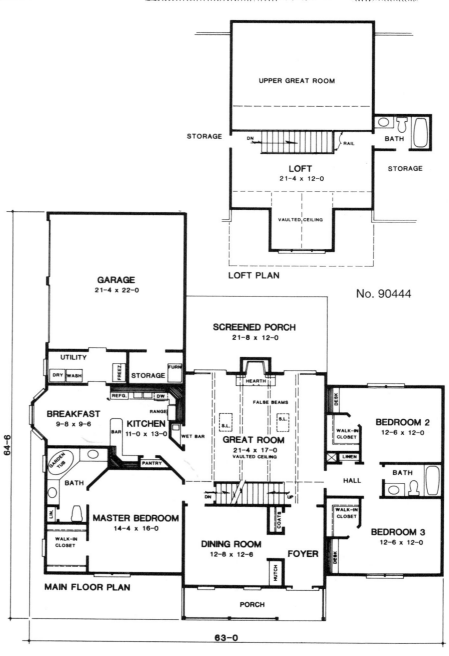

282

No. 91319

All Seasons

■ This plan features:

— Three bedrooms

— Three full baths

■ A wall of windows taking full advantage of the front view

■ An open stairway to the upstairs study and the Master Bedroom

■ A Master Bedroom with a private Master Bath and a walk-in wardrobe

■ An efficient Kitchen including a breakfast bar that opens into the Dining Area

■ A formal Living Room with a vaulted ceiling and a stone fireplace

■ A daylight Basement that includes storage, a laundry room, a mudroom, and a full bath

FIRST FLOOR — 1,306 SQ. FT.
SECOND FLOOR — 598 SQ. FT.
LOWER FLOOR — 1,288 SQ. FT.

TOTAL LIVING AREA:
3,192 SQ. FT.

MAIN FLR.

LOWER FLR.

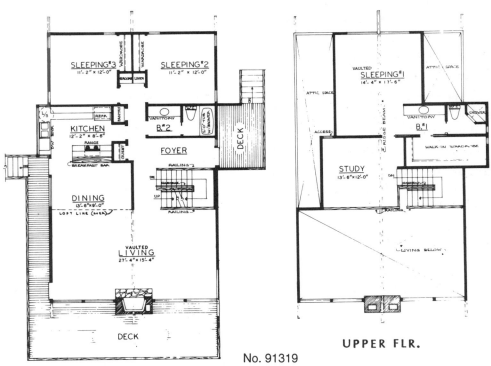

DECK

No. 91319

UPPER FLR.

No. 90423
Your Classic Hideaway

■ This plan features:

— Three bedrooms

— Two full baths

■ A lovely fireplace in the Living Room which is both cozy and a source of heat for the core area

■ An efficient country Kitchen connecting the large Dining and Living Rooms

■ A lavish Master Suite enhanced by a step-up sunken tub, more than ample closet space, and separate shower

■ A screened porch and patio area for outdoor living

■ An optional basement, slab or crawl space foundation — please specify when ordering

FIRST FLOOR — 1,773 SQ. FT.
SCREENED PORCH — 240 SQ. FT.

TOTAL LIVING AREA:
1,773 SQ. FT.

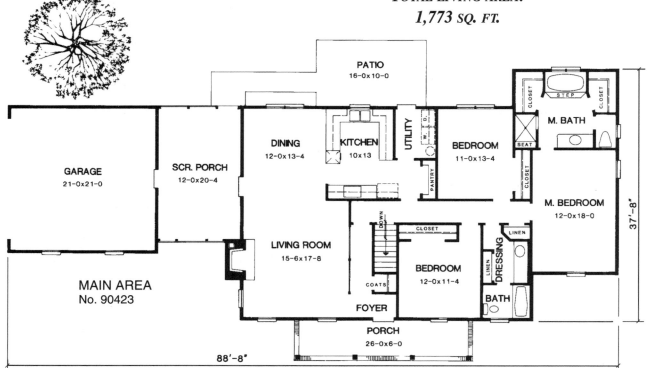

No. 90930

A-Frame for Year-Round Living

■ This plan features:

— Three bedrooms

— Two full baths

■ A vaulted ceiling in the Living Room with a massive fireplace

■ A wrap-around sun deck that gives you a lot of outdoor living space

■ A luxurious Master Suite complete with a walk-in closet, full bath and private deck

■ Two additional bedrooms that share a full hall bath

FIRST FLOOR — 1,238 SQ. FT.
LOFT — 464 SQ. FT.
BASEMENT — 1,175 SQ. FT.
WIDTH — 34'-0"
DEPTH — 56'-0"

TOTAL LIVING AREA:
1,702 SQ. FT.

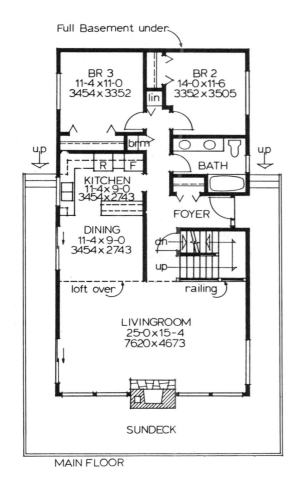

MAIN FLOOR

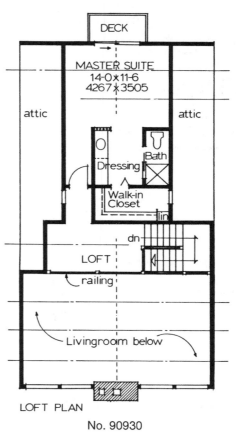

LOFT PLAN

No. 90930

No. 90941

Vaulted Sunken Living Room

- ■ This plan features:
- — Four bedrooms
- — Two full and one half baths
- ■ A dramatic, sunken Living Room with a vaulted ceiling, fireplace, and glass walls to enjoy the view
- ■ A well-appointed, Kitchen with a peninsula counter and direct access to the Family Room, Dining Room or the sun deck
- ■ A Master Suite with a walk-in closet and a private full bath
- ■ A Family Room with direct access to the rear sun deck

FIRST FLOOR — 1,464 SQ. FT.
BASEMENT — 1,182 SQ. FT.
GARAGE — 418 SQ. FT.
WIDTH — 48'-0"
DEPTH — 39'-0"

**TOTAL LIVING AREA:
2,646 SQ. FT.**

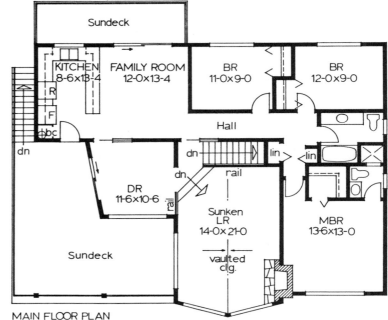

MAIN FLOOR PLAN

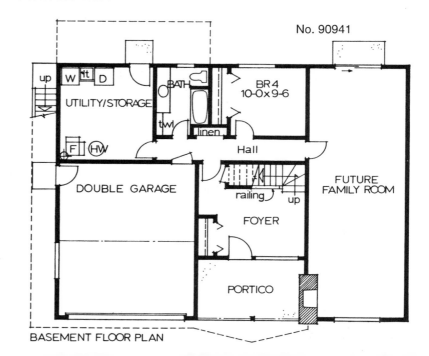

BASEMENT FLOOR PLAN

286

No. 90844

A-Frame Update

■ This plan features:

— Three bedrooms

— Two full and one half baths

■ A wrap-around deck adding outdoor living space

■ Two-story glass walls in the Dining Room and Living Room

■ A Master Bedroom with a private half bath

■ An open loft with an expansive bedroom having its own private deck and full bath

FIRST FLOOR — 1,086 SQ. FT.
SECOND FLOOR — 340 SQ. FT.

TOTAL LIVING AREA:
1,426 SQ. FT.

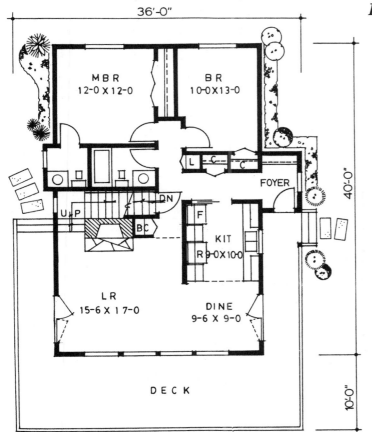

36'-0"

40'-0"

10'-0"

MBR
12-0 X 12-0

BR
10-0 X 13-0

FOYER

DN

U P

BC

F

KIT
R 9-0 X 10-0

LR
15-6 X 17-0

DINE
9-6 X 9-0

DECK

GROUND FLOOR

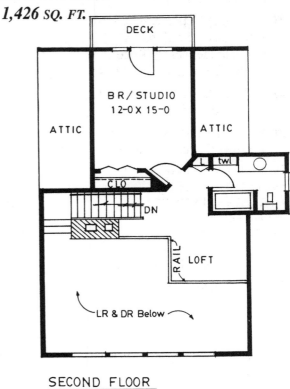

DECK

BR / STUDIO
12-0 X 15-0

ATTIC

ATTIC

CLO

L twl

DN

RAIL

LOFT

LR & DR Below

SECOND FLOOR

No. 90844

No. 90396

Traditional Transom Windows Add Appeal

■ This plan features:

— Three bedrooms

— Two full and one half baths

■ A vaulted ceiling in both the Living and adjoining Dining Rooms, accentuated by a fireplace

■ A well-appointed, sky-lit Kitchen which easily serves the Dining Room

■ A first floor Master Suite with a dramatic vaulted ceiling and private patio access

■ A private Master Bath with double vanity and walk-in closet

FIRST FLOOR — 1,099 SQ. FT.
SECOND FLOOR — 452 SQ. FT.

TOTAL LIVING AREA: 1,551 SQ. FT.

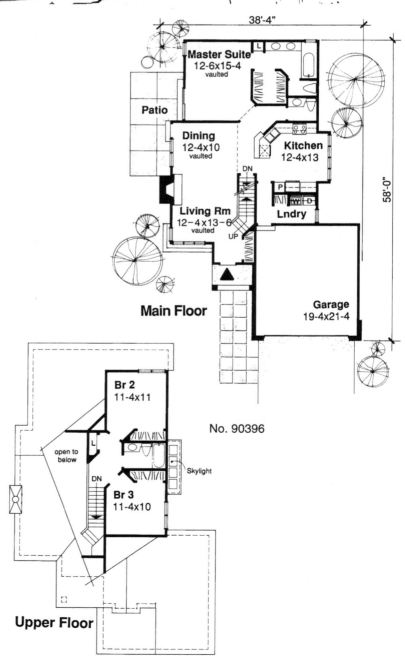

No. 99324

For the Young at Heart

■ This plan features:

— Three bedrooms

— Two full baths

■ Half-round transom windows, divided-light windows, bay windows and a covered entry porch

■ A Great Room with a vaulted ceiling, a fireplace and a transom window

■ A Kitchen with a vaulted ceiling and a Breakfast area with sliding doors to the deck

■ A Master Suite with ample closet space and a private full Master Bath

FIRST FLOOR — 1,307 SQ. FT.

TOTAL LIVING AREA: 1,307 SQ. FT.

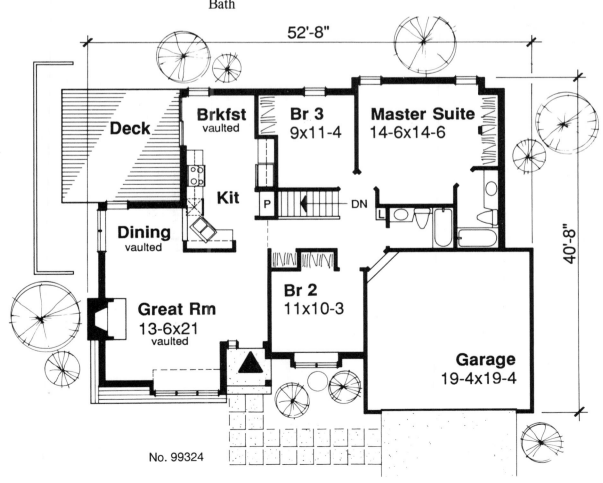

52'-8"

40'-8"

Deck

Brkfst vaulted

Br 3 9x11-4

Master Suite 14-6x14-6

Kit

P

DN

L

Dining vaulted

Great Rm 13-6x21 vaulted

Br 2 11x10-3

Garage 19-4x19-4

No. 99324

No. 90406

Compact Victorian Ideal for Narrow Lot

■ This plan features:

— Three bedrooms

— Two full baths

■ A large, front Parlor with a raised hearth fireplace

■ A Dining Room with a sunny bay window

■ An efficient galley Kitchen serving the formal Dining Room and informal Breakfast Room

■ A beautiful Master Suite with two closets, an oversized tub and double vanity, plus a private sitting room with a bayed window and vaulted ceiling

First floor — 954 sq. ft.
Second floor — 783 sq. ft.

Total living area: 1,737 sq. ft.

FIRST FLOOR

No. 90406

SECOND FLOOR

No. 90445
Old-Fashioned Charm

■ This plan features:

— Four bedrooms

— Three full baths

■ A large Master Suite with a trayed ceiling and a vaulted ceiling in the lavish, private bath

■ Two additional bedrooms sharing the full hall bath

■ A Great Room with a cozy fireplace focal point

■ A bayed formal Dining Room convenient to the galley Kitchen

■ A sunny Breakfast Nook with a convenient laundry area

■ An optional basement, slab or crawl space foundation — please specify when ordering

FIRST FLOOR — 1,030 SQ. FT.
SECOND FLOOR — 1,020 SQ. FT.
BONUS ROOM — 284 SQ. FT.

TOTAL LIVING AREA: 2,050 SQ. FT.

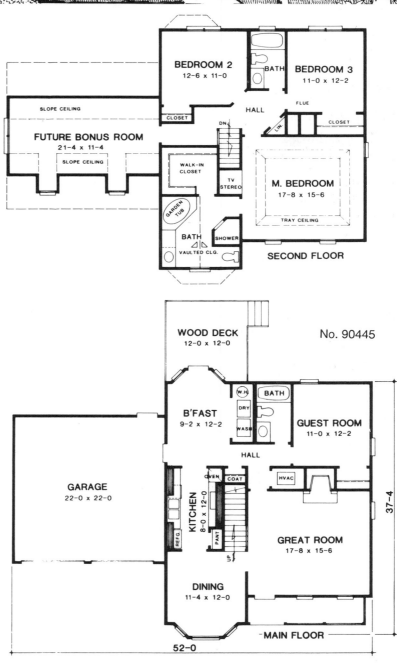

No. 99236

Jeffersonian Colonial Features

■ This plan features:

— Five bedrooms

— Three and one half baths

■ A large, impressive entry courtyard

■ A central, brick-floored foyer leading to a traditional "keeping room", with a fireplace and brick bread oven

■ An efficient and well-appointed Kitchen

■ A formal Living and Dining Room with direct access to the portico and terrace

■ A Guest Suite that could be the perfect in-law quarters with its full bath, spacious walk-in closets and ample privacy

■ An oversized Master Suite including a fireplace and separate dressing and bath areas

■ Three additional bedrooms that share a full hall bath

■ A studio and a lounge area with a fireplace

FIRST FLOOR — 1,152 SQ. FT.
FIRST FLOOR GUEST SUITE/GAME ROOM — 688 SQ. FT.
SECOND FLOOR — 1,152 SQ. FT.
SECOND FLOOR STUDIO — 306 SQ. FT.
STORAGE ROOM ABOVE GARAGE — 525 SQ. FT.
GARAGE — 483 SQ. FT.

TOTAL LIVING AREA:
3,823 SQ. FT.

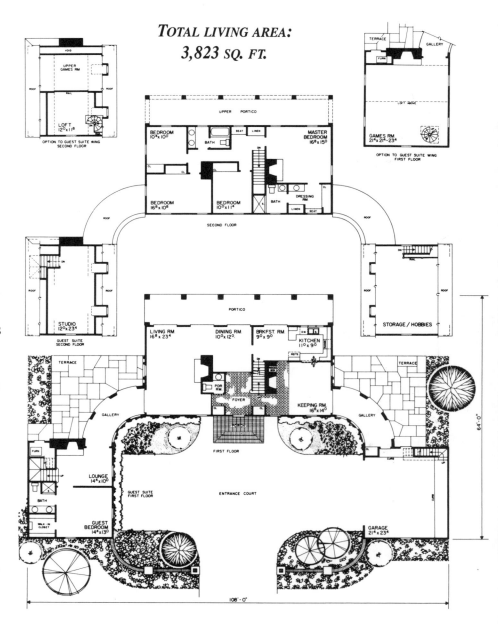

No. 99240
A Master Suite To Love

■ This plan features:

— Three bedrooms

— Two full and two half baths

■ A large Sun Room with a cathedral ceiling and floor-to-ceiling windows

■ An enormous country Kitchen with a center range, double wall ovens, more than ample counter space, and a snack bar

■ A Clutter Room with a walk-in pantry, half bath, and laundry/work area

■ A double-sided fireplace that opens the Kitchen to the Living Room with a wall-length raised hearth

■ A huge Master Suite with his-and-her walk-in closets, dressing or exercise room and private Master Bath

FIRST FLOOR — 3,511 SQ. FT.
SECOND FLOOR — 711 SQ. FT.
GARAGE — 841 SQ. FT.
WORKSHOP/THIRD GARAGE BAY —
231 SQ. FT.

TOTAL LIVING AREA:
4,222 SQ. FT.

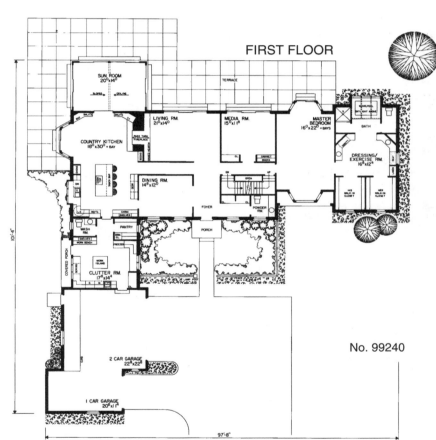

FIRST FLOOR

No. 99240

SECOND FLOOR

No. 99316

Past Meets Present

■ This plan features:

— Three bedrooms

— Two full and one half baths

■ Formal Living and Dining Rooms that are adjacent to the entry with vaulted ceiling

■ An island Kitchen with corner double sink, built-in pantry, and Breakfast area

■ A sunken Family Room with fireplace and a vaulted ceiling

■ A lavish Master Bath with focal tub and shower with curved glass block wall surrounding

■ Two additional bedrooms that share use of a full hall bath

FIRST FLOOR — 1,556 SQ. FT.
SECOND FLOOR — 534 SQ. FT.

TOTAL LIVING AREA: 2,090 SQ. FT.

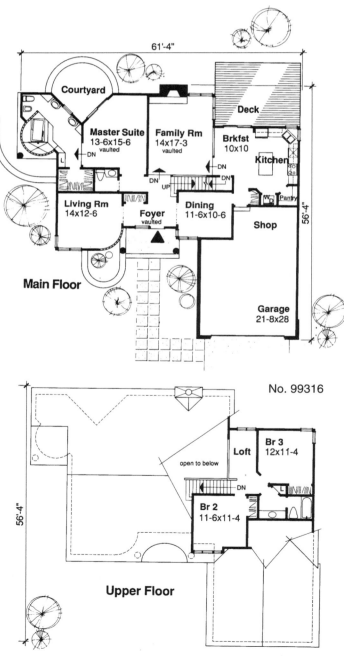

No. 90398

Interior and Exterior Unity Distinguishes Plan

■ This plan features:

— Three bedrooms

— Two full baths

■ A vaulted ceiling Living Room with cozy fireplace

■ Columns dividing the Living and Dining Rooms and half-walls separating the Kitchen and Breakfast Room

■ A luxurious Master Suite with a private sky-lit bath, double vanities and a generous walk-in closet

FIRST FLOOR —1,630 SQ. FT.

TOTAL LIVING AREA: 1,630 SQ. FT.

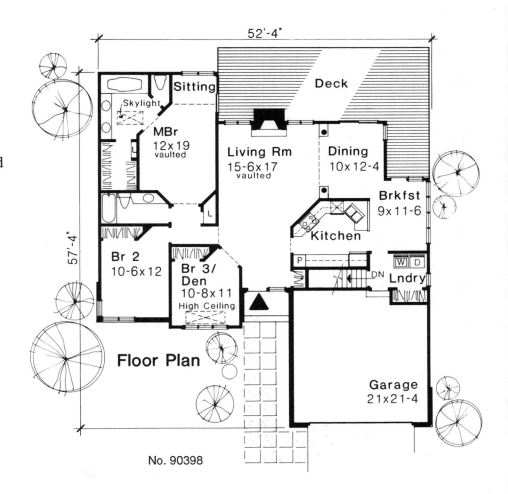

52'-4"

57'-4"

Sitting

Skylight

MBr
12x19
vaulted

Deck

Living Rm
15-6x17
vaulted

Dining
10x12-4

Brkfst
9x11-6

Kitchen

Br 2
10-6x12

Br 3/
Den
10-8x11

High Ceiling

P

W D

DN

Lndry

Floor Plan

Garage
21x21-4

No. 90398

FmHA Home

No. 92026

Inviting Entrance Welcomes All

■ This plan features:

— Two bedrooms

— One full bath

■ A covered front porch

■ A large Living Room/Dining Room combination

■ An efficient U-shaped Kitchen with a double sink and ample cabinet and counter space

■ Two bedrooms that share the full hall bath and have ample storage space

FIRST FLOOR — 863 SQ. FT.

TOTAL LIVING AREA: 863 SQ. FT.

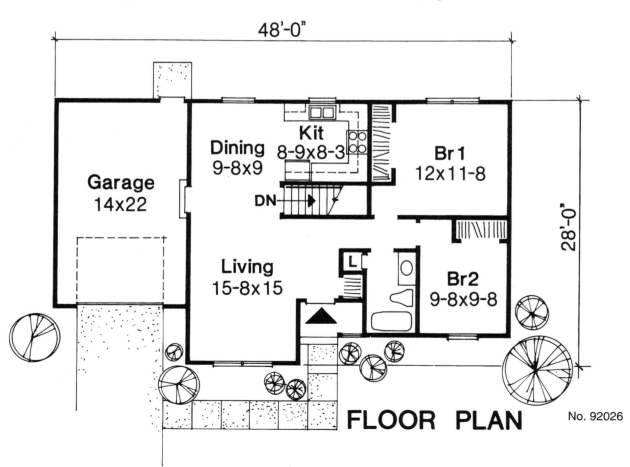

48'-0"

28'-0"

Garage
14x22

Dining
9-8x9

Kit
8-9x8-3

Br 1
12x11-8

DN

Living
15-8x15

L

Br2
9-8x9-8

FLOOR PLAN   No. 92026

No. 91033

Neat and Tidy

■ This plan features:

— Two bedrooms

— Two full baths

■ A two-story Living Room and Dining Room with a handsome stone fireplace

■ A well-appointed Kitchen with a peninsula counter

■ A Master Suite with a walk-in closet and private Master Bath

■ A large utility room with laundry facilities

■ An optional basemen or crawl space foundation — please specify when ordering

FIRST FLOOR — 952 SQ. FT.
SECOND FLOOR — 297 SQ. FT.

TOTAL LIVING AREA:
1,249 SQ. FT.

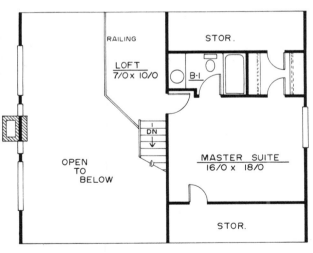

UPPER FLOOR

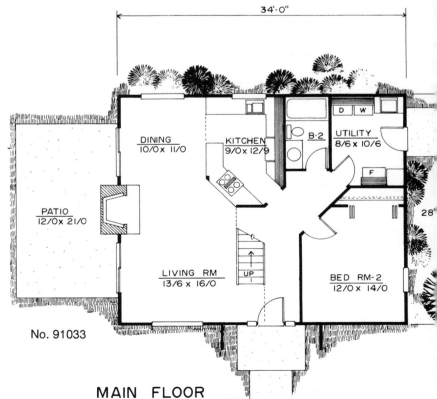

No. 91033

MAIN FLOOR

No. 90966
Stately Manor

■ This plan features:

— Three bedrooms

— Two full and one half baths

■ A porch serving as a grand entrance

■ A very spacious foyer with an open staircase and lots of angles

■ A beautiful Kitchen equipped with a cook top island and a full bay window wall that includes a roomy Breakfast Nook

■ A Living Room with a vaulted ceiling that flows into the formal Dining Room for ease in entertaining

■ A grand Master Suite equipped with a walk-in closet and five piece private bath

FIRST FLOOR — 1,359 SQ. FT.
SECOND FLOOR — 1,038 SQ. FT.
BASEMENT — 1,334 SQ. FT.
GARAGE — 420 SQ. FT.
WIDTH — 52'-0"
DEPTH — 43'-0"

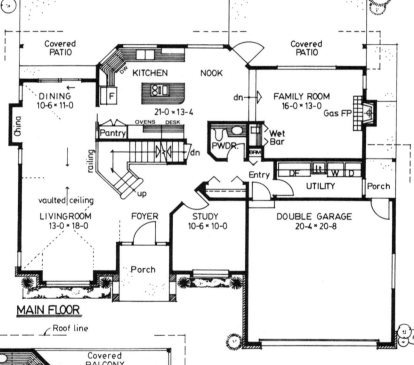

MAIN FLOOR

No. 90966

**TOTAL LIVING AREA:
2,397 SQ. FT.**

SECOND FLOOR

No. 92106

Surrounded by Multi-Level Decks

■ This plan features:

— Three bedrooms

— Two full and one half baths

■ Extra lighting and cabinets in the island Kitchen that opens to a bright and sunny Family Room

■ A unique octagonal-shaped Dining Room that leads to an immense covered Deck and steps down to the Living Room

■ A Master Bedroom with a walk-in closet, Master Bath and a private deck

■ Two additional bedrooms, one with a walk-in closet, that share a full hall bath

FIRST FLOOR — 2,358 SQ. FT.
SECOND FLOOR — 700 SQ. FT.
GARAGE — 954 SQ. FT.

TOTAL LIVING AREA:
3,058 SQ. FT.

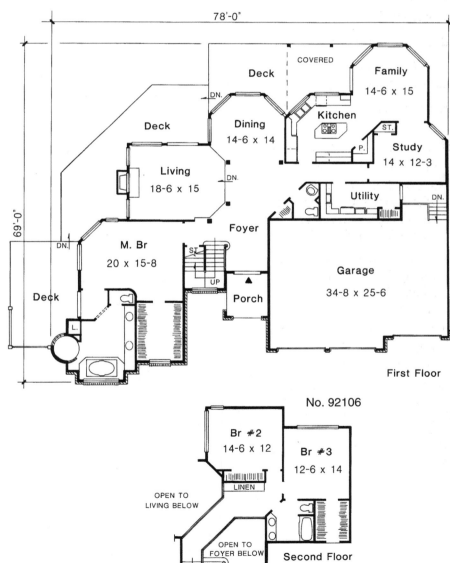

First Floor

No. 92106

Second Floor

No. 90816

Den Can Double as a Home Office

■ This plan features:

— Four bedrooms

— Two full and one half baths

■ A sunken Living Room for formal entertaining

■ A built-in china cabinet in the Dining Room which also has a bay window

■ A built-in pantry and planning area in the efficient Kitchen serving the informal Nook as well as formal Dining Room

■ A sunken Family Room with a cozy fireplace

■ A Master Suite with a Jacuzzi tub and a separate shower

FIRST FLOOR — 1,252 SQ. FT.
SECOND FLOOR — 1,117 SQ. FT.
BASEMENT — 1,245 SQ. FT.
GARAGE — 564 SQ. FT.
WIDTH — 71'-0"
DEPTH — 35'-0"

TOTAL LIVING AREA: 2,369 SQ. FT.

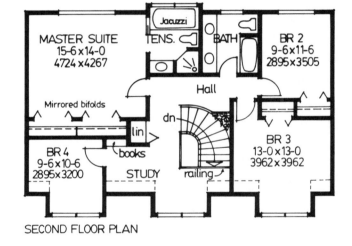

No. 90816

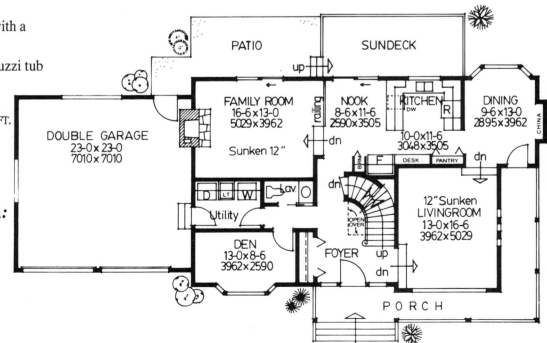

No. 92400

Quaint Starter Home

No. 92400

■ This plan features:

— Three bedrooms

— Two full baths

■ A vaulted ceiling giving an airy feeling to the Dining and Living Rooms

■ A streamlined Kitchen with a comfortable work area, a double sink and ample cabinet space

■ A cozy fireplace in the Living Room

■ A Master Suite with a large closet, French doors leading to the patio and a private bath

■ Two additional bedrooms sharing a full bath

FIRST FLOOR — 1,050 SQ. FT.

TOTAL LIVING AREA: 1,050 SQ. FT.

No materials list available

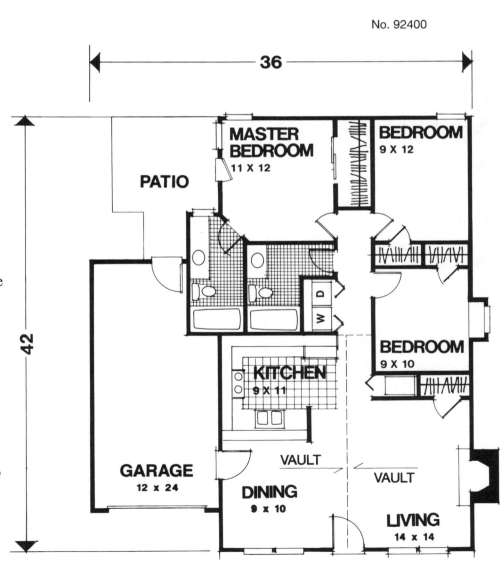

No. 90500

Compact Home for a Small Space

■ This plan features:

— Three bedrooms

— Two full baths

■ A Master Suite with a private Master Bath and a walk-in closet

■ A Living Room with sunny bayed windows and a fireplace focal point

■ A formal Dining Room adjoining the Living Room

■ A bright and sunny Breakfast Nook for informal eating

■ Two additional bedrooms sharing a full hall bath

FIRST FLOOR — 1,299 SQ. FT.

TOTAL LIVING AREA: 1,299 SQ. FT.

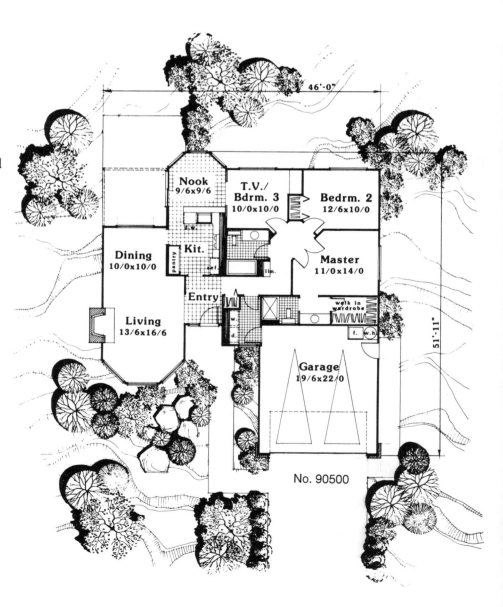

No. 90500

No. 91504
Family Plan

- ■ This plan features:
- — Four bedrooms
- — Two full and one half baths
- ■ A two-story foyer
- ■ A bay window accentuating the formal Living Room
- ■ An island Kitchen that flows into the sunny eating Nook

- ■ A vaulted ceiling in the spacious Family Room warmed by a fireplace
- ■ A Master Suite with an elegant sky-lit bath and a walk-in closet

FIRST FLOOR — 1,105 SQ. FT.
SECOND FLOOR — 950 SQ. FT.

TOTAL LIVING AREA: 2,055 SQ. FT.

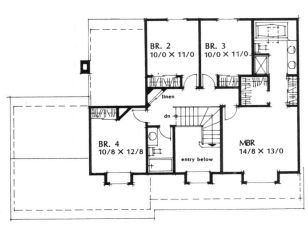

No. 91504

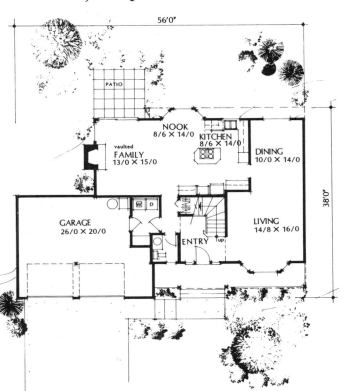

No. 90443

Traditional that has it All

- **This plan features:**

— Three bedrooms

— Two full and one half baths

- A Master Suite with two closets and a private bath with separate shower, corner tub and dual vanities

- A large Dining Room having a bayed window, adjacent to the Kitchen

- A formal Living Room for entertaining and a cozy Family Room with fireplace for informal relaxation

- Two upstairs bedrooms with walk-in closets sharing a full hall bath

- A Bonus Room to allow the house to grow with your needs

- An optional basement or crawl space foundation — please specify when ordering

FIRST FLOOR — 1,927 SQ. FT.
SECOND FLOOR — 832 SQ. FT.
BONUS ROOM — 624 SQ. FT.
BASEMENT — 1,674 SQ. FT.

TOTAL LIVING AREA: 2,759 SQ. FT.

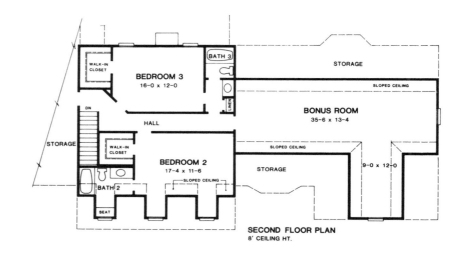

SECOND FLOOR PLAN
8' CEILING HT.

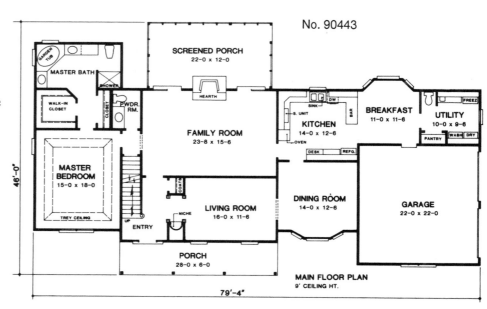

No. 90443

MAIN FLOOR PLAN
9' CEILING HT.

No. 99610
Greek Revival

■ This plan features:

— Three bedrooms

— Two full baths

■ A large front porch with pediment and columns

■ A stunning, heat-circulating fireplace flanked by cabinetry and shelves in the Living Room

■ A formal Dining Room enhanced by a bay window

■ An efficient U-shaped Kitchen with a peninsula counter and informal Dinette area

■ A Master Suite with a private Master Bath and direct access to the private terrace

■ Two additional bedrooms sharing a full hall bath

FIRST FLOOR — 1,460 SQ. FT.
LAUNDRY/MUDROOM — 68 SQ. FT.
BASEMENT — 1,367 SQ. FT.
GARAGE & STORAGE — 494 SQ. FT.

TOTAL LIVING AREA:
1,528 SQ. FT.

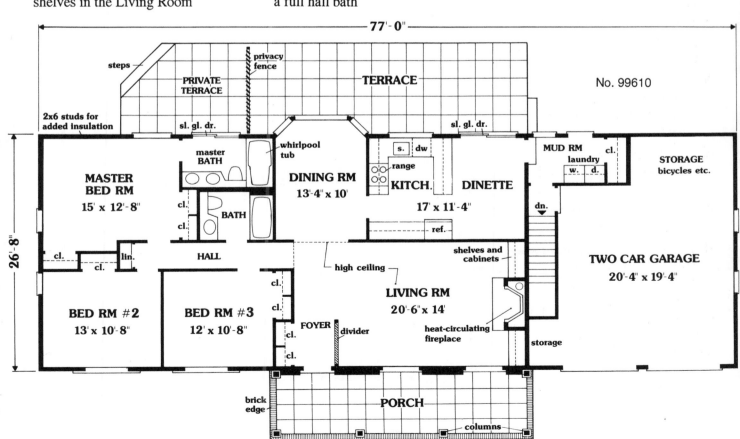

No. 90395

Half-Round Window Graces Attractive Exterior

■ This plan features:

— Three bedrooms

— Two full baths

■ Soaring ceilings in the Kitchen, Living Room, Dining, and Breakfast Rooms

■ An efficient, well-equipped Kitchen with a pass-through to the Dining room

■ Built-in bookcases flanking the fireplace in the Living Room

■ A Master Suite with a private Master Bath and walk-in closet

FIRST FLOOR — 1,452 SQ. FT.

TOTAL LIVING AREA:
1,452 SQ. FT.

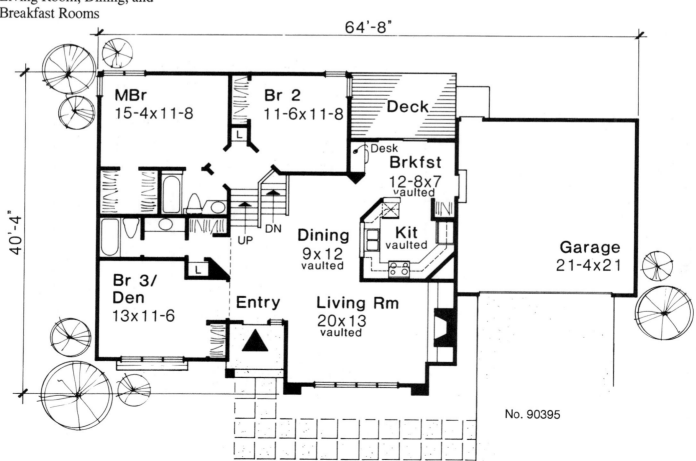

64'-8"

40'-4"

MBr
15-4x11-8

Br 2
11-6x11-8

Deck

Desk

Brkfst
12-8x7
vaulted

DN

UP

Dining
9x12
vaulted

Kit
vaulted

Garage
21-4x21

Br 3/
Den
13x11-6

Entry

Living Rm
20x13
vaulted

No. 90395

No. 99217

Early American Charmer

■ This plan features:

— Three bedrooms

— Two full baths

■ A complete second-floor Master Bedroom Suite with upper Living Room, Studio, and Master Bath

■ A convenient Kitchen with pass-through to a Dining Room

■ A rear Living Room with an elegant fireplace

■ Two first-floor bedrooms that are served by a full hall bath

FIRST FLOOR — 1,425 SQ. FT.
SECOND FLOOR — 704 SQ. FT.
BASEMENT — 1,425 SQ. FT.

**TOTAL LIVING AREA:
2,129 SQ. FT.**

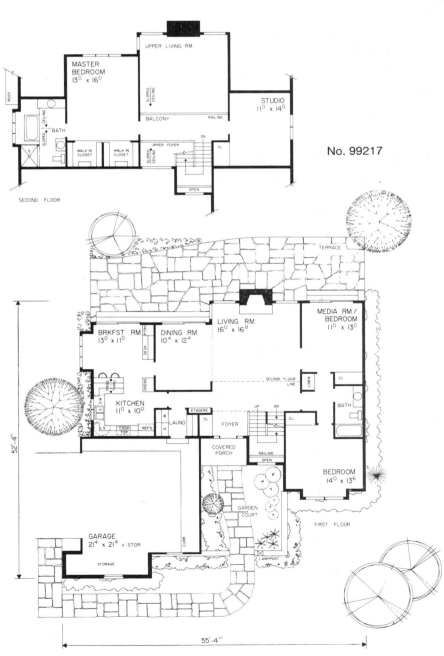

No. 92402

Porch Provides Country-Style Relaxation

■ This plan features:

— Three bedrooms

— Two and one half baths

■ Siding and stacked stone exterior

■ A spacious Family Room with a cozy fireplace and direct access to the rear yard

■ A sunken Great Room with large windows looking out over the country-style porch

■ An efficient Kitchen that serves both the formal Dining Room and the informal Breakfast Room

■ A private Master Suite including a roomy master bath with a double vanity, separate garden tub, shower, commode closet, linen closet and a walk-in closet

■ A convenient second floor laundry room

■ Two additional bedrooms that share a full hall bath

FIRST FLOOR — 1,204 SQ. FT.
SECOND FLOOR — 943 SQ. FT.
BONUS ROOM — 276 SQ. FT.

TOTAL LIVING AREA: 2,147 SQ. FT.

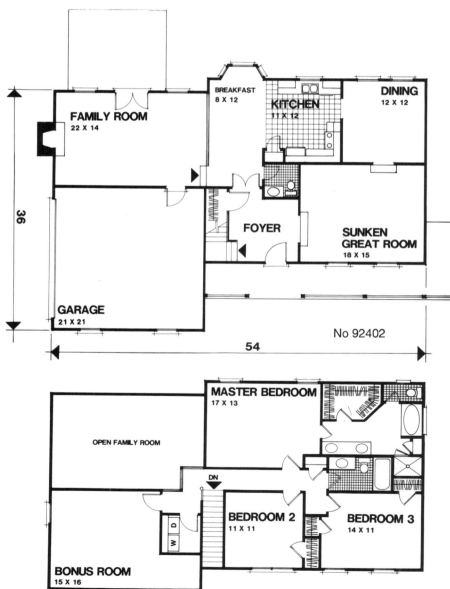

No materials list available

No. 91503
Clapboard Classic

■ This plan features:

— Three bedrooms

— Two full and one half baths

■ A cozy Parlor with a fireplace and direct access to the formal Dining Room

■ A bay window adding natural light to the formal Dining Room

■ A sunny Kitchen with a corner window over a double sink, built-in desk, and a bright eating Nook

■ A Family Room opening off the eating Nook with a lovely fireplace

■ A fabulous Master Suite with a garden spa tub, double vanities and a huge walk-in closet

FIRST FLOOR — 1,285 SQ. FT.
SECOND FLOOR — 1,100 SQ. FT.
BONUS ROOM — 238 SQ. FT.

TOTAL LIVING AREA: 2,385 SQ. FT.

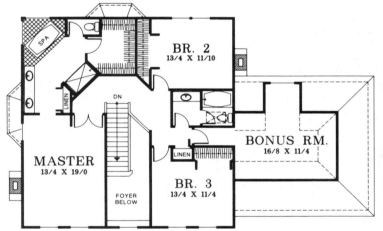

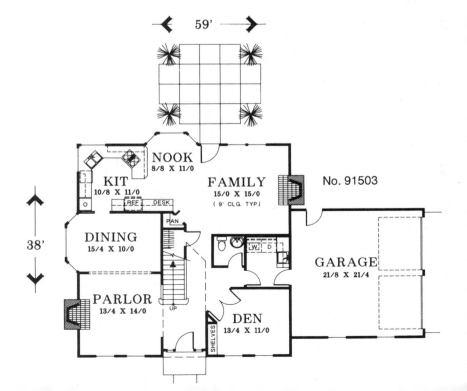

No. 99338

Easy Access; Easy Living

■ This plan features:

— Three bedrooms

— Two full baths

■ A Living Room with a vaulted ceiling, massive fireplace and access to the deck

■ A formal Dining Room with a column arcade dividing it from the Living Room and also having access to the deck

■ A Master Suite with a vaulted ceiling, walk-in closet, and luxurious spa bath

■ Two additional bedrooms that share a full hall bath

FIRST FLOOR — 1,642 SQ. FT.

TOTAL LIVING AREA: 1,642 SQ. FT.

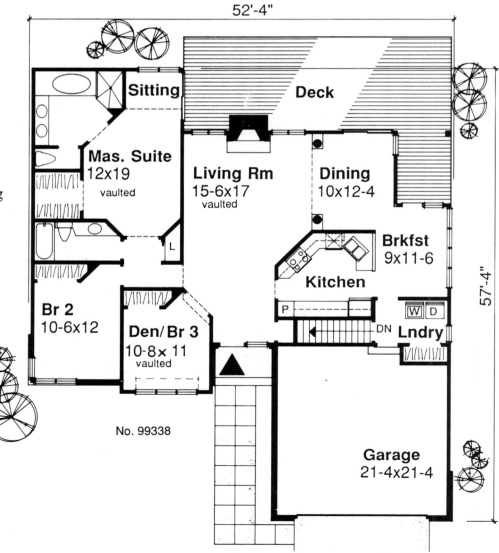

52'-4"

57'-4"

Sitting

Deck

Mas. Suite
12x19
vaulted

Living Rm
15-6x17
vaulted

Dining
10x12-4

Brkfst
9x11-6

Kitchen

L

P

W D

DN Lndry

Br 2
10-6x12

Den/ Br 3
10-8 x 11
vaulted

Garage
21-4x21-4

No. 99338

No. 90821

Vacation Cottage

■ This plan features:

— Two bedrooms

— One full bath

■ An economical, neat and simple design

■ Two picture windows in the Living/Dining Room

■ An efficient Kitchen design

■ A large, cozy loft bedroom flanked by big storage rooms

FIRST FLOOR — 616 SQ. FT.
LOFT — 180 SQ. FT.
WIDTH — 22'-0"
DEPTH — 28'-0"

TOTAL LIVING AREA:
796 SQ. FT.

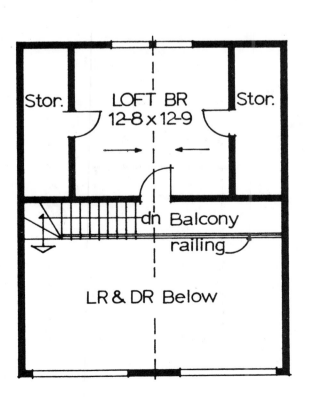

Stor.

LOFT BR
12-8 x 12-9

Stor.

dn Balcony
railing

LR & DR Below

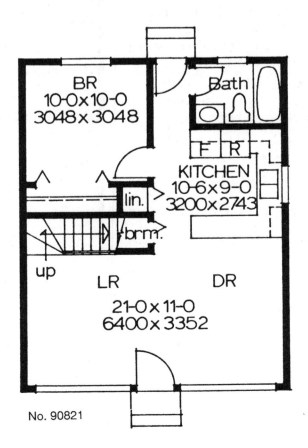

BR
10-0 x 10-0
3048 x 3048

Bath

F   R

KITCHEN
10-6 x 9-0
3200 x 2743

lin.

brm.

up

LR

DR

21-0 x 11-0
6400 x 3352

No. 90821

No. 98316

For the Empty-Nester

■ This plan features:

— Two bedrooms

— Two full baths

■ A Great Room with a 13 foot ceiling and access to the Lanai

■ An island Kitchen with a built-in pantry, desk, and an open layout to the Breakfast area

■ A Master Suite with his and her walk-in closets and a private Master Bath

■ A Den that can function as a third bedroom

FIRST FLOOR — 1,859 SQ. FT.
GARAGE — 393 SQ. FT.

TOTAL LIVING AREA: 1,859 SQ. FT.

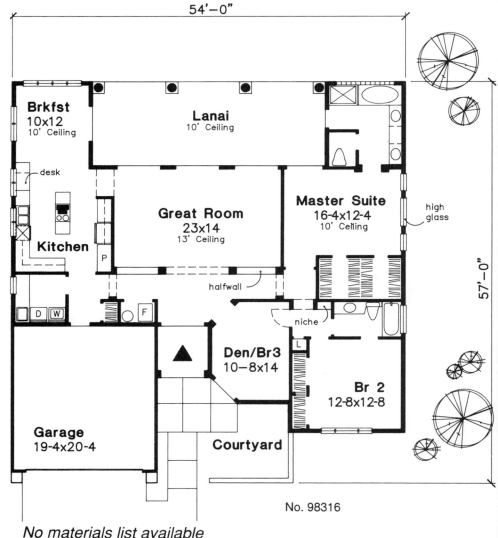

54'-0"

57'-0"

Brkfst 10x12 10' Ceiling

desk

Lanai 10' Ceiling

Master Suite 16-4x12-4 10' Ceiling

high glass

Kitchen

P

Great Room 23x14 13' Ceiling

halfwall

niche

D W

F

Den/Br3 10—8x14

L

Br 2 12-8x12-8

Garage 19-4x20-4

Courtyard

No. 98316

No materials list available

Floor Plan

No. 99339

Contemporary Traditions

■ This plan features:

— Three bedrooms

— Two full baths

■ A vaulted ceiling in the Living Room with a half-round transom window and a fireplace

■ A Dining area flowing into either the Kitchen or the Living Room with sliders to the deck

■ A main-floor Master Suite with corner windows, walk-in closet, and private access to a full bath

■ Two additional bedrooms on the second floor, one with a walk-in closet, having use of a full bath

FIRST FLOOR — 857 SQ. FT.
SECOND FLOOR — 446 SQ. FT.

TOTAL LIVING AREA: 1,303 SQ. FT.

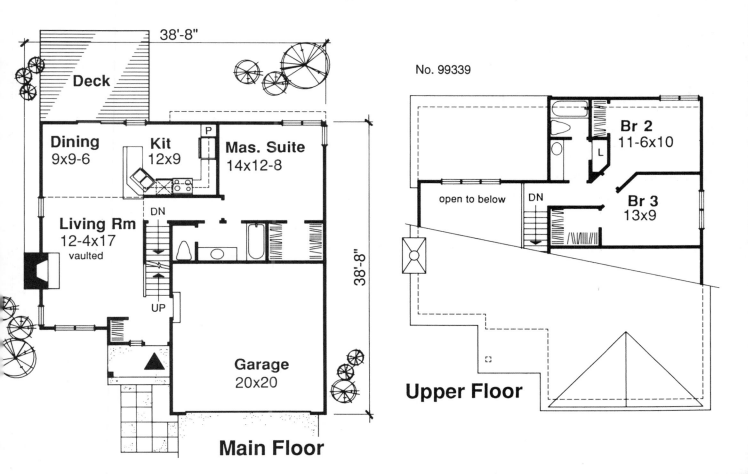

Main Floor

38'-8"

Deck

Dining 9x9-6

Kit 12x9

P

Mas. Suite 14x12-8

Living Rm 12-4x17 vaulted

DN

UP

Garage 20x20

38'-8"

Upper Floor

No. 99339

Br 2 11-6x10

open to below

DN

Br 3 13x9

No. 91650
Master Suite Crowns Plan

■ This plan features:

— Three bedrooms

— Two full and one half baths

■ A stately vaulted ceiling in the foyer accented by a winding staircase

■ A bright bay window and a fireplace enhancing the Living Room

■ A cook-top island Kitchen with corner double sinks, and a built-in pantry

■ A Family Room with a fireplace and direct access to the rear yard

■ An extensive Master Suite with a decorative ceiling, full bath and a walk-in closet

■ Two additional bedrooms that share a full hall bath

FIRST FLOOR — 1,288 SQ. FT.
SECOND FLOOR — 1,094 SQ. FT.
BONUS ROOM — 255 SQ. FT.

TOTAL LIVING AREA: 2,382 SQ. FT.

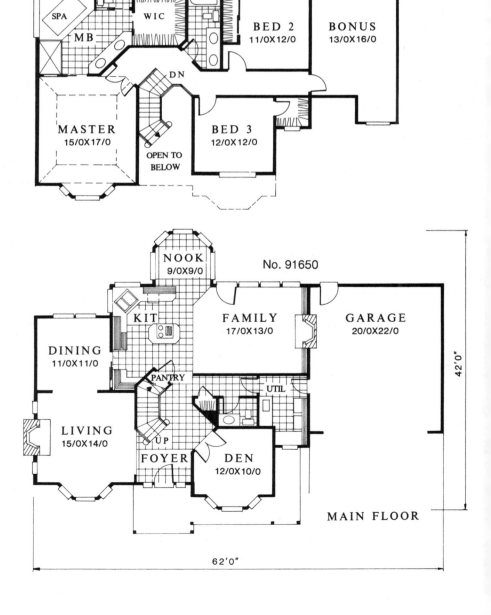

314

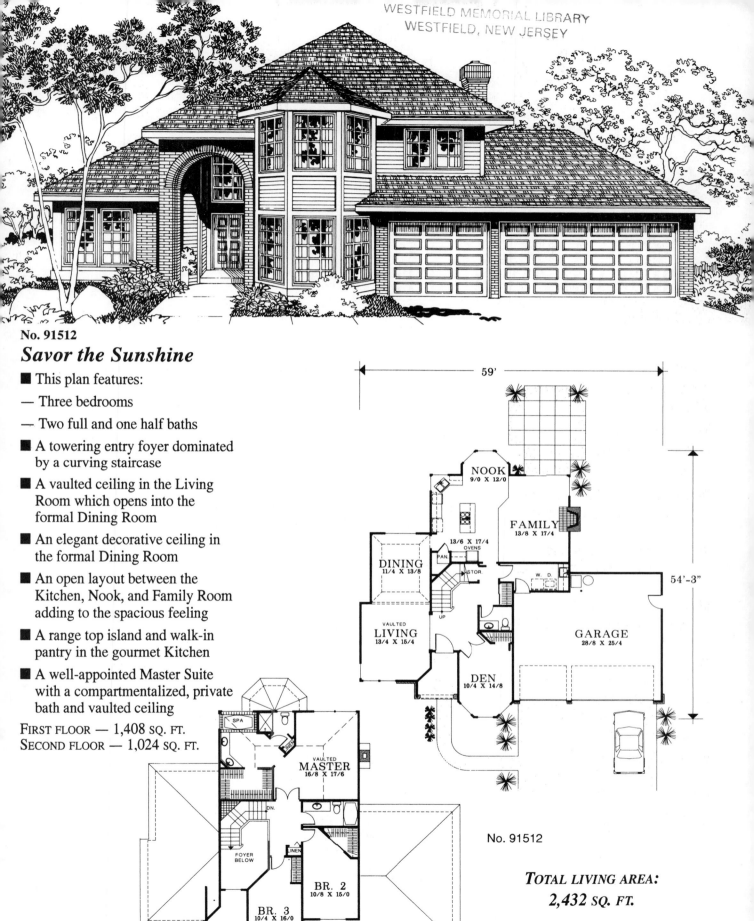

No. 91512

Savor the Sunshine

■ This plan features:

— Three bedrooms

— Two full and one half baths

■ A towering entry foyer dominated by a curving staircase

■ A vaulted ceiling in the Living Room which opens into the formal Dining Room

■ An elegant decorative ceiling in the formal Dining Room

■ An open layout between the Kitchen, Nook, and Family Room adding to the spacious feeling

■ A range top island and walk-in pantry in the gourmet Kitchen

■ A well-appointed Master Suite with a compartmentalized, private bath and vaulted ceiling

FIRST FLOOR — 1,408 SQ. FT.
SECOND FLOOR — 1,024 SQ. FT.

No. 91512

**TOTAL LIVING AREA:
2,432 SQ. FT.**

Everything You Need to Make

You pay only a fraction of the original cost

You've picked your dream home!

You can already see it standing on your lot... you can see your-selves in your new home... enjoying family, entertaining guests, cele-brating holidays. All that remains ahead are the details. That's where we can help. Whether you plan to build-it-yourself, be your own contractor, or hand your plans over to an outside contractor, your Garlinghouse blueprints provide the perfect beginning for putting yourself in your dream home right away.

We even make it simple for you to make professional design modi-fications. We can also provide a materials list for greater economy.

My grandfather, L.F. Garlinghouse, started a tradition of quality when he founded this company in 1907. For over 85 years, homeown-ers and builders have relied on us for accurate, complete, professional blueprints. Our plans help you get results fast... and save money, too! These pages will give you all the information you need to order. So get started now... I know you'll love your new Garlinghouse home!

Sincerely,

HERE'S WHAT YOU GET!

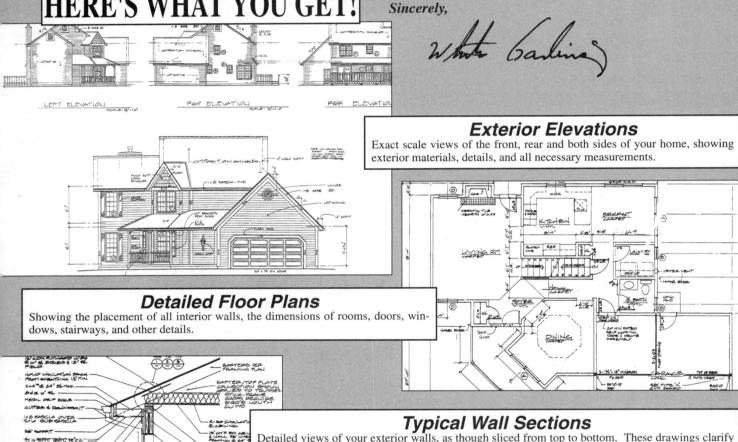

Exterior Elevations

Exact scale views of the front, rear and both sides of your home, showing exterior materials, details, and all necessary measurements.

Detailed Floor Plans

Showing the placement of all interior walls, the dimensions of rooms, doors, win-dows, stairways, and other details.

Typical Wall Sections

Detailed views of your exterior walls, as though sliced from top to bottom. These drawings clarify exterior wall construction insulation, flooring, and roofing details. Depending on your specific geography and climate, your home will be built with either 2x4 or 2x6 exterior walls. Most profes-sional contractors can easily adapt plans for either requirement.

Kitchen and Bath Cabinet Details

These plans or, in some cases, elevations show the specific details and placement of the cabinets in your kitchen and bathrooms as applicable. Customizing these areas is simpler beginning with these details

Your Dream Come True!

for home designs by respected professionals.

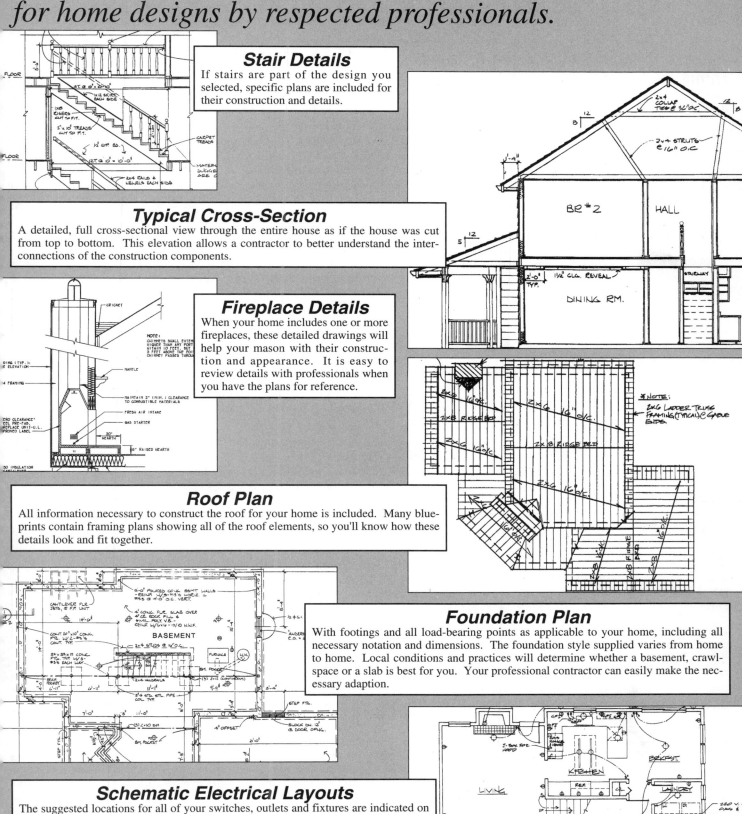

Stair Details

If stairs are part of the design you selected, specific plans are included for their construction and details.

Typical Cross-Section

A detailed, full cross-sectional view through the entire house as if the house was cut from top to bottom. This elevation allows a contractor to better understand the interconnections of the construction components.

Fireplace Details

When your home includes one or more fireplaces, these detailed drawings will help your mason with their construction and appearance. It is easy to review details with professionals when you have the plans for reference.

Roof Plan

All information necessary to construct the roof for your home is included. Many blueprints contain framing plans showing all of the roof elements, so you'll know how these details look and fit together.

Foundation Plan

With footings and all load-bearing points as applicable to your home, including all necessary notation and dimensions. The foundation style supplied varies from home to home. Local conditions and practices will determine whether a basement, crawlspace or a slab is best for you. Your professional contractor can easily make the necessary adaption.

Schematic Electrical Layouts

The suggested locations for all of your switches, outlets and fixtures are indicated on these drawings. They are practical as they are, but they are also a solid taking-off point for any personal adaptions.

Garlinghouse options and extras make the dream truly yours.

*R*eversed Plans Can Make Your Dream Home Just Right!

"That's our dream home... if only the garage were on the other side!"

You could have exactly the home you want by flipping it end-for-end. Check it out by holding your dream home page of this book up to a mirror. Then simply order your plans "reversed". We'll send you one full set of mirror-image plans (with the writing backwards) as a master guide for you and your builder.

The remaining sets of your order will come as shown in this book so the dimensions and specifications are easily read on the job site... but they will be specially stamped "REVERSED" so there is no construction confusion.

We can only send reversed plans with multiple-set orders. But, there is no extra charge for this service.

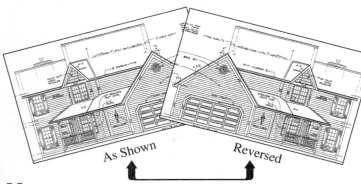

As Shown   Reversed

*M*odifying Your Garlinghouse Home Plan

Easy modifications to your dream home such as minor non-structural changes and simple material substitutions, can be made between you and your builder and marked directly on your blueprints. However, if you are considering making major changes to your design, we strongly recommend that you purchase our reproducible vellums and use the services of a professional designer or architect.

*O*ur Reproducible Vellums Make Modifications Easier

With a vellum copy of our plans, a design professional can alter the drawings just the way you want, then you can print as many copies of the modified plans as you need. And, since you have already started with our complete detailed plans, the cost of those expensive professional services will be significantly less. Refer to the price schedule for vellum costs.

Reproducible vellum copies of our home plans are only sold under the terms of a license agreement that you will receive with your order. Should you not agree to the terms, then the vellums may be returned unopened for a full refund.

*Y*ours FREE With Your Order

FREE SPECIFICATIONS AND CONTRACT FORM provides the perfect way for you and your builder to agree on the exact materials to use in building and finishing your home *before* you start construction. A must for homeowner's peace of mind.

*R*emember To Order Your Materials List

It'll help you save money. Available at a modest additional charge, the Materials List gives the quantity, dimensions, and specifications for the major materials needed to build your home. You will get faster, more accurate bids from your contractors and building suppliers — and avoid paying for unused materials and waste. Materials Lists are available for all home plans except as otherwise indicated, but can only be ordered with a set of home plans. Due to differences in regional requirements and homeowner or builder preferences... electrical, plumbing and heating/air conditioning equipment specifications are not designed specifically for each plan. However, detailed *typical* prints of residential electrical, plumbing and construction guidelines can be provided. Each set of electrical and plumbing prints conforms to the requirements at the National Electrical and Plumbing Codes. The construction prints conform to the Uniform Building Code or BOCA code. These prints can be supplied at a low cost of $14.95 each.

*Q*uestions?

Call our customer service number at 1-203-632-0500.

318